SOVIET RUSSIA TODAY:
PATTERNS AND PROSPECTS

SOVIET RUSSIA *TODAY:*

PATTERNS AND PROSPECTS

EDITED BY

JOHN L. STIPP

Knox College

HARPER & BROTHERS, NEW YORK

SOVIET RUSSIA TODAY: PATTERNS AND PROSPECTS

Copyright © 1956, by Harper & Brothers

Printed in the United States of America

Pages 26–29. From "The 'Religion' of Communism," from Michael T. Florinsky, *World Revolution and the U.S.S.R.*, The Macmillan Company. Copyright 1933 by The Macmillan Company and used with publisher's permission. Pages 30–32; 35–38. From Sir John Maynard, *Russia in Flux*. The Macmillan Company. Copyright 1942 by The Macmillan Company and used with publisher's permission. Pages 33–35. Reprinted from *What Marx Really Meant* by G. D. H. Cole, by permission of Alfred A. Knopf, Inc. Copyright 1934 by G. D. H. Cole. Pages 50–59. Reprinted from *Leninism*, by J. Stalin, by permission of International Publishers. [No co.], 1933. Pages 59–62. Reprinted from *State and Revolution*, by N. Lenin, by permission of International Publishers. Copyright 1932 by International Publishers. Pages 64–77; 254–258. Reprinted from *German Marxism and Russian Communism*, by John Plamenatz, by permission of Longmans, Green & Co., Inc. [No co.], 1954. Pages 77–86. Reprinted from *Dynamics of Soviet Society*, by W. Rostov, by permission of W. W. Norton & Company. Copyright 1953 by Massachusetts Institute of Technology. Pages 92–107; 145–155. Reprinted by permission of the publishers from Barrington Moore, Jr., *Soviet Politics— The Dilemma of Power*, Cambridge, Mass.: Harvard University Press, Copyright 1950 by The President and Fellows of Harvard College. Pages 108–123. Reprinted from *Management in Russian Industry and Agriculture*, by G. Bienstock, S. M. Swarz, and A. Yugow, by permission of Cornell University Press. Copyright 1948 by Cornell University Press. Pages 125–145. Reprinted by permission of the publishers from Merle Fainsod, *How Russia is Ruled*, Cambridge, Mass.: Harvard University Press, Copyright 1953 by The President and Fellows of Harvard College. Pages 155–164. From Julian Towster, *Political Power in the U.S.S.R.*, Copyright 1948 by Oxford University Press. Pages 166–176. Reprinted by permission of the publishers from George Fischer, *Soviet Opposition to Stalin: A Case Study in World War II*, Cambridge, Mass.: Harvard University Press, Copyright 1952 by The President and Fellows of Harvard College. Pages 176–186. From Isaac Deutscher, *Stalin: A Political Biography*, Copyright 1949 by Oxford University Press, Inc. Pages 187–194. Reprinted from "The New Soviet Policy Toward the Satellites" by Isaac Deutscher, *The Reporter*, Dec. 2, 1954, by permission of *The Reporter*. Pages 197–213. From *Little Golden America: Two Famous Soviet Humorists Survey These United States*, by Ilya Ilf & Eugene Petrov, Translated from the Russian by Charles Malateauth, Copyright, 1937, by Rinehart & Company, Inc. Reprinted by permission of Rinehart & Company, Inc., New York, Publishers. Pages 218–226. Abridged from *The Soviet Image of the United States* by Frederick C. Barghoorn, Copyright, 1950, by Harcourt, Brace and Company, Inc. Pages 230–239. Reprinted from Philip E. Mosely, "Russia After Stalin," *Headline Series*, No. 111 (New York, Foreign Policy Association, May–June 1955). Pages 239–244. Reprinted from *The Mind of Modern Russia*, by Hans Kohn, by permission of Rutgers University Press. Copyright 1955 by The Trustees of Rutgers College. Pages 244–248. From: *Mother Russia*, by Maurice Hindus. Copyright 1942, 1943 by Maurice Hindus, reprinted by permission of Doubleday & Company, Inc. Pages 249–253. Reprinted by permission of the publishers from Barrington Moore, Jr., *Terror and Progress, U.S.S.R.*, Cambridge, Mass.: Harvard University Press, Copyright, 1954 by The President and Fellows of Harvard College.

Library of Congress catalog card number: 56–11085

to the tomorrows of
J. E. S.
and his generation

CONTENTS

INTRODUCTION

Winston Churchill in October, 1939, described Soviet Russia as "a riddle wrapped in a mystery inside an enigma." This volume will do much to explain the mystery to the lay reader. Professor Stipp has selected extracts from the best authorities on the various aspects of contemporary Russia, put them in context by a historical introduction, and woven them together with illuminating comments. The whole is a comprehensive, balanced, authoritative and readable guide to Soviet Russia. There are few gilded phrases or slanted adjectives. The reader will feel that he has been given the best that is known about Russia, mostly by scholars of the Western world who have devoted themselves to specialized study of the subject, but on Soviet ideology, the words of the prophets themselves, Marx, Lenin, and Stalin, are presented.

The organization of the volume assures a due proportion of historical background, ideological analysis, description of practical activity, and appraisal of future prospects. Professor Stipp's historical contribution, starting with the proposition that misery tends to revolution but does not necessarily do so, makes clear by historical narration how the Revolution of 1905 and the two of 1917 actually did emerge from the century-old misery and oppression of the Russian peasants, once they had become convinced that the Czar was aligned with the gentry and aristocracy against them.

The analysis of Communist doctrine in its "religious," "scientific," and "historical" aspects may seem confusing, but this is inherent in the material. This doctrine had various objectives when it began with Karl Marx, and it changed radically when it was transferred from Germany to Russia and applied to the peasant conditions of that country. It has been at times a doctrine to explain history, to stimulate social revolution, to industrialize a primitive country, to justify the power of ambitious leaders, and to advance Russian national interests in international politics. It has been a theory of society, of history, and of politics; a philosophy of values; a propaganda of revolution and of nationalism; and a guide to revolutionary economic, political and military strategy and administration. Functioning in such multifarious conditions and with such multifarious goals, consistency is not to be expected.

The section on practical activities and achievements of the Soviet Union suggests that decisions and policies of its government have been based far more on experience, on trial and error, than on theory. The distribution of decision-making authority between central and local organs; the policies on industry and agriculture; the development of economic incentives tending to approach those in a capitalistic economy; the organization of controls—legal, party, secret police, army—; the actions taken on all of these matters have little relation to theory, though the preference inherent in doctrine for centralization, both geographic and functional, and for subordination of the individual and of groups to the state, provided initial guidance which experience has tended to attenuate.

Among the most interesting chapters are those giving the Soviet view of the West and those speculating on the future. The former should provide much food for thought by all Western readers. Professor Barrington Moore's speculation on the future suggests that whether the Soviet Union moves toward more intensive totalitarianism, toward technical rationality, or toward traditional forms of government, depends to a considerable extent on what the West, and particularly the United States, does about it. The final selection by John Plamenatz, while giving due emphasis to the difficulties, strikes the optimistic note that accommodation is possible. "We must," he writes, "look formidable to them and yet not seem to threaten their security. We cannot rely on their good will, but we can, if we act wisely, rely on their patience. Their false philosophy teaches them that time is their ally; and the more they can be persuaded to let time pass quietly, the better for us and for them."

QUINCY WRIGHT

University of Chicago

PREFACE

This book is strictly for "beginners;" scholars and specialists will find nothing in it for them. Its aims, specific and restricted, are these: to present in non-technical language the basic faith and beliefs which undergird Marxism; to show their transformation, under the Bolsheviks, into Russian Communism; to examine the fundamental structures of the USSR's economic and political life; to set forth the difficulties, internal and external, which confront it; to give to us outsiders the picture of ourselves which the Russians see; to evaluate the impact of Communism upon Russian and world history; to essay conjectural answers to the question "what of tomorrow?"

While reference is made to developments as recent as, for example, the Twentieth Party Congress of 1956, this volume deals essentially with topics which have an abiding interest and importance regardless of the flip of this or that leaf of our century's calendar, or of the purge of this or that Russian leader. Hence, just as this work is not meant for specialists who already know the answers it provides, neither is it intended for sensation lovers seeking exposés of yesterday's developments—for answers, in short, nobody really knows including, probably, some participants in those developments.

It must be said, finally, that this book disclaims two other common aims. It is designed neither as apologia nor as criticism; but only as an account. The editor does not disparage devotees of either the pro or con argument on the great Russian Question. He simply says what they are looking for is not found here. The volume's basic purpose is not to inflame anyone, but only to instruct those who feel in need of instruction.

Grateful appreciation is herewith expressed to Dean Hermann R. Muelder of Knox College, for suggesting the idea for Chapter Eight; to Miss Amy Vandersall, competent graduate assistant in the history department of Mount Holyoke College, for cheerfully exploring a blind alley which otherwise would have been the scene of my own fruitless labor; to Professor Wilma Pugh, chairman of the history department of Mount Holyoke College, for administrative arrangements which freed me from much routine paper work; to Professor Peter Viereck, of Mount Holyoke College, who will know why; and to my brother, Mr. Eugene L. Stipp, whose help at one point permitted me to maintain the schedule I had set for myself.

Formal acknowledgements to authors and publishers are made elsewhere. Here it need only be said that I am fully aware this is not my book, and that I am profoundly grateful to those who really made it. My fear—a serious one—is that I have not done justice to them and to their readers.

August, 1956

I

RETROSPECT

CHAPTER 1

Why Communism Came to Russia

The course of Russian history has been one long road to revolution.

The recorded history of mankind makes clear that unrelieved mass misery inevitably produces revolution. It also teaches that the longer the misery continues and the greater it becomes, the vaster will be the explosive character of the upheaval.

Virtually all reputable historians agree that no people, involved in western society and whose state later became a "Great Power," has suffered—in span of centuries and depth of degradation— the miseries suffered by the Russian people. The record comes close to the unbelievable, especially if those asked to believe are common-sense Americans whose heritage is founded upon Anglo-Saxon concepts of human freedom and dignity.

But to say that revolution was expected in Russia is not to say that a *Communist* revolution was inevitable. For a half century before Bolshevism came to power, numerous Russians of all classes were fearing or despairing of or hoping for a destruction of Tsarist autocracy. When it came no one was surprised. But that a tiny handful of radical Marxists would inherit the fruits of the revolution was distinctly a surprise, shared, perhaps, by those Marxists themselves.

What were the features of Russian history which produced revolution? What were the conditions which gave a few Communists control of it?

3

From the beginning of its history, in the eighth or ninth century, until today, Russia has been primarily a land of workers of the soil. Since 1917 the ratio of city to rural dwellers has increased, but population preponderance still lies with the latter. As late as the beginning of World War I, over seventy-five percent of all Russians were peasants.

Until 1861 most of these workers were serfs who owned no land, had little control over the produce of the soil, and remarkably little management of their own personal lives. Even after the much-heralded Emancipation Act—anticipating Lincoln's proclamation by two years—the status of the peasant was little changed.

For most of his history the peasant was a serf. In the 1500's he was, by ukase of the Tsar, attached to the soil and prohibited from leaving it save by special permission of the squire or lord. All land was, until the eighteenth century, the property of the Tsar who, from time to time, gave estates to those lords who best served him—and took them back when it suited. In 1762 private ownership of land was granted to the gentry and, a few years later, legal right of the latter to sell his serfs with the land. About this time, too, the Tsar decreed that no serf was to be allowed to register complaints against his lord. Those who did were lashed for their insolence, or sent into exile at hard labor.

The granting of land to the gentry produced a curious belief in peasant minds which sheds light upon the whole framework of peasant mentality, a framework which held steadfast until the revolution of 1905. News of the Tsar's decree seeped down, of course, to the serf. But he refused to believe what he had heard. The land, he was told, or much of it, had been relinquished from Tsar to lord. So far, good; this was an act of mercy long expected of the all-powerful and all-merciful Autocrat. But undoubtedly the Little Father had ordered, at the same time, that substantial portions of the land be likewise handed over to the serf, and his serfdom ended. The lord, however, cleverly had kept this part of the decree from the peasant. Both the serf and the well-meaning Tsar had been cheated by the avaricious gentry. The strange illusion of an all-merciful Autocrat, swindled by landlords who likewise swindled the peasant, constituted one of the main threads of the pattern of the serf's dimly sensed way of life. For well over one hundred years the "plain people"—as distinguished from the landed "persons"—nursed this supposed grievance, and yearned for the day when the Tsar and his people together would with fierce vengeance destroy the fraud that made the whole land a dark one.

In reality, of course, the Tsar was the fountainhead of the system. To maintain his power he needed the gentry. To further their strength, from which he drew, he encouraged the landlords to keep their toilers in serfdom, to tie them to the land, to prevent them from acquiring property or even completely possessing their chattels. To this end he sanctioned a society in which the masses were virtually slaves, unable to marry by their own will alone, kept by deliberate policy ignorant, and deprived of those elementary choices which long since the West had designated as perquisites of human dignity.

A development which occurred in the reign of Peter the Great (1672–1725) served to widen substantially and permanently the gulf between "people" and "persons." Peter, anxious to westernize his slavic country, forced Europeanization upon his lords. As a consequence their dress, habits, and way of life generally conspicuously set them apart from the peasant masses. They "became to the peasant a stranger, a domestic foreigner."

For the serf there was virtually no law. His law was what the elder of his village, or the squire, or the government official, or the police said it was. This is not rhetorical language but a literal statement of fact. These agents had full disciplinary authority over him. The most commonly used instrument of this authority was the whip. Flogging came to be so common and so commonly accepted that a nineteenth century writer, quoted by Jan Khucharzewski in his *Origins of Modern Russia*, could with a straight face declare:

The former serf [this was written after the Emancipation Act of 1861], beaten and lashed for centuries, is accustomed to birching and patriarchal punishment. He does not at all feel its disgrace and offers his back without shame. His mind is still too realistic and positive not to perceive the merits of this type of punishment; and he appreciates birching without prejudice. Birching costs neither time nor money. After birching a man works and sleeps better—says an old proverb.

Khucharzewski also cites the case of a woman who, bringing dinner to the fields late, was given a beating by her father-in-law. Appealing to an official for redress, the woman was beaten a second time by order of the official, who felt that if women began complaining of the whip, a serious breach in the authoritarian structure would be invited.

Serf fathers often sold their daughters in marriage—with the permission of the squire. From seventy to a hundred rubles was a common price. So great was the gulf between serf and master that common standards of moral behavior were frequently inapplicable to the former. From the source cited above this illustration is given. A certain member of the gentry owned an estate made up of two small villages. Each year he visited his estate for a two or three week period. Before these visits his estate manager would draw up a list of the girls and young women in the villages. Each girl in succession then served two or three days as the lord's "maid." There was nothing particularly clandestine about such an arrangement. The "people" were different.

From the produce of their estates the gentry took what they could and left what they had to for serf subsistance. In times of famine, and these were not uncommon (in the 1840's, for example, there were three serious ones in a single decade), the "black people" were reduced to eating acorns, bark, and grass. Even in normal times the primitive agricultural methods and the notoriously low yield per acre kept the peasant forever hungry and filled with smoldering hate for the "robber lord."

In the middle of the nineteenth century the typical peasant hut was a fifteen by fifteen wooden structure without a chimney; a clay stove served for heating and cooking. Eating utensils were hardly more advanced than those used by pre-Columbian Indians. Splinters of fir lighted the hut at night, and the occupants slept on straw on the floor and, not infrequently, on the stove. Birch sandals were the common footwear and so rare was a cloth coat that often one was shared by a whole village.

Out of such a milieu it was not to be expected that an educated youth could develop. In the first place the government, while never, of course, officially saying so, and, indeed, making token efforts to provide elementary schools, was suspicious of education as a process and saw in it a kind of enemy. Education could "arouse social appetites," it could provide tools to analyze a situation the powers of the *status quo* did not want analyzed. As one writer has put it, the government and gentry, by curbing education, could "curb the social aspirations of the peasant, and thus keep him in a patriarchal state for the security of both the empire and the possessing class."

As late as 1897 in Kharkov province—an area considerably larger than Denmark—there were but 523 elementary schools. The published plans of the government respecting the development of these schools were such that it would have taken until the year 2114 before primary education would have become available to all boys in the province. Schooling for girls was not even contemplated. This, it should be noted, was thirty-six years after the "Great Reform." By comparison Denmark had, in 1897, just under 3000 elementary schools. In Württemberg, an area equal to but two of Kharkov's counties, there were in the corresponding period 4031 elementary schools. When the Kharkov *zemstvo*—the local governing body—was shamed into voting an annual appropriation of 200,000 rubles for peasant education, the administrative authorities, at the behest of the *zemstvo's* more powerful gentry, vetoed the appropriation.

Plagued by the trinity of famine, illiteracy, and poverty, many peasants allowed themselves to drift into complete hopelessness. Many others, however, did not. In the 1770's a serious uprising, under the famous Pugachev, demonstrated clearly the latent power and hate of the exploited serf. A little earlier, when Catherine II's accession was announced, riots occurred in seventeen provinces. By the nineteenth century, uprisings had assumed an almost epidemic nature. In 1845 there were riots on thirty-two estates in seventeen provinces; in 1846, twenty-seven riots in sixteen provinces; in 1847, thirty-five in twenty-five provinces; in 1848, fifty-four in twenty-seven provinces. During the whole reign of Nicholas I (1826–1854) there were, by official admission, 556 revolts. The quelling of these uprisings in each case was swift and savage. When, in 1847, peasants refused to obey their master, Prince Golitzin, troops were sent to administer mass floggings. So unmercifully was the knout used that some peasant women threw themselves into ponds. A few years earlier (1834) in the province of Viatka, each of the principal agitators received 6000 lashes in the presence of the summoned peasants.

After Alexander II came to the throne in 1854, an attempt was made to ameliorate the lot of the "black people." For several years the Tsar's advisors had, at his direction, studied the problem of freeing the serf and, in 1861, by imperial ukase, emancipation was proclaimed. Since then a great body of literature has developed explaining, expounding, and interpreting the intricate directives and developments involved in this complex Act. For centuries the peasant had protested to his lord, "We are yours, but the land is ours." Now, overnight as it were, a beneficent Tsar had given, with a stroke of the pen, the people both their "personhood" and the legal right to own land. But whatever the literature on the subject may say, sober study of the actual historical development since emancipation shows the serious inadequacy of the Act.

For one thing, the law required that compensation be made to the squire. Always the peasant had believed that both God and common sense had given the land to those who worked it; the scheming squire had somehow circumvented both. Now the Little Father himself had acquiesed in the evil absurdity, and the peasants were alternately puzzled and outraged. Many finally came to believe that the Tsar's decree had actually given them the land without *obrok*—the name of the compensatory fee— but the lord again had outwitted both the Crown and the people by withholding publication of this provision.

Secondly, the fee—commonly called redemption dues—was fixed, in the majority of cases, at a level beyond the possibility of peasant payment. As a result, arrears immediately piled up which seemed to postpone ownership forever.

Further, a provision stipulated that those serfs who preferred could, without compensation at all, receive a fourth of the land otherwise to be allotted to them. Hundreds of thousands took this seemingly simple way out, only to discover that their pauper lot, as it came to be called, was altogether insufficient to provide minimum subsistence.

Then, large portions of the land were made exempt from the Act and remained in the hands of the lords. Often this turned out to be pasture land, without which the peasant could not feed his cattle.

A further provision required the Mir—the loosely organized village community electing its own officials and having much to say about land, crops, and general administration (always, however, subject to the lord's veto)—to be held responsible as a unit for individual payments of its former serf's allottment. This obviously restricted quite severely the mobility and choices of the individual peasant. For example, peasant A, wanting to leave the village and having finally paid his redemption dues in full, might be prevented from doing so by the elder and his advisors who might feel that the Mir would be penalized without the labor of A. Until *all* former serfs of the Mir had paid their redemption dues, each was obligated, legally, to its decisions.

Sir John Maynard—probably the West's foremost authority on the Russian peasant—has evaluated the Emancipation Act thus:

Generally speaking, the serfs received less land than they had held before Emancipation. In Russia as a whole the reductions (the *ostryeski*, or "cuttings") played an important part in subsequent history. . . . But the most intimate and comprehensive of the restrictions upon the freedom of the liberated serf was the absence of any demarcation of his legal rights and duties. He was as completely at the command of every representative of the executive power as the bullock or horse which he drove to the fields was at the command of the switch he carried. He was expected to do what he was told, and he was beaten if he failed to do it.

Thus the "Great Reform" failed to relieve both the centuries-old land hunger of the peasant, and his unceasing urge to find a "release of energy" in more than a kind of sub-human existence.

At this time—that is, just after Emancipation—there occurred a development constituting one of the most puzzling ironies of Russian history. A number of "conscience-stricken gentlemen" —landlords who, through their reading, had come into contact with western life and thought (who had, in short, finally brushed the spirit of the Enlightenment)—began to preach "going to the people." In this they were joined—indeed, led—by the remarkable phalanx of Russian intellectuals which the nineteenth century produced. For a full generation Russian huts were invaded by solicitous lords and intelligentsia who preached that "the people" were really, despite their crudeness, their ignorance, and their "sin," a kind of redeeming Christ. In them somehow resided the secret of Russia's salvation, and neither arguments nor the peasant's often ill-concealed hostility could serve to destroy the illusion. Thus as the twentieth century dawned the masses and many of Russia's best minds were bound, in what might be called a marriage of inconvenience, in a strange, passive struggle against the frightened lords and their even more frightened Autocrat. A year of reckoning was coming, a time of troubles, that might last long and perhaps remind one of Lincoln's words at the time of our own civil strife: ". . . if God wills that it continue until all the wealth piled by the bondsman's two hundred and fifty years of unrequited toil shall be sunk, and until every drop of blood drawn by the lash shall be paid by another drawn by the sword, as was said three thousand years ago, so still it must be said 'the judgments of the Lord are true and righteous altogether.' " Lermontov, one of Russia's great poets of the mid-nineteenth century, looked ahead and saw just such a time. In his *Prophecy* he said:

A year, a black year for Russia will come, when the crown will fall off the Tsar's head. The people will forget their old love for them, and the masses will feed on blood and murder. The destroyed law will protect neither women nor innocent children. And the fetid corpses will cause pestilence in the desolate villages and call the victims from the huts. Famine will torment the unfortunate country and rivers will be red with the reflexes of fires.

At this point a question may occur. "How, in the life of a Great Power, could such conditions become fixed and prevail for so long?" Full development is too long and involved to be essayed here, but the basic features of the answer may be sketched.

Of all the large European nations Russia alone missed the Renaissance. It is impossible, of course, to say what the history

of western man would have been if the "awakening" had not occurred. But it is certain that it helped mightily to develop in
western man the consciousness of his individual worth, and to
enable him to construct that vast edifice of inquiry which liberated him, in part, from ancient error and, as well, from mediaeval
inertia. It is quite reasonable to suppose that Russia would have
experienced, in some degree at least, this stimulus to self reëxami-
nation had not, at that very moment in history, a "golden horde"
from the eastern steppes overrun the country and deflected its
life from the main stream of western development. If Russia is
different from other European Great Powers, certainly the Mon-
gol invasion, which lasted from the thirteenth to the fifteenth
centuries, is one of the basic reasons for this difference.

Likewise Russia missed the stimulus of the Reformation and
the corrective it brought in the form of a curb to the repressive
force of ecclesiastical power over the peasant. And it missed, of
course, the Counter Reformation which had done so much to
reinvigorate the mind and learning of the Roman Catholic cleric.
In this connection it is worthwhile to remember that the evil
Rasputin, the so-called monk who wielded tremendous power in
the Russian empire just prior to the Great Revolution, had no
counterpart in western Europe.

Geography and history combined to cut Russia off from development in the western tradition. Adjacent to the East, she
easily absorbed its mystic fatalism and absolutism. Converted by
the eastern church, she thereby "went without the Latin language,
the common tongue of European thought and learning, without the rationalistic training of the Roman mentality . . . and
without the scholastic philosophers who applied reason to doctrine."

Finally, she missed the original impetus of the Industrial Revolution and lingered long outside its influence. Thereby she failed
to fashion a strong middle class, always and everywhere the class
which introduces economic and political liberalism—though it
may later come to regret its championing of the latter.

Unlike the peasant, who has been present in Russia from its
beginnings, the industrial worker came late upon the scene. And

when he did appear, he still held close ties with his old Mir and
hence tended to remain peasant-oriented in his thought and feelings. As late as 1914 the industrial workers formed under fifteen
percent of the total population. In their grievances, proletariat
and peasant shared alike.

After the Emancipation peasants began to drift, in substantial
numbers, to the cities. About 4,000,000 serfs had been made
landless as a result of the Tsar's "beneficence," and from this
group, especially, the migrants came.

In the 1870's and 1880's the working day in the factory for
men, women, and children averaged somewhere from twelve to
sixteen hours. Wages were so low that Americans, particularly,
find it hard to credit the truth. At the outbreak of World War I
the average factory worker's wage was 300 rubles a year, or about
$150. Many of the factories built workers' barracks where prole-
tarian life centered. If this suggests a military atmosphere, the
full truth makes it explicit, for under Count Witte—Russia's
leading exponent of industrialization, and the Tsar's Minister of
Finance in the closing years of the nineteenth and opening years
of the twentieth century—the state became the chief entrepreneur; and state and army were really one.

Sometimes the worker was paid in kind, or partially so. At no
time, however, from the beginnings of Russian industrialization
until the Revolution (or after it, for that matter) did the factory
worker receive a wage sufficient to maintain a living standard
which, by western measure, could be called even modest.

Until a few years before the Revolution all union activity was
forbidden by the state. Many times workers sought to elect a
"headman" to lead them in efforts to raise wages or to better
working conditions. Invariably the government crushed these
efforts and sent the leaders to prison or into exile. Thus union
activities were forced underground. So much agitation of this
kind was carried on, and so harassing to officialdom did it become
that in 1900 the government took a fantastic step. It inaugurated what later came to be called "police socialism." Zubatov,
head of the police system, was entrusted with the task of setting
up unions supervised by police officials. The aim was to divert
worker unrest into manageable channels. Americans might think

of such a system as one of "official company unions." The idea backfired when the movement passed out of the hands of police-unionists and headed toward what was thought of as "worker extremism." By 1904, Zubatovism had run its course. In its wake was left a reservoir of worker union experience later to prove of high value to trained organizers.

Out of these conditions arose the "soviet," a non-communist invention. The original soviets were worker organizations, headed by a factory "elder"; the idea and pattern were copied directly from the peasant Mir. Subsequently the Communists—at first suspicious of the soviets—absorbed them into their pattern of activity and, still later, identified the name exclusively with themselves. The average American, as a consequence, has come to think of the soviet as an original Communist device. This is an unfortunate misconception, for it tends to blur the basic peasant nature of this organization and renders more difficult the understanding of its role in the revolutions of 1917.

By necessity, much of its work was carried on in an atmosphere of restriction and secrecy. On the other hand, the work of these factory groups was facilitated by a paradox in Russian industry. Although this industry was greatly retarded in general scope, compared with that of western nations, it contained a higher concentration of workers per factory—in proportion to total workers involved—than any other country. For example, by 1905 "the proportion employed in large works having more than a thousand hands apiece was in Russia three times as great as in Germany." For the Russian worker these soviets, springing up in numerous cities in and after 1905, proved to be the seedbed of revolutionary activity. And since, in 1917, many if not most of the factory workers were raw recruits from the land, the soviets served all the more as a strong, albeit strange, link binding proletariat and peasant together.

By the opening decade of the twentieth century, Russian peasants and Russian workers shared a deep and abiding hatred of the autocratic machine and all its parts. For over a half century, furthermore, the greatest minds of Russia had been preaching the revolutionary doctrines of the West in the face of a censorship more irritating than effective. Marxism had been introduced, by Plekhanov, in the 1870's. Revolutionary parties of various hues and aims had been organized. The two major ones were the Social Revolutionary Party, slanted toward the peasant and imbued with the philosophy of "going to the people," and the Social Democratic Party, oriented in the direction of the city worker and convinced that the revolution, when it came, would be directed and managed by professional revolutionaries. Shortly after 1900 the latter party came to be split into two parts. One part preached violent revolution spearheaded by a disciplined "vanguard" of the party. This section was headed by Lenin and a small group of colleagues; it took the name of Bolsheviks. The second part, called Mensheviks, was larger (contrary to the literal meaning of the Russian words used to differentiate the two) and, though it consisted of revolutionaries too, believed in a stricter interpretation of Marx and consequently a slower tempo. Other groups were formed from time to time, ranging from liberal parliamentarians to terroristic anarchists.

By the turn of the new century, no knowing person believed Russia could ultimately escape revolution. The only questions were *when* and *what kind.*

As history spelled out the answers, the Great Revolution is seen as a drama of three acts. Act One was staged in 1905; the other two followed each other in rapid succession in 1917.

The background of the First Act was the war with Japan which lasted from February, 1904, to August, 1905. The world had expected the great Russian bear to defeat the Nipponese pygmies with little trouble. Instead, Russia received a decisive defeat. As its armed forces, made up of peasants and proletariat, suffered rout and death, the home front suffered privation and humiliation.

The basic weakness of the regime, unmasked for all to see, invited expression of the pent-up fury of the long-suppressed masses. In the villages burning of manors and confiscation of farm machinery and, in many localities, of the land itself, spontaneously took place. Strikes in the larger cities—especially in St. Petersburg, under the leadership of Trotsky and the worker-soviets—occurred. Massed demonstrators paraded the grievances of centuries.

One demonstration and its aftermath had particular importance for subsequent events. In January, 1905, Father Gapon, priest, and formerly of the "socialist police," led a huge demonstration in St. Petersburg, peacefully seeking redress of workers' wrongs. The demonstrators congregated in front of the Winter Palace, residence of the Tsar. They were met with bullets. Dozens were killed, hundreds wounded. The people had gone directly to the Little Father for justice; they were given death. The myth of a beneficent Tsar betrayed by an avaricious gentry and bureaucracy was destroyed. The Tsar stood revealed for that which he had always been, the fountainhead of autocratic oppression. The people, bitter in their disillusionment, were to remember the Winter Palace scene twelve years later.

During these violent times the Crown and its supporting groups were much frightened. The Tsar's most influential minister, Count Witte, frankly told his sovereign, after defeat by Japan was recognized, that he had either to grant a constitution to appease popular passion or set up a military dictatorship to crush it. Typically, the Tsar wavered. Under the leadership of Trotsky the St. Petersburg Soviet had taken the lead in calling a general strike which threatened to paralyze the country. Peasants were burning and sacking. Some appeasement of the masses seemed imperative. Still, to the Tsar constitutional government was a betrayal of divine commands laid upon him. As Christ's vicar he dared not license mob rule and anarchy. The things that were Caesar's must be guarded.

His "solution" was the Manifesto of October 30, 1905. This promised the calling of a legislative body—the Duma—and, among other things, a measure of free speech. But the basic absolutism of the autocracy was not compromised, and the laws regulating the right to vote showed clearly that the "little people" were to have virtually no voice in the framing of statutes. For that matter, the Crown reserved to itself the right to veto absolutely, and, further, the right to initiate, by decree, such laws as it wished. The first Duma elected proved too radical for the Tsar, even under the highly restricted franchise, and he dissolved it within a month. The second was even more radical, and it too was soon sent home. Thereupon the Tsar tightened even more severely the voting right and finally, in 1906, found the third Duma a sufficiently conservative group of representatives.

His next move was to give to Stolypin, one of his ministers, the authority (*sans* Duma approval) to put into operation a program the latter believed would regain stability for the regime. The essence of this program was the creation of a peasant class of the "strong and sober" (kulaks); free farmers who would cleave to the Crown and act as a bulwark against revolution. The execution of this program did indeed bring such a body into existence, but the price was further alienation of the masses of poor and middling peasants. Stolypin, moreover, carried out his plans with such utter ruthlessness that the numerous hangings which the program's execution entailed—"Stolypin's Neckties," they were dubbed—set off a new wave of peasant uprisings.

But by this time the government had—now that the war with Japan was over—regained its nerve; by this time, too, the spontaneous revolutionary fervor had lost its edge, and the inexperienced leaders of the insurrection could not reform and redirect the movement. The First Act ends, then, with the autocracy weakened but still ruling, at least on the surface, substantially as before.

Act Two has a long prologue which can only be sketched here. In 1911 Stolypin was assassinated, and his program virtually abandoned. Three years later, in August, 1914, Russia went to war again; this time not against little Japan, but Greater Germany. Within two years the Russian armies, badly trained, poorly led, ill-fed, and under-equipped, were smashed by the Kaiser's efficient war machine. Great Britain and France, Russia's allies (and later the United States) tried to persuade the staggering bear to stay on his feet. Promises were made, some aid was sent, but the situation was hopeless. Some troops, for example, were sent into battle without rifles; bare fists were supposed to stand, somehow, against German cannon and machine guns. Internally, transportation facilities, none too good to begin with, were in a chaotic state. Soldier-peasants began deserting by regiments to escape certain annihilation; and in the cities, workers were starving. City starvation, indeed, was the immediate cause of the actors taking up their roles in the Second Act. And under the skin of the city worker, it must be remembered, was the beaten flesh and seared soul of the Russian peasant.

The Tsar himself was in a pitiable condition. Lacking a strong character, he leaned more and more heavily upon his hysterical wife who was, herself, under the influence of the "mad monk," Rasputin. Under such conditions the formation—to say nothing of the execution—of a strong and consistent policy was impossible. So bad had things become in the House of the Autocrat that even the gentry was appalled. As for the moneyed middle class, its partnership with the Crown had always been reluctant and of a tenuous nature.

The Second Act began February 23 (according to the calendar then used in Russia; by the western calendar the date was March 8) with a celebration of International Women's Day. Some fifteen years later one of the chief revolutionary figures of this period—Trotsky, second only to Lenin while the latter lived —wrote thus of this day:

On February 23, under the flag of "Woman's Day," began the long-ripe and long-withheld uprising of the Petrograd [as it was then called] working masses. The first step of the insurrection was the strike. In the course of three days it broadened and became general. . . . Becoming more and more aggressive, the strike merged with the demonstrations, which were bringing the revolutionary mass face to face with the troops. This raised the problem as a whole to the higher level where things are solved by force of arms.

On February 26 the Tsar sent an order dissolving the Duma. The deputies accepted the order of dissolution but remained in the capital awaiting developments. By this time thousands of workers—yesterday's peasants—were in the streets. The next day, February 27, a significant scene took place. The Tsar's capital guards, numbering some 150,000 soldiers, not only refused to fire upon the insurrectionists but, finally, joined them. Trotsky later, quoting another's words, explained the phenomenon simply.

. . . the regiments of the Guard which on February 27 overthrew the Russian throne, came without their officers . . . not the army but the workers began the insurrection; not the generals but the soldiers came to the State Duma. The soldiers supported the workers not because they were obediently fulfilling the commands of their officers, but because . . . they felt themselves blood brothers of the workers as a class composed of toilers like themselves. The peasants and the workers—those are the two social classes which made the Russian revolution.

By the evening of that day the capital garrison had dissolved into the ranks of the insurrectionists. By March the Tsar's authority had simply melted away. The strangest thing about the March revolution was its unrevolutionary character. There were no long-lasting bloody riots, little pillaging, little noise and bombast. Soldiers quit fighting, trains stopped running, policemen vanished—the state, in short, quietly collapsed. The Tsar looked on sadly. His wife, it is true, raised a shrill voice. Its message was the one she had been harping on for some months and is best expressed in a letter she wrote to her royal husband in late 1916, while he was at army headquarters. "Be Peter the Great, Ivan the Terrible, Emperor Paul—crush them all under you—*now don't you laugh, naughty one!*" The absurd beginning of Autocracy's end is epitomized in this fantastic admonition. The cartoon shapes itself: "The Autocrat's wife—crying in the wilderness."

The Tsar possessed the confidence of no substantial section of the nation. Soldiers, peasants, workers, a large portion of the middle class, and even some of the gentry agreed that the Tsar had to go.

Meantime the factory soviets had become active. Soon they were led by professional revolutionaries; Lenin had arrived from Switzerland, Trotsky from America, Stalin from exile in Siberia. More and more they assumed, in the cities, a quasi-governmental function. In the country newly formed "Canton Committees," roughly equivalent to the soviets (and soon to call themselves that), took over a large part of local control. On the battlefield soldier-soviets were forming.

On March 2, 1917, the Tsar of All the Russias signed a simple statement saying, ". . . we have recognized that it is for the good of the country that we should abdicate the Crown of the Russian State. . . ." The Second Act had ended. The Autocracy, established in the fifteenth century, had surrendered to "the plain people." A provisional government took its place.

But the new government already had a rival in the loose network of soldiers', workers', and peasants' soviets, and there followed a confused interlude.

It was at this point in the drama that American, British, and French spectators had expected a model of their own bourgeois democracy to be set up. To them it seemed the logical next step. Landed aristocrats had stepped out of power; middle class democrats would fill the void left by this abdication.

For the next seven months the provisional government, consolidating finally under the leadership of Kerensky, tried indeed to fill the void in much that way. But for middle class democracy to succeed, there must first be a sizable middle class. Further, there must exist leaders in its ranks who possess political experience and a workable program. In tumultuous times an added ingredient is needed—iron will. None of these existed in 1917 Russia save the iron will, and that was to be found in another, infinitesimally small party—the Bolshevik Party.

Kerensky was almost as vacillating as the Tsar. Himself a Social Revolutionary, he tried to work with both the moderate liberals called Cadets, who wanted a constitutional monarchy, and with the Mensheviks, who wanted, as a first step toward the final revolution, a bourgeois republic. With the Bolsheviks, whose cry was "All Power to the Soviets" (which by then they dominated), he alternately adopted opposing policies, now attacking, now tolerating them.

Perhaps his biggest mistake was trying to continue the war against Germany. Soldiers, sailors, workers, and peasants, all demanded an end to the impossible situation. But Kerensky felt honor bound to go on with the fighting. The cities demanded bread, the villages land and a decent price for their produce. About all Kerensky and his quarreling colleagues could do was make promises. Consequently desertion at the front and chaos at home continued.

Meantime the chief figures of the Third Act were cueing themselves into the drama. The provisional government promised peace, but only after victory; it promised land and factory reform, but only after a Constituent Assembly should meet and draw up a constitution—and the date for its meeting had already been postponed several times. It neither crushed the soviets nor supported them. Lenin and his Bolshevik colleagues, on the other hand, were sharp, sure, and simple in their basic strategy and propaganda—almost the only leaders in all Russia who were. Their slogans said what the people wanted to hear: "Peace," now; "Bread," for the cities; "Land," to be taken from the gentry and given to the peasant; "All Power to the Soviets," as the vehicle to effect these aims. Bread to the starving workers, the soil to land-hungry peasants, and peace for the battle and home fronts—this program increasingly won mass support as the Kerensky government talked of peace after victory and reform sometime in the future. (That the implementation of this program meant to the Bolsheviks something different from what it meant to the masses Lenin never hesitated to emphasize—privately. Bread would be given to the city workers—but by forceful requisition, if need be; land would be "given" to the peasant —but under the ownership of the state; and peace would very probably entail—as in actuality it did—large sacrifices of Russian soil.)

In their strategy the Bolsheviks were as direct and simple as in their propaganda—control of the soviets and overthrow of the provisional government.

From March to October in 1917 the overall situation drifted ever closer to pure anarchy. In September Kerensky launched the last Russian offensive which, after a faint flicker of success, faded and failed. The Third Act opened.

It was brief, virtually bloodless, and big with consequence. Bolshevik leaders were already in controlling positions within the key soviets. Even so, Lenin had to prod his comrades into action; most of them thought the time was not quite ripe; Lenin was sure that it was. Under his overpowering will, therefore, the second revolution of the year was staged.

In October the Petrograd Soviet, the largest and most powerful in the country, called a Congress of Soviets into meeting. On the night of the 27th it passed a resolution, immediately pub-

lished, declaring all land to the peasants and all power to the soviets. Back of the Congress stood the peasant-worker army. The provisional government offered feeble resistance (though in Moscow, Kiev, and several other large cities some sanguinary fighting took place), and within the week Lenin and his compatriots were in power. The Third Act was over.

By July, 1918, the new free farmer began to understand some of the implications of the Bolshevik program. Shortly thereafter, led by Tsarist generals and supported by foreign governments, millions of Russia's peasants joined in a fierce struggle against the Bolshevik—now called Communist—government. For three years civil war raged, and intervention continued. Red armies, supported by city workers as well as some segments of the peasantry, defeated their opponents one after another. By 1921 the fighting was over and the Communists settled down to the business of transforming the whole of Russian society.

History had supplied some answers to some questions: "Why a revolution?"; "Why 1917?"; "Why Communist?"

What answers to certain present problems history will supply tomorrow will substantially depend upon what understanding is had or can be gotten today of the basic features of the new society the Russian revolution has produced.

History is a jealous teacher; in the past she has been harsh to those who chose not to know.

II

THE WORD

CHAPTER 2

The Marxian Faith

Communists believe there exists one method, one tool, one key which opens to man the riddles of human life—and one alone. Its awkward name is Dialectical Materialism. However intelligent and knowledgeable men may be, unless they possess and use this key all intelligence and all other knowledge avail nothing. With it one may, provided his thought and will are strong, discern the "curve of history"—always and everywhere conditioned by economic forces—and thus be able to fit himself meaningfully into his destiny. Without it, all is sound and fury, signifying nothing. No dedication to high ideals, no love of man for his fellow man can take its place or change its working.

Karl Marx, the father of Dialectical Materialism, was none too exact in defining its basic features. Since his time Communists and non-Communists alike have compounded the original confusion until today the experts disagree and most others shrug and ignore it—or have never heard of it. Disagreement among the experts, probably inevitable, is not too serious. But that an elementary understanding of this concept is almost wholly lacking among average citizens is not only deplorable, it is dangerous, and may be fatal. However much the Western world in general, and Americans in particular, may wish to the Devil the whole business of Communist ideology the fact remains that it shapes a large part of the world today and indirectly influences the rest. The leaders of Communist Russia, unlike their counterparts in the non-Communist world, study deeply and know thoroughly the philosophy which underlies their way of life, and they scru-

pulously and strictly apply it. From time to time, it is true, interpretations vary; but the principle holds even when interpretations differ.

Superimposed on our ignorance of Dialectical Materialism is a careless and casual subscription to broad, and often untrue or only partly true, generalizations on the Russian world. One of these generalizations is that Communism is a religion. From here it is easy and fairly common to form superficial judgments as to what are the proper reactions and counterdevelopments. All too often, as a consequence, they turn out to be not proper at all, and the world scene becomes more unclear and perplexing.

The following expositions seek to answer, simply and yet accurately, these questions: Is Communism a religion? And, what is Dialectical Materialism?

The author of the first selection is Michael T. Florinsky, internationally known scholar whose understanding and integrity are universally acknowledged. The selection is taken from his WORLD REVOLUTION AND THE U.S.S.R.

FROM

Michael T. Florinsky
WORLD REVOLUTION AND THE U.S.S.R.

THE bewildering spectacle of Holy Russia suddenly embracing the materialistic teaching of Marx and the missionary zeal which undoubtedly animates many of the disciples of Lenin has lead numerous authors writing on Soviet conditions to describe communism as a religion. This statement, like so many other broad generalizations, may be either true or misleading: it all depends on the exact meaning which we choose to give to the word religion. The assertion itself is usually based on a rather unwarranted assumption that, hitherto, the Russian people have always been devout adherents of the Greek Orthodox Church. It seems extremely doubtful whether this statement could be adequately proved, and the remarkable ease with which the Soviet Government succeeded [in its early years] in stamping out religious practices within the borders of the U.S.S.R. would suggest the necessity of greater caution than is displayed by most writers when pronouncing upon the religious feelings of both Russia's peasantry and Russia's educated classes.

If we use religion in the ordinary sense of the term, meaning "human recognition of superhuman controlling power, and especially of a personal God entitled to obedience and the effect of such recognition on conduct and mental attitude," to quote the definition of the Oxford Dictionary, it will appear at once that the comparison is not valid. The communist teaching is primarily a materialistic doctrine from which any idea of superhuman control or, much more, of a personal God is rigidly excluded and, indeed, branded as vulgar superstition. The sphere of action of communism ends where the real sphere of religion begins; at that mysterious but inevitable boundary which every human being has to cross, that line which separates our earthly existence from what is beyond. Communism can win the sincere and wholehearted support of multitudes by promising them a better existence, one from which the inequality, misery, unhappiness, and debasement which we find everywhere in the capitalist world will be eliminated. But it can do nothing to meet that irresistible urge which has it in its power to bring men and women willingly to abandon the comforts, satisfactions, and joys of this world in order to achieve what they believe to be eternal salvation. The materialistic doctrine of Marx and Lenin and the teaching of the churches appeal therefore to entirely different human emotions; and in this deeper and more fundamental aspect the two have nothing in common.

Viewed, however, from a different angle and in its more superficial aspects, the comparison of communism with religion is both justifiable and useful. Like most intellectual movements with a broad social appeal, especially movements controlled by small but well-organized groups with large means at their disposal, the Russian Communist Party has been eminently successful in spreading its teaching and inspiring at least some of its followers with a missionary zeal which compares not unfavorably with that of the early Christians. It displayed a militant spirit and an intolerance towards all who did not share its gospel which will compare with the most outstanding examples offered by religious struggles. It chastised the heretics in its ranks with a ruthless savagery which may be likened, without fear of exaggeration, to that of the Roman Inquisition, although here again the ultimate motives are very different: In disposing of the undesirable and erring members of the Party, communists are concerned with the advancement of their purely secular purposes, while the ultimate aim of the Inquisition was the salvation of the souls of the very men and women they sent to the stake. Like the monastic orders, the Russian Communist Party seeks to impose upon its members a severe discipline with a view to controlling not only their behavior but also their way of thinking. In all these respects, no doubt, communism and religion have a great deal in common. But this would be largely true of any popular social movement, as, for instance, to take a familiar example, that of Prohibition in the United States.

There is, however, one aspect of the present situation in the Soviet Union which seems to indicate a particularly close kinship between communism and religion. This is a truly religious cult which has grown up, and which now enshrines the memory and work of Lenin, the great leader of the Bolshevik revolution. It would be dangerous to draw definite conclusions from those lone lines of people who wait for hours to file by his tomb in the Red Square. There is no way of determining whether the motives of these communist pilgrims are similar to those of Russian peasants of pre-revolution days who journeyed hundreds of miles to visit a holy icon in an ancient monastery, or whether the psychology involved is more like that of some contemporary crowd in New York or London which maintains a long vigil and endures great discomfort to obtain a glimpse of Charlie Chaplin, Greta Garbo, or some heavyweight champion of the world. One must remember that there are no movie stars in U.S.S.R., and that the life of the ordinary Soviet citizen is very drab.

But if the popular attitude toward the memory of Lenin and its outward manifestations are open to more than one interpretation, there can be no question as to the supreme authority with which his writings have been clothed by the intellectual leaders of the communist movement. Strange as this may appear to anyone who is at all familiar with the Marxian dialectics, the great controversy over the question of world revolution, like all other discussions in the Soviet Union, turns largely on the interpretations of the pronouncements of the Master. The speeches and writings of the Soviet leaders bristle with quotations from Lenin. Every scrap of his work is collected, studied, annotated, and published with a zeal truly religious by a staff of learned experts of the Lenin Institute in Leningrad. The whole spirit as well as the external form of the discussions is clearly theological; and it is imbued with that intolerance and bitterness which is characteristic of disputes over religious dogmas. The proof of something is the fact that Lenin held that particular view. To be convicted of misrepresenting his opinions is to be convicted of heresy with all its inescapable consequences. It is never suggested in a communist discussion that Lenin might have made a mistake, or failed to foresee some future development. His writings are the source of all inspiration; they supply the only reliable guide in any new political situation. He supersedes Marx and Engels as the prophet of the modern world and of the world to come. He is the sole and only Fountain of Truth.

Florinsky does not include Stalin in this section because, at the time of its writing, the Stalin Cult had not yet developed. As it turns out, however, the omission is unimportant, for since Stalin's death Communist leaders have made a special effort to de-emphasize the Stalin "myth" and to speak again of Marxism-Leninism. Further reference to this is made below, in Chapter 6.

In the following section excerpts from the works of two students of Communist thought are used. Sir John Maynard, whose careful scholarship and penetrating insights have won the admiration even of those who disagree with his conclusions, answers the question, what is Dialectical Materialism? This answer, as here given, is from his RUSSIA IN FLUX. *Inter-*

spersed between parts of his answer is a clear account of the place of the human mind in the working out of man's history, as Marxian theory views it. The author of this account is Professor G. D. H. Cole, Chichele Professor of Social and Political Theory in the University of Oxford. It is from his WHAT MARX REALLY MEANT.

FROM

Sir John Maynard
RUSSIA IN FLUX

THE Hebrew prophets proclaimed a vision of history and of its inevitable continuation into the future. There was in Karl Marx something of the passion for justice which inspired their utterances. But he was more than a Prophet, because he initiated the world into his method. He claimed to be scientific where the Hebrew Prophets claimed to have a revelation, and to show how Man could carry the work of Prophecy further, and play a part in its realization.

Earlier Socialists had for the most part depicted the desirable, and had assumed that the idea of the desirable would win its way to acceptance, and reform the world according to its own image. They had not asked for the help of history to tell them what conditions were in the process of development, and there-fore actually capable of realization. Marx called his own Socialism scientific, and the earlier Socialism Utopian, because he made a new departure in this respect. *He plotted the curve* of history, as mathematicians say, and his prophecy was its continuation. Whether the curve was correctly or incorrectly plotted can only be decided by the event.

It is this plotting of the curve of history that is the essence of the Marxian method. And the method is more important than any of the results so far attained by it. For, without the method, prophecy degenerates into dogma, and, if right, is only right by accident or by inspiration. With the method, if it be sound, there is a vista of further results, ascertaining, perhaps controlling, the evolution of human society. They may even contradict Marx himself, as the Hegelian dialectic, in the hands of the young Hegelians, ultimately contradicted Hegel.

But there can be no plotting of the curve of history without the assumption that history follows laws of its own. At the back of the Marxian method lies this assumption. It adopts from the biological sciences the conception of evolution, and applies it to the life of human societies. History, in the sense of the activity of social man, enters the domain of law and becomes the subject of scientific investigation. Accidents, in the sense of events which have historic consequences but no historic cause (earthquakes, for instance) may deflect its course. Great personalities are accidents, but the field in which they operate has been prepared by history, and is not accidental. Just as we have to assume, for working purposes, that the order of nature continues unchanged, so it is assumed that the "accidents" will not suffice to disturb more than temporarily the working of the laws of history, and that the curve of human affairs can be plotted. But, as an Einstein arose to enlarge the work of a Newton, so some later thinker may teach us that the curve is to be plotted otherwise than Marx plotted it. Neither Marx nor Engels fancied that they had completed their own theory: any more than the theory of the origin of species had been completed by Darwin.

In plotting his curve, Marx went back to a very ancient theory of the universe. He accepted the doctrine that all things are permanently in flux, always in a state of becoming, that every form contains in itself the germ of its own destruction, but that the destruction is only the birth of a new form, which in turn must be destroyed and give place to a newer. This doctrine that all things are in flux he extended to the forms of social life. It is evident that we ought to change our metaphor and, instead of the plotting of a curve speak rather of observing a stream of historical tendency, and of tracking it where the natural configuration of the country suggests that it must flow; but the nature of the soil offers possibilities of erosion and avulsion, which may modify its course, and sudden alterations of level may quicken it into a destructive torrent.

Behind all this there is a philosophy, going down to the very roots of being and of thought: but Marx and Engels never formulated such a philosophy in separate form. Their followers and commentators have done it for them (as they have done much else): but there is no doubt of its general character. One group of philosophers puts the idea before the thing. Philosophies of the great Religions, at all events of all the Religions which postulate a Divine Creator of the Universe, inevitably put the idea before the thing. Another group puts the thing before the idea, existence before consciousness. Hegel, of whom Marx in his early days was a worshipper, and whom he never ceased to admire even when he had, in his own language, turned him upside down, conceived that there was a logical idea at the basis of life, and that this logical idea developed itself progressively, and was the cause of all change, as a theologian might speak of a power within us, not ourselves, that makes for righteousness. The mature Marx rejected this pre-existent or co-existent idea, and substituted, as a cause of growth and change, social facts of an entirely different order, arising out of social life and social relations, and having no mystical character.

We are now prepared to consider what we mean by Dialectical Materialism. It owes a sad grudge to its godparents for a name wholly unintelligible to most of us and of doubtful intelligibility to all. . . . It does not mean that History is mechanistic, but rather that it is to be treated as a branch of Biology. The present writer takes the materialism of Marx to consist primarily in the fact that he belonged to the group of philosophers who put the thing before the thought, who did not believe in the mystical pre-existence of the idea, who believed that thought grew out of a particular form of motion in matter, that there was no Divine Creator who "thought" of the universe before it came into existence. It is materialism, secondarily, because it explains social life in terms of economic relations. In the Marxian view, history is, in the final resort, always to be explained by the social relations arising out of material production: though the connection of these relations with the fact is frequently obscured by a layer of intermediate causation.

Now Professor Cole, in his WHAT MARX REALLY MEANT, *speaks of the place, in the operation of history, of man's mind and will.*

FROM

G. D. H. Cole

WHAT MARX REALLY MEANT

MARX'S so-called materialism, which was in fact Realism, upheld actual mind equally with actual matter against the Absolute which was greedy to engulf them both. He did not pose the question of mind [versus] matter at all, because he conceived it to be wholly without meaning for the world of men. For in the world of men and things, mind and matter are so interpenetrated and at one that it is futile to ask which counts for more. Mind cannot exist save in the material substance of the brain, or receive impressions save through the material avenues of the sense-organs; and the material objects external to man amid which he lives and works, from the soil itself to the steam-engine and the electrical generator, owe their form in nature and productive power so largely to man's activity as to be essentially products of mind, constantly evolving and changing under the influence of man's inventive power.

When therefore we speak, in Marxian terms, of "the powers of production" as the fundamental forces responsible for social evolution, the phrase has no meaning unless it applies not only to the natural forces which are at man's disposal, but also to the artificial forces which men have made by their use, and not only to all these forces, natural and artificial, taken together, but also to men's knowledge of how to apply them. The Realist Conception of History is so far from representing men as merely the sport of things that it stresses more than any other theory the creative function of men in making the world after the pattern of their own knowledge. The outcome of the Realist Conception is not to dethrone the mind of man, but on the contrary to assert that men make their own history against those who hold that

God or the Absolute make it for them, or that the whole course of human events is no more than a stream of undirected chance.

Men make their own history; but they make it primarily in the economic sphere. The great history-makers are those who by invention or experiment, or by enlarging the boundaries of human knowledge, alter the character of the powers of production, and therewith the ways in which men get their living and organize themselves for economic ends, or those who by destroying civilizations and sweeping away the works and knowledge accumulated by generations of toil and experiment drive men back to painful new beginnings of economic and cultural activity. This is not to say that the dominant role in history belongs to great scientists and to inventors on the one hand and to great captains of destruction on the other; . . . Emphatically, "the great man" theory of history does not hold good: but to deny its validity is not to deny that great men do count for both good and ill. There is no warrant for the view that the Russian Revolution would have followed the same course without Lenin, or the French Revolution without Napoleon, or that someone else would have been bound to hit on just the same inventions as Watt and Siemens and Marconi at just the same time even if these particular individuals had not been born.

Great men do count; but they count because their greatness fits in with the opportunities of their time. What forms world history above all else is the continual interaction between what is given to men as their social inheritance, natural or acquired, and the minds of men in each generation.

In considering how men's social heritage acts upon them, and how men act upon it, in any particular epoch, it is irrelevant how much of this heritage is natural and how much the product of the activity of earlier generations of men.

This view of history does not, as many people appear to suppose, imply any sort of fatalism. It does not say that, given a certain objective situation *apart from the human beings who have to handle it*, there is only one possible outcome, so the next phase of human history is utterly predestined however human beings may behave. It does insist that, as history is a chain of connective development, the next phase must be of such a nature that it can be developed out of its predecessor, and that men's power of influencing the course of history is limited to a choice between alternatives which are possible in the face of the objective situation.

Marxism is deterministic, but not fatalistic. No one who reads Marx's political writings, or his elaborate plannings of Socialist strategy, can reasonably suppose that he considered the victory of Socialism to be predestined as to both time and place, and the behavior of men in the objective situations which faced them to be limited to an inevitable reaction to economic circumstances. He clearly held that it made a quite vitally significant difference to the prospects of Socialism how Socialists behaved, and that their behavior was capable of being influenced by instruction and exhortation and example.

Maynard then picks up where he left off:

This is why Dialectical Materialism is Materialistic. Why is it Dialectical? We must expel from our minds all associations of the word with local variations of language, and get back to its original significance of the art of discussion, of conversation and dispute, of the interchange of arguments, where A takes one view, B takes another, and finally, if they are reasonable people not too wedded to their preconceived opinions, they agree on something which is not precisely what either of them said at the beginning of the discussion. The Dialectic may thus be conceived as consisting of a statement, and a contradictory statement, and a third statement which reconciles or embodies the other two. Let us now remember that in the view of Marx, to which he succeeded as the heir of a long line going back to the Greek Heraclitus, nothing is static, all things are in flux, in process of becoming. In such conditions a simple Yes or No is not the answer to any question. Yes is still true, while No is becoming true, and No is already passing into something that is neither Yes nor No. The Dialectic is a syllogism of a growing and a changing world, where truth also is a rushing river. He who argues dialectically must travel with that river, not stand on its bank and observe it as a stationary phenomenon.

Mr. H. G. Wells, little as he likes the Marxian doctrine, gives us precisely the appropriate metaphor in his autobiography, when he speaks of "running as hard as I can by the side of the marching facts, and pointing to them." We see him, in the light of this metaphor, as an enthusiastic collegian running by the side of his college boat, along the towpath of time, and pointing out from moment to moment how B gains on A, until C comes up from behind and successfully bumps B. At each moment his bulletin of information is correct, and at each moment it is contradicted and made untrue by the next phase of the eternal spectacle, fulfilling perhaps what the intelligent amateur has foreseen of the temporary issue. This is just what happens to the user of the dialectical method.

* * * * *

As the conversation, which gives its name to the dialectic, proceeded by statement, counter-statement, and agreement upon a third statement, which reconciled or included the other two, so the dialectic is conceived as proceeding, in this eternally changing universe, by thesis, antithesis and synthesis: each synthesis serving in turn for a new phase in a further similar process. Each successive phase in the process contains in itself a contradiction which must ultimately destroy it, and cause it to give place to the new phase. It is the disruptive force of the eternally repeated contradiction which makes the world and makes its history. If I may be pardoned for adding yet another metaphor to those which I have already ventured to employ, a contradiction is the force which produces the explosion and the series of explosions is the motive power which impels the machine. Thus if we consider, for a moment from the Marxian standpoint, that particular balance of economic forces known as the Capitalistic system, we see that, as the result of an earlier dialectical process, it superseded the Feudal system, because it provided an immensely greater range of economic satisfactions to man. No sooner has it done so, than internal contradiction begins to make itself apparent. The Capitalist system, as Marx sees it, is increasingly unable to find markets for its own products at prices profitable to itself, is compelled to restrict production, and becomes a fetter upon the growth of wealth. It therefore perishes and gives place to a new synthesis, that of Socialism, which does not need to demand a separate profit in each portion of the field of production, so long as outgoings are balanced by incomings over the field taken as a whole.

Truth itself is not something absolute or static. It is a perpetually shifting goal, to be approached only by successive approximations, each of which requires to be verified by practice.

In the particular example taken, the new synthesis, of Socialism, is not an automatic product of self-determining forces, independent of the will and action of man. There must be a concurrent activity of thought, feeling, and will, and Man must, so to speak, bring himself into the balance, in order to determine the result. The Capitalists and their supporters may prefer a smaller output of wealth for society as a whole, in consideration of retaining a larger share of it, and a dominating position for themselves. They may make a fight for it, with the help of the tremendous machinery of modern warfare, and defy the less-well organized majority. In short, they may make the synthesis something other than Socialism, and may be successful in the making of the alternative, if the conditions are right for their success. This is where the power of man to make his own history comes into the dialectical process. He has that power, but it is not an absolute power, because he can only win that for which the course of history has prepared the conditions. The Capitalist's victory will be only a temporary set-back if a system other than the capitalistic one is the one which fits the conditions of the time and gives the greater scope for the development of the productive forces.

If we assume, for the moment, that Socialism is the synthesis, and that, as a further development of the dialectical process, a classless society, which is a Marxian aim, is attained, we are not to infer that this is the end of the process. It was not the affair of Karl Marx or of Friedrich Engels to follow the future of man beyond the termination of his economic antagonisms. Their purview extends to the attainment of the social constitution which gives scope to the forces of production, and their task ends there. But the dialectical process continues to infinity in the development of human personality. Set at liberty from economic pre-occupations man has set before him a limitless future, which it is for the eyes of others to explore. As Lenin put it, the immanent contradictions will remain, and their continuance is a necessary pre-supposition of further development. The whole of history is nothing but the progressive transformation of human nature, first unconscious and afterwards conscious. . . .

But this is not the point which concerns us at the moment. I have tried to convey my notion of what is meant by Dialectical Materialism. The operator—for he is more than an investigator —proceeding with the assistance of the dialectical method seeks to foretell the historical process by using economic relations as his clue through the darkness of the labyrinth, and by observing the internal contradictions whose function it is to produce a new phase by the destruction of the old: and he seeks to complete the process according to his own aim. Human will (it is human will conditioned by economic relations and environment) is one of the factors in the production of change; but only one of them.

Such is the method, which might be described as a method of induction assisted by certain special clues and accompanied by effort.

This then, is the Marxist faith—that Dialectical Materialism is the key, the only key, to unlocking the door to an understanding of human history and human destiny. From this faith certain basic doctrines have developed to which attention must now be turned.

CHAPTER 3

Marxian Doctrines

The basic Marxian doctrines deal with these developments: a decline of the landed aristocracy; the rise and dictatorship of the bourgeoisie; the rise of the proletariat; class warfare between the bourgeoisie and the proletariat; the proletarian revolution; the dictatorship of the the proletariat; the coming of the classless society; the consequent "withering away" of the state. Marxism holds that the key of Dialectical Materialism permits the above stages of human societal evolution to be discerned and prepared for.

For exposition of these doctrines no better sources are available than the words of the two founders and the two chief developers of the Marxist system of thought: Karl Marx, Friedrich Engels, N. Lenin, and J. Stalin. Consequently this section is taken from their work. The first selection, which takes us down to the last three of the phases listed above, is from the famous COMMUNIST MANIFESTO, *composed by Marx and Engels in February, 1848. The second excerpt is from Stalin's* LENINISM, *and the third from Lenin's* STATE AND REVOLUTION.

FROM

Marx and Engels
COMMUNIST MANIFESTO

THE history of all hitherto existing society is the history of class struggles.

Free man and slave, patrician and plebeian, lord and serf,

guild-master and journeyman, in a word, oppressor and oppressed, stood in constant opposition to each other, carried on an uninterrupted, now hidden, now open fight, a fight which each time ended, either in a revolutionary reconstitution of society at large, or in the common ruin of the contending classes.

In the earlier epochs of history we find almost everywhere a complicated arrangement of society into various orders, a manifold gradation of social rank. In ancient Rome we have patricians, knights, plebeians, slaves; in the Middle Ages, feudal lords, vassals, guild-masters, journeymen, apprentices, serfs; in almost all of these classes, again, subordinate gradations.

The modern bourgeoisie society that has sprouted from the ruins of feudal society has not done away with class antagonisms. It has but established new classes, new conditions of oppression, new forms of struggle in place of the older ones.

Our epoch, the epoch of the bourgeoisie, possesses, however, this distinctive feature: it has simplified the class antagonisms. Society as a whole is more and more splitting up into two great hostile camps, into two great classes directly facing each other—bourgeoisie and proletariat.

From the serfs of the Middle Ages sprang the chartered burghers of the earliest towns. From these burgesses the first elements of the bourgeoisie were developed.

The discovery of America, the rounding of the Cape, opened up fresh ground for the rising bourgeoisie. The East Indian and Chinese markets, the colonization of America, trade with the colonies, the increase in the means of exchange and in commodities generally, gave to commerce, to navigation, to industry, an impulse never before known, and thereby, to the revolutionary element in the tottering feudal society, a rapid development.

The feudal system of industry, in which industrial production was monopolized by closed guilds, now no longer sufficed for the growing wants of the new markets. The manufacturing system took its place. The guild-masters were pushed aside by the manufacturing middle class; division of labor between the different corporate guilds vanished in the face of division of labor in each single workshop.

Modern industry has established the world market, for which the discovery of America paved the way. This market has given an immense development to commerce, to navigation, to communication by land. This development has, in its turn, reacted on the extension of industry; and in proportion as industry, commerce, navigation, railways extended, in the same proportion the bourgeoisie developed, increased its capital, and pushed into the background every class handed down from the Middle Ages.

We see, therefore, how the modern bourgeoisie is itself the product of a long course of development, of a series of revolutions in the modes of production and exchange.

Each step in the development of the bourgeoisie was accompanied by a corresponding political advance of that class. An oppressed class under the sway of the feudal nobility and armed in self-governing association in a medieval commune, here independent urban republic as in Italy and Germany, there taxable third estate of the monarchy as in France, afterwards in the period of manufacture proper serving either the semi-feudal or the absolute monarchy as a counterpoise against the nobility and, in fact, cornerstone of the great monarchies in general, the bourgeoisie has at last since the establishment of modern industry and of the world market, conquered for itself in the modern representative state exclusive political sway. The executive of the modern state is but a committee for managing the common affairs of the whole bourgeoisie.

The bourgeoisie, historically, has played a most revolutionary part.

The bourgeoisie, wherever it has gotten the upper hand, has put an end to all feudal, patriarchal, idyllic relations. It has pitilessly torn asunder the motley feudal ties that bound a man to his "natural superiors" and has left no other nexus between man and man than naked self-interest and callous "cash payment." It has drowned the most heavenly ecstasies of religious fervour, of chivalrous enthusiasm, of Philistine sentimentalism, in the icy water of egotistical calculation. It has resolved personal worth into exchange value, and in place of the numberless indefeasible chartered freedoms, has set up that single unconscionable freedom—Free Trade. In one word, for exploitation, veiled by religious and political illusions, it has substituted naked, shameless, direct, brutal exploitation.

The bourgeoisie has stripped of its halo every occupation hitherto honored and looked up to with reverent awe. It has converted the physician, the lawyer, the priest, the poet, the man of science, into its paid wage laborers.

The bourgeoisie has torn away from the family its sentimental veil, and has reduced the family relation to a mere money relation.

The bourgeoisie has disclosed how it came to pass that the brutal display of vigor in the Middle Ages, which reactionaries so much admire, found its fitting complement in the most slothful indolence. It has been the first to show what man's activity can bring about. It has accomplished wonders far surpassing Egyptian pyramids, Roman aqueducts, and Gothic cathedrals; it has conducted expeditions that put in the shade all former exoduses of nations and crusades.

The bourgeoisie cannot exist without constantly revolutionizing the instruments of production, and thereby the relations of production, and with them the whole relations of society. Conservation of the old modes of production in unaltered form, was, on the contrary, the first condition of existence for all earlier industrial classes. Constant revolutionizing of production, uninterrupted disturbance of all social conditions, everlasting uncertainty and agitation distinguish the bourgeois epoch from all earlier ones. All fixed, fast, frozen relations, with their train of ancient and venerable prejudices and opinions, are swept away. All new-formed ones become antiquated before they can ossify. All that is solid melts into air, all that is holy is profane, and man is at last compelled to face with sober senses his real conditions of life and his relations with his kind.

The need of a constantly expanding market for its products chases the bourgeoisie over the whole surface of the globe. It must nestle everywhere, establish connections everywhere.

The bourgeoisie has through its exploitation of the world market given a cosmopolitan character to production and consumption in every country. To the great chagrin of reactionaries, it has drawn from under the feet of industry the national ground on which it stood. All old-established national industries have been destroyed or are daily being destroyed. They are dislodged by new industries, whose introduction becomes a life and death question for all civilized nations, by industries that no longer work up indigenous raw material, but raw material drawn from the remotest zones; industries whose products are consumed, not only at home, but in every quarter of the globe. In place of the old wants, satisfied by the production of the country we find new wants, requiring for their satisfaction the products of distant lands and climes. In place of the old local and national seclusion and self-sufficiency, we have intercourse in every direction, universal inter-dependence of nations. And as in material, so also in intellectual production. The intellectual creations of individual nations become common property. National one-sidedness and narrow-mindedness become more and more impossible, and from the numerous national and local literatures there arises a world literature.

The bourgeoisie, by the rapid improvement of all instruments of production, by the immensely facilitated means of communication, draws all, even the most barbarian, nations into civilization. The cheap prices of its commodities are the heavy artillery with which it batters down all Chinese walls, with which it forces the barbarians' intensely obstinate hatred of foreigners to capitulate. It compels all nations, on pain of extinction, to adopt the bourgeoisie mode of production; it compels them to introduce what it calls civilization into their midst, i.e., to become bourgeoisie themselves. In one word, it creates a world after its own image.

The bourgeoisie has subjected the country to the rule of the towns, it has created enormous cities, it has greatly increased the urban population as compared with the rural, and has thus rescued a considerable part of the population from the idiocy of rural life. Just as it has made the country dependent on the towns, so it has made barbarian and semi-barbarian countries dependent on the civilized ones, nations of peasants on nations of bourgeoisie, the East on the West. It has agglomerated population, centralized means of production, and has concentrated property in a few hands. The necessary consequence of this was political centralization. Independent or but loosely connected provinces, with separate interests, laws, governments, and systems of taxation, became lumped together into one nation, with one government, one code of laws, one national class interest, one frontier and one customs tariff.

The bourgeoisie, during its rule of scarce one hundred years, has created more massive and more colossal productive forces than all preceding generations together. Subjection of nature's forces to man, machinery, application of chemistry to industry and agriculture, steam navigation, railways, electric telegraphs, clearing of whole continents for cultivation, canalisation of rivers, whole populations conjured out of the ground—what earlier century had even a presentiment that such productive forces slumbered in the lap of social labor?

We see then: the means of production and of exchange, on whose foundation the bourgeoisie built itself up, were generated in feudal society. At a certain stage in the development of these means of production and exchange, the conditions under which feudal society produced and exchanged, the feudal organization of agriculture and manufacturing industry, in one word, the feudal relations of property became no longer compatible with the already developed productive forces; they became so many fetters. They had to be burst asunder; they were burst asunder.

In their place stepped free competition, accompanied by a social and political constitution adapted to it, and by the economic and political sway of the bourgeoisie class.

A similar movement is going on before our own eyes. Modern bourgeoisie society with its relations of production, of exchange and of property, a society that has conjured up such gigantic means of production and of exchange is like a sorcerer who is no longer able to control the powers of a nether world whom he has called up by his spells. For many a decade past the history of industry and commerce is but the history of the revolt of modern productive forces against modern conditions of production, against the property relations that are the conditions for the existence of the bourgeoisie and of its rule. It is enough to mention the commercial crises that by their periodic return put the existence of the entire bourgeoisie society on its trial, each time more threateningly. In these crises a great part, not only of the existing product, but also of the previously created productive forces, are periodically destroyed. In these crises there breaks out an epidemic that, in all earlier epochs, would have seemed an absurdity—the epidemic of over-production. Society suddenly finds itself put back into a state of momentary barbarism; it appears as if a famine, a universal war of devastation had cut off the supply of every means of subsistence; industry and commerce seem to be destroyed. And why? Because there is too much civilization, too much means of subsistence, too much industry, too much commerce. The productive forces at the disposal of society no longer tend to further the development of the conditions of bourgeoisie property; on the contrary they have become too powerful for these conditions, by which they are fettered, and so soon as they overcome these fetters, they bring disorder into the whole of bourgeois society, endanger the existence of bourgeois property. The conditions of bourgeoisie society are too narrow to comprise the wealth created by them. And how does the bourgeoisie get over these crises? On the one hand, by enforced destruction of a mass of productive forces; on the other, by the conquest of new markets, and by the more thorough exploitation of the old ones. That is to say, by paving the way for more extensive and more destructive crises, and by diminishing the means whereby crises are prevented.

The weapons with which the bourgeoisie felled feudalism to the ground are now turned against the bourgeoisie itself.

But not only has the bourgeoisie forged the weapons that bring death to itself; it has also called into existence the men who are to wield those weapons—the modern working class—the proletarians.

In proportion as the bourgeoisie, i.e., capital, is developed, in the same proportion is the proletariat, the modern working class, developed—a class of laborers, who live only so long as they find work, and who find work only so long as their labor increases capital. These laborers, who must sell themselves piecemeal, are a commodity and consequently exposed to all the vicissitudes of competition, to all the fluctuations of the market.

Owing to the extensive use of machinery and to the division

of labor, the work of the proletarians has lost all individual character, and, consequently, all charm for the workman. He becomes an appendage of the machine, and it is only the most simple, most monotonous, and most easily acquired knack, that is required of him. Hence, the cost of production of a workman is restricted, almost entirely, to the means of subsistence that he requires for his maintenance, and for the propagation of his race. But the price of a commodity, and therefore also of labor, is equal to its cost of production. In proportion, therefore, as the repulsiveness of the work increases, the wage decreases. Nay, more, in proportion as the uses of machinery and division of labor increases, in the same proportion the burden of toil also increases, whether by prolongation of the working hours, by increase of the work exacted in a given time, or by increased speed of the machinery, etc.

Modern industry has converted the little workshop of the patriarchal master into the great factory of the industrial capitalist. Masses of laborers, crowded into the factory, are organized like soldiers. As privates of the industrial army they are placed under the command of a perfect hierarchy of officers and sergeants. Not only are they slaves of the bourgeoisie class, and of the bourgeoisie state; they are daily and hourly enslaved by the machine, by the overlooker, and above all, by the individual bourgeoisie manufacturer himself.

*   *   *   *   *

The lower strata of the middle class—the small tradespeople, shopkeepers, and retired tradesmen generally, the handicraftsmen and peasants—all these sink gradually into the proletariat, partly because their diminutive capital does not suffice for the scale on which modern industry is carried on, and is swamped with the competition with the large capitalists, partly because their specialized skill is rendered worthless by new methods of production. Thus the proletariat is recruited from all classes of the population.

The proletariat goes though various stages of development. With its birth begins its struggle with the bourgeoisie. At first the contest is carried on by individual laborers, then by the work of people in a factory, then by the operatives of one trade, in one locality, against the individual bourgeois who directly exploits them. They direct their attacks not against the bourgeois conditions of production, but against the instruments of production themselves; they destroy imported wares that compete with their labor, they smash to pieces machinery, they set factories ablaze, they seek to restore by force the vanished status of the workmen of the Middle Ages.

At this stage the laborers still form an incoherent mass scattered over the whole country, and broken up by their mutual competition. If anywhere they unite to form more compact bodies, this is not yet the consequence of their own active union, but of the union of the bourgeoisie, which class, in order to attain its own political ends, is compelled to set the whole proletariat in motion, and is moreover yet, for a time, able to do so. At this stage, therefore, the proletarians do not fight their enemies, but the enemies of their enemies, the remnants of absolute monarchy, the landowners, the non-industrial bourgeoisie, the petty bourgeoisie. Thus the whole historical movement is concentrated in the hands of the bourgeoisie; every victory so obtained is a victory of the bourgeoisie.

But with the development of industry the proletariat not only increases in number; it becomes concentrated in greater masses, its strength grows, and it feels that strength more. The various interests and conditions of life within the ranks of the proletariat are more and more equalized, in proportion as machinery obliterates all distinctions of labor, and nearly everywhere reduces wages to the same low level. The growing competition among the bourgeoisie, and the resulting commercial crises, make the wages of the workers ever more fluctuating. The unceasing improvement of machinery, ever more rapidly developing, makes their livelihood more and more precarious; the collisions between individual workmen and individual bourgeoisie take more and more the character of collisions between two classes. Thereupon the workers begin to form combinations (trade unions) against the bourgeoisie; they club together in order to keep up the rate of wages; they found permanent associations in order to make provision beforehand for the occasional revolts. Here and there the contest breaks out into riots.

Now and then the workers are victorious, but only for a time. The real fruit of their battle lies, not in the immediate results, but in the ever expanding union of the workers. This union is helped on by the improved means of communication that are created by modern industry, and that place the workers of different localities in contact with another. It was just this contact that was needed to centralize the numerous local struggles, all of the same character, into one national struggle between classes. But every class struggle is a political struggle. And that union, to attain which the burghers of the Middle Ages, with their miserable highways, required centuries, the modern proletarians, thanks to railways, achieve in a few years.

This organization of the proletarians into a class, and consequently into a political party, is continually being upset again by the competition between the workers themselves. But it ever rises up again, stronger, firmer, mightier. . . .

Altogether, collisions between the classes of the old society further in many ways the course of development of the proletariat. At first with the aristocracy; later on, with those portions of the bourgeoisie itself, whose interests have become antagonistic to the progress of industry; at all times with the bourgeoisie of foreign countries. In all these battles it sees itself compelled to appeal to the proletariat with its own elements of political and general education, in other words, it furnishes the proletariat with weapons for fighting the bourgeoisie.

Further, as we have already seen, entire sections of the ruling classes are, by the advance of industry, precipitated into the proletariat, or at least threatened in their conditions of existence. These also supply the proletariat with fresh elements of enlightenment and progress.

Finally, in times when the class struggle nears the decisive hour, the process of dissolution going on within the ruling class, in fact within the whole range of old society, assumes such a violent, glaring character, that a small section of the ruling class cuts itself adrift, and joins the revolutionary class, the class that holds the future in its hands. Just as, therefore, at an earlier period, a section of the nobility went over to the bourgeoisie, so now a portion of the bourgeoisie goes over to the proletariat, and in particular, a portion of the bourgeois ideologists, who have raised themselves to the level of comprehending theoretically the historical movement as a whole.

Of all the classes that stand face to face with the bourgeoisie today, the proletariat alone is a really revolutionary class. The other classes decay and finally disappear in the face of modern industry; the proletariat is a special and essential product.

The lower middle class, the small manufacturer, the shopkeeper, the artisan, the peasant, all these fight against the bourgeoisie, to save from extinction their existence as fractions of the middle class. They are therefore not revolutionary, but conservative. Nay, more, they are reactionary, for they try to roll back the wheel of history. If by chance they are revolutionary, they are so only in view of their impending transfer into the proletariat; they thus desert not their present, but their future interests; they desert their own standpoint to place themselves at that of the proletariat.

The "dangerous class," the social scum, that passively rotting mass thrown off by the lowest layers of old society, may, here and there, be swept into the movement by a proletarian revolution; its conditions of life, however, prepare it far more for the part of a bribe tool of reactionary intrigue.

The conditions of the proletariat, those of old society at large, are already virtually swamped. The proletarian is without property; his relation to his wife and children has no longer anything in common with the bourgeoisie family relations; modern industrial labor, modern subjection to capital, the same in England as in France, in America as in Germany, has stripped him of every trace of national character. Law, morality, religion, are to him so many bourgeoisie prejudices, behind which lurk in ambush just as many bourgeoisie interests.

All the preceding classes that got the upper hand, sought to fortify their already acquired status by subjecting society at large to their conditions of appropriation. The proletarians cannot become masters of the productive forces of society, except by abolishing their own previous mode of appropriation, and thereby also every other previous mode of appropriation. They have nothing of their own to secure and to fortify; their mission is to destroy all previous securities for, and insurances of, individual property.

All previous historical movements were movements of minorities, or in the interests of minorities. The proletarian movement is the self-conscious, independent movement of an immense majority, in the interest of the immense majority. The proletariat, the lowest stratum of our present society, cannot stir, cannot raise itself up, without the whole superincumbent strata of official society being sprung into the air.

Though not in substance, yet in form, the struggle of the proletariat with the bourgeoisie is at first a national struggle. The proletariat of each country must, of course, first of all settle matters with its own bourgeoisie.

In depicting the most general phases of the development of the proletariat, we traced the more or less veiled civil war, raging within existing society, up to the point where that war breaks out into open revolution, and where the violent overthrow of the bourgeoisie lays the foundation for the sway of the proletariat.

Stalin now explains the nature of the proletarian revolution and the dictatorship of the proletariat. The reference to Kamenev is to one of the original Bolsheviks who mildly disputed leadership with Stalin after Lenin's death. He was subsequently "purged" by Stalin.

FROM

J. Stalin

LENINISM

What are the characteristic features that distinguish the proletarian revolution from the bourgeoisie revolution?

The differences between the two may be reduced to five basic points.

1. The bourgeois revolution usually begins when more or less finished forms of the capitalist order already exist, forms which have grown and ripened within the womb of feudal society prior to the open revolution; whereas the proletarian revolution begins at a time when finished forms of the socialist order are either absent, or almost completely absent.

2. The fundamental task of the bourgeoisie revolution reduces itself to seizing power and operating that power in conformity with the already existing bourgeoisie economy; whereas the main task of the proletarian revolution reduces itself to building up the new socialist economy after having seized power.

3. The bourgeois revolution is usually completed with the seizure of power; whereas for the proletarian revolution the seizure of power is only its *beginning*, while power is used as a lever for the transformation of the old economy and for the organization of the new one.

4. The bourgeois revolution limits itself to substituting one group of exploiters by another in the seat of power and therefore has no need to destroy the old state machine; whereas the proletarian revolution removes all groups of exploiters from power, and places in power the leader of all the toilers and exploited, the class of proletarians, and therefore it cannot avoid destroying the old state machine and replacing it by a new one.

5. The bourgeois revolution cannot for any length of time rally the millions of the toiling and exploited masses around the bourgeoisie, for the very reasons that they are toilers and exploited; whereas the proletarian revolution can and must link them up precisely as toilers and exploited in a durable alliance with the proletariat, if it wishes to carry out its fundamental task of consolidating the power of the proletariat and building the new socialistic economy.

Here are some of Lenin's fundamental postulates on the subject:

One of the basic differences between the bourgeois revolution and the socialist revolution . . . is that, in the case of the bourgeois revolution, which grows out of feudalism, the new economic organizations are gradually created within the womb of the old order, and by degrees modify all the aspects of feudal society. The bourgeois revolution had but one task to perform: to sweep away, to fling aside, to destroy all the fetters of the previous society. Fulfilling this task, every bourgeois revolution fulfills all that is demanded of it: it stimulates the growth of capitalism. But the socialist revolution is in an altogether different position. The more backward the country in which, thanks to the zigzag course of history, the socialist revolution has to be begun, the more difficult for it is the transition from the old capitalist relations to socialist relations. Here, to the tasks of destruction there are added new organizational tasks of unheard of difficulty. . . .

If the creative force of the masses, in the Russian revolution . . . which went through the great experience of the year 1905, had not created soviets already in February 1917, then these soviets could not under any circumstances have seized power in October, for success depended upon the existent organizational forms of a movement which embraced millions of people. The soviets were such a finished organizational form, and that is why the striking successes and triumphal procession that we experienced awaited us in the political field, for the new political form was already at hand, and all we had to do was by a few decrees transform the Soviet power from the embryonic condition in which it existed during the first months of the revolution, into the form legally recognized and confirmed in the Russian state—the Russian Soviet Republic. . . .

There still remained two tasks of enormous difficulty, the solution of which could, under no circumstances, be the same triumphal procession that our revolution was. . . .

First, there was the task of internal organization which faces every socialist revolution. The difference between the socialist revolution and the bourgeois revolution is precisely that, in the latter case, finished forms of capitalist relationships already exist, whereas the Soviet power, the proletarian power, does not get these relationships, if we leave out of account the most developed forms of capitalism which, as a matter of fact, embraced only a few peaks of industry and affected agriculture only to a very slight extent. The organization of accounting, the control over large-scale enterprises, the transformation of the whole state economic mechanism into a single great machine, into an economic organism which shall work in such a way that hundreds of millions of people shall be directed by a single plan, such is the tremendous organizational task which lay on our shoulders. Under the existing conditions of labor it under no circumstances allowed solution in the "hurrah" fashion in which we were able to solve the problems of the civil war. . . .

The second enormous difficulty was . . . the international question. If we were able to cope so easily with Kerensky's bands, if we so easily established our power, if the decree on the socialization of the land, and on worker's control, was secured without the slightest difficulty—if we obtained all this so easily it was only because for a brief space of time a fortunate combination of circumstances protected us from international imperialism. International imperialism, with all the might of its capital and its highly organized military technique, which represents a real force, a real fortress of international capital, could under no circumstances, under no possible conditions, live side by side with the Soviet Republic, both because of its objective situation and because of the economic interests of the capitalist class which was incorporated in it, could not do this because of commercial ties and of international financial relationships. A conflict is inevitable. This is the greatest difficulty of the Russian revolution, its greatest historical problem: the necessity to solve international problems, the necessity to call forth the world revolution.

Such is the inner character and the basic idea of the proletarian revolution.

Can such a radical transformation of the old bourgeois system of society be achieved without a violent revolution, without the dictatorship of the proletariat?

Obviously not. To think that such a revolution can be carried out peacefully within the framework of bourgeois democracy, which is adapted to the domination of the bourgeoisie, means one of two things. It means either madness, and the loss of normal human understanding, or else an open and gross repudiation of the proletarian revolution.

It is necessary to insist on this all the more strongly, all the more categorically, since we are dealing with a proletarian revolution which has for the time being triumphed in only one country, a country surrounded by hostile capitalist countries, a country the bourgeoisie of which cannot fail to receive the support of international capital.

That is why Lenin states that:

. . . the liberation of the oppressed class is impossible not only without a violent revolution, *but also without the destruction* of the apparatus of state power which was created by the ruling class. . . .

Let the majority of the population at first, while private property is still maintained, that is while the power and oppression of capital are maintained, declare itself for the party of the proletariat. Only then can it, and should it, take power. That is what is said by *petty-bourgeois democrats who call themselves "socialists" but are really the henchmen of the bourgeoisie.*

But we say: let the revolutionary proletariat first overthrow the bourgeoisie, break the yoke of capital, break up the bourgeois state apparatus. Then the victorious proletariat will speedily gain the sympathy and support of the majority of the toiling non-proletarian masses by satisfying their wants at the expense of the exploiters.

In order to win the majority of the population to its side the proletariat must first of all overthrow the bourgeoisie and seize state power and, secondly, it must introduce Soviet rule, smash to pieces the old state apparatus, and thus at one blow undermine the rule, authority and influence of the bourgeoisie and of the petty-bourgeoisie compromisers in the ranks of the non-proletarian toiling masses. Thirdly, the proletariat must *completely and finally destroy* the influence of the bourgeoisie and of the petty-bourgeoisie compromisers among the *majority* of the non-proletarian toiling masses by the *revolutionary* satisfaction of *their* economic needs *at the expense of the exploiters.*

Such are the characteristic symptoms of the proletarian revolution.

If it be admitted that the dictatorship of the proletariat is the basic content of the proletarian revolution, what then are the fundamental characteristics of the dictatorship of the proletariat?

Here is the most general definition of the dictatorship of the proletariat, given by Lenin:

The dictatorship of the proletariat is not the end of the class struggle but its continuation in new forms. The dictatorship of the proletariat is the class struggle of the proletariat which has achieved victory and has seized political power against the bourgeoisie who have been defeated but not annihilated, who have not disappeared, who have not ceased their resistance, who have increased their resistance.

Replying to those who confuse the dictatorship of the proletariat with "popular," "elected" and "non-class" government, Lenin states:

The class that has seized political power has done so conscious of the fact that it has seized power alone. This is implicit in the concept of the dictatorship of the proletariat. This concept has meaning only when one class knows that it alone takes political power into its own hands, and does not deceive either itself or others by talk about "popular, elected government, sanctified by the whole people."

This does not mean, however, that the rule of this one class, the class of the proletarians, which does not and cannot share this rule with any other class, does not need an alliance with the toiling and exploited masses of other classes for the attainment of its objectives. On the contrary, this rule, the rule of a single class, can be firmly established and exercised to the full only by means of a special form of alliance between the class of proletarians and the toiling masses of the petty-bourgeoisie classes, especially the toiling masses of the peasantry.

What is this special form of alliance? What does it consist of? Does not this alliance with the toiling masses of other, non-proletarian classes generally contradict the idea of the dictatorship of one class?

This special form of alliance lies in that the leading force of this alliance is the proletariat, that the leader in the state, the leader within the system of the dictatorship of the proletariat is *a single* party, the party of the proletariat, the party of the Communists, *which does not and cannot share* that leadership with other parties.

As you see, the contradiction is only apparent, a seeming one.

The dictatorship of the proletariat . . . is a *special form of class alliance* between the proletariat, the vanguard of the toilers, and the numerous non-proletarian strata of toilers (the petty bourgeoisie, the small masters, the peasantry, the intelligentsia, etc.), or the majority of these; it is an alliance against capital, an alliance aiming at the complete overthrow of capital, a complete suppression of the resistance of the bourgeoisie and at any attempt on their part at restoration, an alliance aiming at the final establishment and consolidation of socialism. It is a special type of alliance, which is being built up under special circumstances, namely, in the circumstances of furious Civil War; it is an alliance between the firm supporters of socialism and its wavering allies and sometimes "neutrals" (when the agreement to fight becomes an agreement to maintain neutrality). *It is an alliance between classes which differ economically, politically, socially and ideologically.*

In one of his instructional reports, Comrade Kamenev, disputing such a conception of the dictatorship of the proletariat, states: "the *dictatorship is not* an alliance between one class and another."

I believe that Comrade Kamenev had in view, above all, a passage in my pamphlet *The October Revolution and the Tactics of the Russian Communists*, where it is stated:

The dictatorship of the proletariat is not simply the governing upper stratum "cleverly" "selected" by the careful hand of an "experienced strategist," and "sensibly" relying on the support of one section or another of the population. The dictatorship of the proletariat is a class alliance between the proletariat and the toiling masses of the peasantry, for the purpose of overthrowing capital, for bringing about the final victory of socialism, an alliance based on the condition that its leading force is the proletariat.

I completely endorse this formulation of the dictatorship of the proletariat, for I think that it wholly and fully corresponds to Lenin's formulation, just quoted.

I maintain that Comrade Kamenev's declaration that "the *dictatorship is not* an alliance between one class and another," in the categorical form in which it is made, has nothing in common with the Leninist theory of the dictatorship of the proletariat.

I maintain that only those who have never understood the meaning of the bond, the idea of the alliance between the workers and the peasants, the idea of the *hegemony* of the proletariat within this alliance, can speak in such a fashion.

Such statements can only be made by those who have failed to grasp Lenin's thesis that:

Nothing but an agreement with the peasants can save the socialist revolution in Russia until the revolution has taken place in other countries.

Such statements can only be made by those who have failed to grasp Lenin's proposition that:

The supreme principle of the dictatorship is the preservation of the alliance between the proletariat and the peasantry, in order that the proletariat may continue to retain the leading role and state power.

Pointing to one of the most important aims of the dictatorship, namely, the suppression of the exploiters, Lenin states:

The scientific concept, dictatorship, means nothing more nor less than power that directly rests on violence, that is not limited by any laws or restricted by any absolute rules. . . . Dictatorship means [. . . .] unlimited power, resting on violence and not on law. During civil war, victorious power can only be dictatorship.

But, of course, the dictatorship of the proletariat does not merely mean violence, although there is no dictatorship without violence.

Dictatorship . . . does not mean violence alone, although it is impossible without violence. It likewise signifies a higher organization of labor than that which previously existed.

The dictatorship of the proletariat . . . is not merely the use of violence against the exploiters, and is not even mainly the use of violence. The economic basis of this revolutionary violence, the guarantee of its vitality and success, is that the proletariat represents and introduces a higher type of social organization of labor compared with capitalism. That is the essential point. This is the source of the strength of Communism and the guarantee of its inevitable complete victory.

Its quintessence (i.e., of the dictatorship—J. S.) lies in the organization and discipline of the advanced detachment of the toilers, of its vanguard, its sole leader, the proletariat. Its aim is to establish socialism, to put an end to the division of society and to classes, to make all members of society toilers, to remove the soil for the exploitation of man by man. This aim cannot be achieved at one stroke. It demands quite a protracted period of transition from capitalism to socialism, because the reorganization of production is a difficult matter, because time is needed for radical changes in all spheres of life, and because the enormous force of habit of petty-bourgeoisie and bourgeoisie management can be overcome only by a long stubborn struggle. That was why Marx spoke of a dictatorship of the proletariat as of a whole period, a period of transition from capitalism to socialism.

Such are the characteristic features of the dictatorship of the proletariat.

Hence there are three fundamental aspects of the dictatorship of the proletariat.

1. The utilization of the power of the proletariat for the suppression of the exploiters, for the defense of the country, for the consolidation of the ties with the proletarians of other lands, and for the development and the victory of the revolution in all countries.

2. The utilization of the power of the proletariat in order to detach the toiling and exploited masses once and for all from the bourgeoisie, to consolidate the alliance of the proletariat with these masses, to enlist these masses for the work of socialist construction, and to insure the state leadership of these masses by the proletariat.

3. The utilization of the power of the proletariat for the organization of socialism, for the abolition of classes, and for the transition to a society without classes, to a society without a state.

The dictatorship of the proletariat is a combination of all three aspects. None of these three aspects can be advanced as the *sole* characteristic feature of the dictatorship of the proletariat. On the other hand, it is sufficient for one of these three characteristic features to be lacking, for the dictatorship of the proletariat to cease being a dictatorship in a capitalist environment. Therefore not one of these three features can be omitted without running the risk of distorting the concept of the dictatorship of the proletariat. Only all these three features taken together give us a complete and fully rounded off concept of the dictatorship of the proletariat.

The dictatorship of the proletariat has its periods, its special forms, its diversified methods of work. During the period of civil war, the coercive aspect of the dictatorship is especially conspicuous. But it by no means follows from this that no constructive work is carried on during the period of civil war. The civil war itself cannot be waged without constructive work. On the other hand, during the period of socialist construction, organizational and cultural work of the dictatorship, revolutionary law, etc., are especially conspicuous. But here, again, it by no means follows that during the period of construction, the coercive side of the dictatorship has fallen away, or could do so. The organs of suppression, the army and other organizations, are as necessary now in the period of construction as they were during the civil war. Without these institutions, constructive work by the dictatorship with any degree of security would be impossible. It should not be forgotten that for the time being the revolution has been victorious in only one country. It should not be forgotten that as long as we live in a capitalist encirclement, so long will the danger of intervention, with all the resultant consequences continue.

Finally, Lenin explains what is meant by "the withering away of the state."

FROM

N. Lenin
STATE AND REVOLUTION

Engels' words regarding the "withering away" of the state enjoy such popularity, they are so often quoted, and they show so clearly the essence of the usual adulteration by means of which Marxism is made to look like opportunism, that we must dwell on them in detail. Let us quote the whole passage from which they are taken.

The proletariat seizes state power, and then transforms the means of production into state property. But in doing this, it puts an end to itself as the proletariat, it puts an end to all class differences and class antagonisms, it puts an end also to the state as a state. Former society, moving in class antagonisms, had need of the state, that is, an organization of the exploiting class at each period for the maintenance of its external conditions of production; therefore, in particular, for the forcible holding down of the exploited class in the conditions of oppression (slavery, bondage or serfdom, wage-labor) determined by the existing mode of production. The state was the official representative of society as a whole, its embodiment in a visible corporate body; but it was this only insofar as it was the state of that class which itself, in its epoch, represented society as a whole: in ancient times, the state of the slave-owning citizens; in the Middle Ages, of the feudal nobility; in our epoch, of the bourgeoisie. When ultimately it becomes really representative of society as a whole, it makes itself superfluous. As soon as there is no longer any class of society to be held in subjection; as soon as, along with class domination and the struggle for individual existence based on the former anarchy of production, the collisions and excesses arising from these have also been abolished, there is nothing more to be repressed, and a special repressive force, a state, is no longer necessary. The first act in which the state really comes forward as a representative of society as a whole—the seizure of the means of production in the name of society—is at the same time its last independent act as a state. The interference of a state power in social relations becomes superfluous in one sphere after another, and then becomes dormant of itself. Government over persons is replaced by the administration of things and the direction of the processes of production. The state is not "abolished," *it withers away*. It is from this standpoint that we must appraise the phrase "people's free state"— both its justification at times for agitational purposes, and its ultimate scientific inadequacy—and also the demand of the so-called Anarchists that the state should be abolished over night.

Without fear of committing an error, it may be said that of this argument by Engels so singularly rich in ideas, only one point has become an integral part of Socialist thought among modern Socialist parties, namely, that, unlike the Anarchist doctrine of the "abolition" of a state, according to Marx the state "withers away." To emasculate Marxism in such a manner is to reduce it to opportunism, for such an "interpretation" only leaves the hazy conception of a slow, even, gradual change, free from leaps and storms, free from revolution. The current popular conception, if one may say so, of the "withering away" of the state undoubtedly means a slurring over, if not a negation, of revolution.

Yet, such an "interpretation" is the crudest distortion of Marxism, which is advantageous only to the bourgeoisie; in point of theory, it is based on a disregard for the most important circumstances and considerations pointed out in the very passage summarizing Engels' ideas, which we have just quoted in full.

In the first place, Engels at the very outset of his argument says that, in assuming state power, the proletariat by that very act "puts an end to the state as a state." One is "not accustomed" to reflect on what this really means. Generally, it is either ignored altogether, or it is considered a piece of "Hegelian weakness" on Engels' part. As a matter of fact, however, these words express succinctly the experience of one of the greatest proletarian revolutions—the Paris Commune of 1871. . . . As a matter of fact, Engels speaks here of the destruction of the bourgeois state by the proletarian revolution, while the words about its withering away refer to the remains of *proletarian* statehood *after* the Socialist revolution. The bourgeoisie state does not "wither away," according to Engels, but is "put an end to" by the proletariat in the course of the revolution. What withers away after the revolution is the proletarian state or semi-state.

Secondly, the State is a "special repressive force." This splendid and extremely profound definition of Engels' is given by him here with complete lucidity. It follows from this that the "special repressive force" of the bourgeoisie for the suppression of the proletariat, of the millions of workers by a handful of the rich, must be replaced by a "special repressive force" of the proletariat for the suppression of the bourgeoisie (dictatorship of the proletariat). It is just this that constitutes the destruction of "state as the state." It is just this that constitutes the "act" of "the seizure of the means of production in the name of society." And it is obvious that such a substitution of one (proletarian) "special repressive force" for another (bourgeoisie) "special repressive force" can in no way take place in the form of a "withering away."

Thirdly, as to the "withering away" or, more expressively and colorfully, as to the state "becoming dormant," Engels refers quite clearly and definitely to the period *after* "the seizure of the means of production [*by the state*] in the name of society," that is *after* the Socialist Revolution. We all know that the political form of the "state" at that time is complete democracy. But it never enters the head of any of the opportunists who shamefully distort Marx that when Engels speaks here of the state "withering away," or "becoming dormant," he speaks of *democracy.* At first sight this seems very strange. But it is "unintelligible" only to one who has not reflected on the fact that democracy is *also* a state and that, consequently, democracy will *also* disappear when the state disappears. The bourgeoisie state can only be "put an end to" by a revolution. The state in general, *i.e.*, most complete democracy, can only "wither away."

These were the doctrines which caught fire in the minds of certain Russian intellectual radicals as the nineteenth century—the Century of Progress—drew to a close. Based upon the Dialectic, and enfused with a "religious" fervor, these doctrines formed the pattern of action on the part of a few Russian Bolsheviks which was to shape the tomorrows of both Russia and a large part of the world.

But if they were to shape events, events were also to shape them. For Marx only preached; Lenin and his colleagues practiced. And they practiced not in the milieu of quiet and books in which Marx wrote, but in the flux and flow of moving life. Inevitably the Marxist pattern underwent change; perforce the doctrines were modified. German Marxism changed into Russian Communism.

At no time, from the days when they came into power until the present, have Communist leaders been willing to admit this change, these modifications. But the facts cannot be verbalized out of existence. To understand Russia it is necessary, therefore, to know not only the original frame of thought and action which guided its Communist leaders, but the modifications made of it.

CHAPTER 4

The Transformation of German Marxism into Russian Communism

The following selections clearly and fully limn these changes and make possible an understanding of the present world of Communist thought.

The first selection, by John Plamenatz, Oxford historian whose grasp of his subject is equaled only by his ability to make it clear to others, is a model exposition of how the master's plan developed in the hands of Lenin. It is taken from his GERMAN MARXISM AND RUSSIAN COMMUNISM. *The second, by W. Rostow, carries the story of metamorphosis through Stalin, and succinctly shows how Russian traditions and history bore upon the changes wrought by the Communists. It is taken from* THE DYNAMICS OF SOVIET SOCIETY. *The "Bernstein" referred to below is Eduard Bernstein, influential German socialist, who held that Marxism could be achieved through a gradual, evolutionary development obviating the need for violent revolution.*

The years "1902 until 1926" mark the period which began with Lenin's decision to marry the Russian peasant to the Russian proletariat and to lead both by means of an elite "vanguard," and ended with Stalin's decision—not implemented until 1928—to begin the forced collectivization of Russian agriculture.

Mention of the "October Manifesto and the constitutional regime established by it in 1905" refers to the uprising of that year brought on by the disastrous war with Japan, in which the seething masses forced the Tsar to abandon, at least to a slight degree, his practice of complete autocracy. The Manifesto turned out to hold much less promise for the development of a democratic parliamentary regime than was originally hoped. Reference is also made to "Socialist-Revolutionaries," "Mensheviks," and the Russian "Social-Democratic Party." The first was a peasant party headed by radical intellectuals who placed much faith in the saving genius of the "Plain Folk." At one time Kerensky was numbered in this group. The Mensheviks were Marxists who believed that the master's blueprint must not be changed, that a bourgeois revolution was a sine qua non for the inevitable revolution of the proletariat, and that a highly disciplined vanguard was both unnecessary and harmful. Their opposites were the Bolsheviks who, under Lenin's leadership, formed a small, amorphous group in 1903 and, in 1912, formally declared themselves the Marxist party. The Social-Democratic Party was the name used to describe the party of Marxian socialists before the split into Mensheviks and Bolsheviks. After the formation of the two factions, both sides felt free to use the label for themselves.

FROM

John Plamenatz
GERMAN MARXISM AND RUSSIAN COMMUNISM

HAD the influence of Marxism been confined to the West, it would probably have done much good and little harm. Its authors thought it a revolutionary creed, but its effect among the advanced peoples has been, on the whole, to make revolution unnecessary. Marx and Engels condemned premature violence; they prescribed many years of preparation before the ultimate revolution, and wanted it made in the fullness of time by an immense and politically organized working class. Their influence served therefore in their own day more to prevent violence than to encourage it; and their program for the working class, had it been fulfilled, would have made violence unnecessary in the future. The political organization of the proletariat in the industrial countries of the West has proved so vast an enterprise that it could only be achieved in free societies; and in them, every large organized group, just because it is organized and large, possesses great political influence. The political organization of the working class has quite transformed the free societies which have made it possible; it has led to so many drastic reforms in the interest of the working class that the capitalistic economy known to Marx no longer exists. This great and peaceful social revolution was not foreseen by Marx, but the influence of his doctrine has been one, and not the least important, among its causes.

Marxism has in western Europe been the socialism of the post-revolutionary epoch. In France it had little influence until after 1871, when the long series of French revolutions was over and the workers could elect deputies to free parliaments. In Germany the socialist movement which survived Bismarck's mild persecutions very quickly became the largest party of its kind in the world. That party condemned Bernstein's attempt to revise Marxism, but the future was nonetheless with Bernstein. Indeed not more the future than the present, for though the leaders who condemned Bernstein were true to the letter of Marx's teachings they were no longer, except in name, revolutionary socialists. Marxism has in the West been a parliamentary socialism, and has flourished only in countries where the regime denounced by Marxists as a "bourgeois sham" has been more or less firmly established. Indeed, the western Marxist parties, before they began to be affected by Bolshevism, were among the most responsible, intelligent and enterprising of socialist movements. They had their faults, but they were not ruthless, or avid for power, or indifferent to freedom. They were competitors for power, but also convinced democrats who competed strictly according to the rules, because they knew—whatever they might sometimes affect to believe—that those rules were as profitable to themselves as to their rivals. Their Marxism was wearing thin, and they would probably soon have let it slip quietly from them. They had in the past profited by it, but it was likely, if they kept fast hold of it, to prove in the future more embarrassing than useful. Bernstein's theories were twice officially condemned, but their influence was quickly growing. Marxism as an active force in politics was dying a slow and natural death, and a death that was honorable. For what more can a fallible mortal ask than that his doctrines should have a great and beneficial effect on mankind for some fifty years?

But Marxism went to Russia and was there transformed. It became the doctrine, not of a working class party in a highly industrialized and literate society, but of a group of intellectual malcontents in a country which, though still primitive, was profoundly affected by the spread of western industrialism and western social and political ideas. Bolshevism is the distorted Marxism of a backward society exposed to the impact of the West.

This is not a condemnation of it, it is a mere statement of fact. Since Marxism, as it left the hands of Marx and Engels, was as much compounded of error as of truth, a distortion of it may well be no more, or even less, open to criticism than it is itself. In any case, Bolshevism is only one kind of distorted Marxism among several; for no social and political theory can be used by practical men in the shape given by its authors; it must always be greatly simplified and often considerably changed.

The process of distortion has been a long one, and the additions and alterations made have therefore been numerous. From 1902 until 1926 German Marxism—the doctrine of Marx and Engels— was gradually transformed into what is nowadays called Communism. This comparatively new doctrine, though it has adherents all over the world, is specifically Russian; its other (and perhaps less misleading) name is Bolshevism. For Bolshevism, though some of its roots are in Marxism, is not really the kind of doctrine that can properly be called either communist or socialist in any of the older nineteenth-century meanings of those words.

Western communism and socialism, before they began to be affected by the Russian "experiment," used always to advocate either extreme democracy or anarchy, whereas Bolshevism is the creed of ruthless and irresponsible minorities who use the state power to transform society in the ways that seem to them best. It is still in some parts of the world a revolutionary creed but has to all intents and purposes ceased to be democratic.

As soon as a Marxist group arises in a primitive and undemocratic country, it is at once faced with two problems: it must decide what its mission is, and also how to order its ranks to be able to execute that self-imposed mission with as little interference as possible from the government. The German Marxist doctrine was put together by its authors for the use of the working class in countries that were already capitalist and accustomed to constitutional and fairly mild, if not exactly democratic, government. The Russian Marxist had to decide what a Marxist group must do in a country not yet capitalist, and also how to set about doing it in defiance of a Tsarist autocracy and secret police. Whatever the first decision—unless it were to do nothing—the second must be to engage in clandestine activities. Any Marxist party in Russia, no matter how mild its program, would have had to be, at least until 1905, a secret political organization; and it was impossible for a free organization of that kind to be democratic. Nor would it have been easy for it, even after 1905, to become democratic, for the constitutional regime established by the October Manifesto was precarious, and the secret police active and oppressive without interruption until March 1917. The socialist movement in Russia had perforce, whatever the theoretical preferences of its leaders, to be undemocratic. Had it been a purely intellectual activity, had it consisted only of conversations in academic and polite circles, it need never have been organized; but as soon as the Russian socialists decided to influence the classes in whose welfare they were interested, they had to organize themselves into a political party, and that party could not be democratic. This was as true of the Socialist-Revolutionaries as of the Marxists.

The peculiarity of the Bolsheviks was not that they recognized that an effective socialist party could not be democratic in the

Tsarist police state; it was that they wanted a more strictly disciplined and exclusive party than the Mensheviks were willing to tolerate. It is one thing to admit that in a police state a socialist party, if it is to be active on any considerable scale, cannot resort to many of the practices needed to keep the party internally democratic; but it is quite another to want to make it an exclusive elite devoted to an agreed body of doctrine. Though the Socialist-Democratic party could not, because it was always watched and harrassed by the police, be properly democratic, most of the Mensheviks in it were by temperament inclined to democracy, whereas the Bolsheviks were not. Not that the Bolsheviks were in principle opposed to the democratic organization of the party; they willingly admitted that, had Tsarist Russia enjoyed even as much freedom as Imperial Germany, the party ought to have been democratically organized. But they accepted the situation as they found it without regretting the expedients that it seemed to impose on them; though they were democratic in principle, it was without reluctance that they acted un-democratically. They wanted the party to be a unified, disciplined, active and irresponsible elite, indoctrinating the workers and teaching them how to fight their oppressors. The party was not to be the only organized group, but the first among many and in control of the others. It was to be the select vanguard of a growing army. The Bolsheviks believed that the condition of Russia made it their duty to create such a party, and they welcomed the opportunity its existence would give them. They thought doctrine important, but they were impatient of doctrinal disputes and tender consciences. Lenin knew that the party could not do without intellectuals, but wanted it so organized that they could always be called to order.

The Bolsheviks also decided—or, rather, Lenin decided for them—to take a leading part in what they chose to call the Russian bourgeois revolution. When that decision was taken by Lenin in 1905, he explained that the Russian working class, weak though they were, had two peculiar advantages: they had to reckon with a middle class who, while they wanted to put an end to Tsarist autocracy, were yet too few and too easily frightened of the socialists to the left of them to dare stake the future on a revolution; and the workers could, if they acted in time, make a political alliance with the peasants, who were not in Russia (what they were in the West) humble and inarticulate supporters of the established order, but a restless, resentful and land-hungry class willing, should the need arise, to use force to get what they conceived to be justice. Lenin did not suppose that Russia was in 1905 ripe for a proletarian revolution; she had still, he thought, to have her bourgeois revolution, and was indeed only just beginning to have it. But why, he asked, should not the proletariat, allied with the peasantry, take control of the bourgeois revolution, and then govern Russia while she passed through the bourgeois phase of her development? Was it not evident that the Russian middle class lacked the courage to do in their country what the French bourgeois had done in France during the great revolution, and that the brunt of the attack on Tsardom was already borne—and not only in the streets—by the workers and their political vanguard? Why should not the workers and peasants destroy the Tsarist autocracy, not to give power to the bourgeois, but to set up their own dictatorship? These questions, had historical materialism been true, would have been foolish; for only the bourgeois can make a bourgeois revolution and govern a bourgeois society. And yet, in the conditions prevailing in Russia, they were not foolish. Marxism was an ideology that first saw the light of day in capitalistic society, and could hardly have done so elsewhere; but its influence could not be confined to the region of its birth. Neither Marxism, nor capitalism, its matrix, could have emerged from inside the Russia of the late nineteenth century; but both could be brought in from outside. They were so brought, and there therefore arose in Russia a situation not accounted for by the Marxism of Marx. Russia acquired a proletariat while she was yet, in most ways, socially and economically more primitive than the West had been when capitalism first arose there. Russia had by 1905 both a proletariat and a Marxist party, and the leaders of that party had to decide what to do in a situation not predicted by the philosophy of history they had put their faith in. Lenin, being a bold, ambitious and shrewd man, caring more for power than consistency, did not mind putting these questions, and could even find in Marx's *Address to the Communist League* texts to support the answers he gave.

It was not Lenin's habit to push an explanation further than was needed to justify the course of action he proposed. He believed in 1905 that Russia's next revolution must be "bourgeois," and he was also certain that the Social-Democrats, if he could knock some of his own sense and courage into them, could use it to establish a "dictatorship of the proletariat and peasantry," with the latter as subordinate allies of the former. He said no more about this dictatorship than that it would serve to get Russia through her bourgeois phase as quickly as possible, and bring her to the point where she could be made socialist. Just how she could be bourgeois and at the same time have dictatorship of the proletariat and peasantry, he did not properly explain. Would the workers and peasants, while they ruled Russia, allow her to develop a capitalistic economy on the Western model? If they could govern, why should they not also control the national economy? And if they could control it, why have a bourgeois phase at all? Lenin spoke of "uninterrupted revolution," of a continuous and rapid transition to socialism, but never put or answered these questions clearly and fairly. He took many liberties with Marxism, but tried always to take no more than were needed to justify whatever decisions seemed to him important at the time. All the rest he left vague and undecided. He never looked far ahead, and possessed to an astonishing degree the faculty of shutting his eyes to what it did not suit him to see. Though not a peasant, he had a large share of that almost willful stupidity which is an essential part of peasant cunning.

Lenin did not even inquire what kind of government a "dictatorship of the proletariat and peasantry" might be in the Russia of 1905. He welcomed the soviets as organs of popular democracy, but did not explain how in a country where the peasants greatly outnumbered the urban worker and both classes were mostly illiterate, it would be contrived that the latter class and not the former should be the senior and controlling partner in the alliance between them. Since both workers and peasants were ignorant, it was not possible for them, however many the soviets at their disposal, to govern Russia. Their "dictatorship" would therefore have to be exercised in their name by whatever parties could plausibly plan to speak for them. Would the Socialist-Revolutionaries, who had as good a right to speak for the peasants as the Social-Democrats to speak for the workers, accept a subordinate role? And if they were somehow obliged to accept it, could they still presume to speak for the peasants?

When Lenin, in 1902, had urged that the Russian Social-Democratic party could not, while the Tsarist police state lasted, be democratic, he had implied that it must become so when that state was destroyed. He had spoken with the approval of the German Socialist party, and had explained why it could be democratic. He had then looked forward to a time when Russia would be what Germany always was—a bourgeois society allowing at least as much freedom as would enable a socialist party to be truly responsible to the working class. But in 1905 he was proposing a "dictatorship of the proletariat and peasantry" at a time when his own party, which he called "the party of the proletariat" was still by his own admission far from being responsible to the proletariat. It was not even a united and disciplined party, for Lenin had not succeeded in imposing his will upon it. If the "bourgeois" revolution of 1905 were to lead to a "dictatorship of the proletariat and peasantry," what could that dictatorship be? The workers and peasants were manifestly incapable of governing Russia or even of contriving that the parties claiming to do so in their name should be responsible to them; the Socialist-Revolutionaries would not willingly accept a subordinate part in a political alliance with the Social-Democrats. What, then, in the Russia of 1905, could the dictatorship that Lenin clamored for amount to except irresponsible power of the Social-Democratic party? Lenin, of course, admitted no such thing. He was less interested in the probable consequences of the policy he advocated than fearful lest the Russian Marxists should not rise to a great occasion; and other people's fears, discordant with his own, merely annoyed him. His instinct was to urge bold courses on the timid, and to let the future take care of itself.

Though Lenin did not know it, the course he chose for his country in 1905 was impossible. There could be no "dictatorship of the proletariat and peasantry" among an illiterate people un-

accustomed to all the processes of organized power. Neither the
workers nor the peasants could rule, in alliance or separately.
The ignorance which put it out of their power to rule their
country also made it impossible for any political party to act for
them. In a large country, no class can rule except through deputies; and there cannot be deputies unless institutions exist to
insure that persons supposed to be responsible to others really
are so; and these institutions cannot function properly except
where there is freedom. There can be no freedom unless the
people—more particularly that part of them active in public
affairs—have acquired the habits and prejudices of the democrats.
Lenin spoke of his party and of the class to whose service that
party was bound as if they were so intimately related that the
rule of the party was, to all intents and purposes, the rule of
the class. It did not suit him to understand that so intimate a
relationship could not bind political leaders to their followers in
a country like Russia, precisely because there existed neither the
institutions nor the habits that make up democracy. No party
can justly claim to speak for a class except in a democracy; and
no modern democracy has known for more than a few years what
could properly be called "the party of a class." Indeed, it is a
thing dangerous to democracy, although democracy alone makes
it possible.

Russia has never had a "party of the proletariat." Were this
name given the British Labor party, it would describe it falsely;
and yet not so falsely as it describes the party of Lenin. The
Russian Social-Democrats were disunited and quarrelsome from
1902 until after the Bolshevik revolution, and the relations that
bound them to the workers were always uncertain and precarious. Nor were their quarrels the effects of dissensions within
the class whose "vanguard" they called themselves; they related
mostly to matters of doctrine beyond the understanding of the
Russian workers. The Russian Social-Democrats no more had
the right to call themselves "the party of the proletariat" than a
man has the right to call himself a woman's husband merely
because, although she does not know it, he intends to marry her.
If a man believes a magician who foretells his marriage to this
woman, it is perhaps difficult for him not to think of her as al-

ready his wife, and not to anticipate his rights. It is the common error of hopeful men to behave as if the future were already in some way present; but it is an error nevertheless, and no woman is a man's wife merely because he has his reasons, unknown to her, for believing that his offer must be accepted in the end. The Russian workers were for the most part not even aware of the kind of relations that the Social-Democrats hoped would eventually unite them to their class. They knew only that the Social-Democrats were well disposed to them, and that it was sometimes worth their while accepting their support and their advice; and the Bolsheviks, when they at last in 1912 formed a party of their own, were certainly no closer than the Mensheviks to the workers. Not until the eve of the October Revolution did they enjoy the confidence of anything like the majority of the industrial workers; and even that confidence was limited, for it was given merely because Lenin's promises were attractive, and not because the workers understood and cared for the doctrines and ambitions of the Bolsheviks. The party of Lenin had some shrewd and bold ideas about what to do with the workers in their own supposed interest, but was never, except in this meager sense, "the party of the proletariat."

The decision to seize power once made, the Bolsheviks were driven to all the courses which, in the eyes of their critics, have made nonsense of their professed Marxism. But—and this too ought always to be remembered about them—they would never, had they not been Marxists, have been driven to these courses. The revolution they attempted was "premature," and yet their excuse for it was Marxian, for they said they were only anticipating in backward Russia what would happen in other countries, where it would be, not premature, but a timely and long step forward, bringing great benefits both to the advanced peoples and to the others who were necessarily dependent upon them. Having taken power in the name of the Russian proletariat, the Bolsheviks quickly discovered that the class whose vanguard they claimed to be would not always follow them; and, seeing that the class was ignorant of what seemed obvious to themselves did not scruple to drive where they could not lead. They had spoken of a "revolutionary dictatorship of the proletariat and peasantry," and had therefore made allies of the Left Wing Socialist-Revolutionaries, who stood to the peasants as they did to the workers; but, when they found that their allies would not accept the minor role allotted to them by Lenin, they set about suppressing them.

The Bolsheviks, applying their principles to the contemporary world, made a number of calculations about what was possible in Russia and probable elsewhere, and then decided that it was their duty, as good Marxists, to become rulers of their own country. Their calculations were partly right and mostly wrong; they were about right enough to enable the Bolsheviks to get power, but not to precipitate the world revolution they hoped for, nor yet to use power in Russia to establish what Marx or Engels (or even Lenin before 1917) would have called a "dictatorship of the proletariat." They watched the course of events in the world, saw only a small part of what was happening, interpreted that part in the light of their faith and to serve their ambition, and then decided to intervene in the world's affairs at the moment most propitious to themselves. It was only afterwards that they discovered they had foreseen almost none of the obstacles standing in the way of their using power to reach the ends for whose sake they had taken it. The world has been greatly changed by them, though not in the ways they had intended; and it has also greatly changed them. They are no longer today the Bolsheviks of 1917. If we are to count them successful, it must be, not as Marxian socialists, but as ambitious men and lovers of power. They have played a great part in the world, but what that part was to be they did not know when they took control of one of the world's two largest states. They looked only a short way into the future, and made several bad guesses.

As Marx saw it, the progress of mankind toward communism is by successive stages, each presided over by a different class, and every passage from stage to stage marked by a revolution made by the only class capable, at that point of the progress, of making it. The stuff of history is a succession of class conflicts, the victor in each (except the last) being the vanquished in the next; and the succession itself is the effect of a long process of economic development, a process for the most part ignored or misunderstood by the warring classes. The proletariat, and therefore *a fortiori* a party of that class, can make only the last revolution.

The Bolsheviks have changed all that. They believe that wherever Marxism finds lodgement in the minds of men banded together in the service of their faith, those men—provided only they are orthodox—are, whatever the society they live in, the "party of the proletariat." Not for them to wait until society has progressed so far that it is ripe for proletarian revolution. On the contrary, it is their duty, using every means in their power, to force progress upon it, whatever the stage of its development. No society can be so primitive that, if there are Communists inside it, there is nothing for them to do; for every society having Communists must have been affected in one way or another, by world capitalism and the social conflicts it engenders. No society can live any longer to itself alone, but is always considerably dependent upon the rest of the world; that dependence must continually increase. The great conflict now in the world is between "proletarian" and "bourgeois" states, and every class in every society is already, or must soon become, a party to that conflict. Therefore, the duty of Communists everywhere is either to push their country into the community of proletarian states or else, should this not prove possible, so to divide and weaken it that its alliance is of little value to the enemies of the Soviet Union. Whenever, in a primitive society, Communists have a chance to get power, they must take it, and then use it to create economic and social conditions that Marx and Engels had thought must exist before they could get it; they must establish a "dictatorship of the proletariat" in order to make their country what, according to Marx and Engels, it must already have become before there could have been any dictatorship.

The Communists, self-styled "party of the proletariat," believing themselves possessed of a doctrine that explains how society must normally develop, suppose themselves competent to control the destinies of every society. Marx, they believe, discovered how any society, unaffected by societies more advanced than itself, must develop; and they, since Marx's time, have discovered how contact with advanced societies affects the development of backward ones. That development is "abnormal" but is also in principle calculable by anyone possessed of Marxian philosophy and knowing the relevant facts. Seeing that capitalism now affects—always more strongly—every part of the world not dominated by the Communists, the development of all backward societies is, from the Marxian point of view, abnormal. It therefore appears to the Communists their duty, wherever they find themselves, to seize power if they can get it, because they alone possess the science enabling them to control the abnormal (but also, if properly controlled, much swifter) progress of backward societies toward the goal common to all societies—which is communism. The Communists believe that, whatever the appearances against them, they have a better right than other people to call themselves the "party of the proletariat," even in countries where there is no proletariat, or one so small as to be insignificant, or one that mistrusts them and turns elsewhere for guidance; for the business of the Communists is always and everywhere to prepare the coming of the classless society—the task assigned by Marx and Engels to the proletariat.

To us it may seem obvious that the Communists are doing the opposite, but they, like other fanatics before them, cherish nothing more obstinately than their illusions. The more successfully they control the development of a backward society and the more quickly they endow it with industries and "collectivize" its peasants, the more proletarian they think they make it. They therefore do for the workers what they, had they been literate, organized and numerous enough, would have done for themselves; and the better they do it, the more their government comes to look like a "dictatorship of the proletariat." In this double sense, though neither is quite literal, they are (so they imagine) the party of the proletariat. They look upon themselves as the only competent midwives of every society, because they alone understand the interworkings of every social process. They believe that they are come, not to deny Marx, but to fulfill him; and have taken it upon themselves to accomplish in a few decades what he thought might occupy many generations.

Nevertheless, though they choose to think otherwise, they have denied him. They have not merely declared possible what must be impossible, they have also created new kinds of inequality and oppression as extensive and self-perpetuating as the old. They have used force, not to assist what the old Marxists would have called a timely and natural birth, but to refashion society from the foundations upward; they have not been midwives but surgeons, and have not been able to foretell the results of their operations. The world they have so greatly transformed is as much a surprise to them as to their enemies. They never imagined it, and still do not understand how their actions have helped make it. It would be presumptuous to call them blinder than their neighbors; their sight is perhaps as good but no better; and yet they claim to see much further. It is mostly this that makes them so great a nuisance in the world. Life in a house where everyone's sight is weak becomes burdensome to all when one of the inmates insists upon behaving as if he had the eyes of a lynx. The Communists are altogether too enterprising in a world whose processes are but slightly known to any of us. Their greatest fault is their immense and inextinguishable conceit.

Professor Rostow, in the following section, describes the effect of Russian traditions upon the developing Marxism administered by Lenin and Stalin.

FROM

W. Rostow

THE DYNAMICS OF SOVIET SOCIETY

LENIN'S thinking reflects three qualities which can be traced in a good many of his Russian predecessors:

1. The notion that there were unique problems and possibilities in Russia's position which required to make possible an evolution different from that of Western Europe.

2. A feeling that a gap existed between the mass of the Russian people and the intellectuals, which the intellectuals had, somehow, to fill.
3. The conception that a phase of violence, even destructive violence, might be required in order to put Russia on the right political and social path—a conception founded in the hard fact of the recurrent triumph of brute force in the long sweep of Russia's history.

It should be strongly emphasized that there were other vital strands in the evolution of Russian political thought before 1917. Russia generated its own version of the Western democratic tradition. Up to 1914, and even to 1917, these more familiar elements were the predominant forces making for change in Russian politics. Although such speculation is not very fruitful there is good cause to be made for the view that Russia would have moved into a phase of fairly familiar Western democracy, had not World War I and its attendant disasters intervened. It is to be remembered that, in their only relatively free election, that of November 25, 1918, the Russian citizens gave at least 58 per cent of their votes to a party representing a moderate socialism, to be executed by parliamentary means. This was the predominant direction of Russian development in the country before 1914, and it was the trend which the Bolsheviks frustrated and repressed. Nevertheless Lenin's view of appropriate political practice had some national roots.

In his perceptive little volume, *The Origin of Russian Communism*, Nicholas Berdyaev says: "The Russian cultured class was suspended over an abyss, crushed by two fundamental forces, autocratic monarchy above and an unenlightened mass of peasantry beneath. Russian thought, without basis and rebellious, in the nineteenth century was inwardly free and audacious; it was not chained to a grim past and to a tradition but outwardly it was cramped and even persecuted." Indeed, Russian political thought and speculation of the nineteenth century presents a wide spectrum, ranging from a philosophical anarchism with profound spiritual bases, through conventional Western conceptions of democracy to extreme autocratic and even totalitarian ideas. Despite this range, the persistent influence on intellectuals of the dual frustration isolated by Berdyaev can be discerned: frustration imposed by a backward Tsarist autocracy and by the massive fact of a population consisting of a downtrodden peasantry, to the extent of some 80 per cent. These frustrations largely account for the three Russian elements noted above, which found their way into Lenin's formulation of the mission, strategy, and tactics of the Communist Party.

The sense of Russia's unique problem and possibilities can be traced in many of the nineteenth century writers, of whom one of the earliest and most distinguished was Alexander Herzen (1812–1870), a cultivated and urbane nobleman who was also the first important Russian socialist. After many years of immersion in the Western tradition, he reacted strongly against the "petty bourgeois spirit," which he felt had infiltrated even European socialism. Exiled from his native land, he came to feel that the oppressed Russian peasant had in him potentialities for a grander social and political evolution than the West had seen. The great social revolution which he envisaged would have begun in Russia and then swept over the West. Out of this holocaust would have arisen a purified and better world. Michael Bakunin (1814–1876), Herzen's contemporary and fellow-nobleman, further elaborated this view. He held it to be possible for Russia to escape what he regarded as the horrors of capitalism and, in this respect, he ranks as one of the more important forerunners of Lenin. In general not only Russian political thought but Russian literature as well, from Pushkin forward, reflects a sense of the special destiny of Russia. On the whole, it is fair to relate Lenin's decision in 1917 to forgo a "bourgeois stage" and to move directly for "dictatorship of the proletariat" to this strand in the national pattern of mind.

The struggle of Russian intellectuals to relate themselves to the mass of the Russian people, and their vacillation between romantic efforts at identification and an almost cynical harnessing of the people's energies to purposes the people did not share, is also a long story. The effort of the intellectuals to get close to their fellow-beings, and especially the peasantry, found major expression in the *narodnichestvo*, the populous movement which engaged in one way or another not only such political figures as Herzen and Bakunin, but also Dostoyevsky and Tolstoi. The emotional basis for this effort was exceedingly complex, reflecting, among the other factors, the sense of isolation of the Russian intellectual community and its guilty conscience at the gap between its own civilized life and the brutal poverty in which the mass of Russians lived. Sir John Maynard, in his *Russia in Flux*, aptly entitled one of his chapters "The Intelligentsia and the Worship of the Plain Folk."

By the 1880's, however, the romantic phase of Russian populism had largely played itself out. The most active *narodniks* in Russia were members of a terrorist wing which included Lenin's unfortunate brother Alexander; their sporadic amateur violence had also revealed itself as insufficient to the revolutionary goals they cherished. In this setting, various versions of Marxism, with this unemotional, alleged scientific basis, were gaining in influence. Among many intellectuals (whom it is easy to overestimate, looking backward from the fact of the November Revolution) there was disappointment with the efficacy of the gradualist efforts at Russian reform, and a tendency to look harder at the facts of political power and ways to achieve it. Lenin, born in 1870, came to maturity at a period of reaction against this back-to-the-people movement, strengthened in his case by his brother's execution. Lenin's doctrine of Communist Party leadership, if necessary against the will of the proletariat, obviously bears the mark of a fairly widespread disillusion with the populist approach in particular and a concept of peaceful political evolution in general.

The third of these Russian elements in Leninism—the persistence of a faith in violence as an instrument for the seizure of power—obviously owes a great deal to the inflexibility of Tsarist autocracy over the pre-1914 century. There were, indeed, important changes and concessions in the operation of Russian autocracy in these years. But reform came slowly, and against the background of a chronic, often brutal, reassertion of autocratic rights and privileges. The failure of the Decembrist Revolt in 1825, with its conception that a military few might achieve quick, drastic, social reform through dictatorship, down through Herzen,

Bakunin, the Nihilists of the 1860's, the terrorist wing of the populous movement, to revolutionary Marxism itself, this theme —that violence would be required—runs through much Russian political thought.

The conception of the Communist Party defined and applied by Lenin owes something, then, to Russian history as well as to the Hegelian strand in Marx and to the hard experience of conspiratorial practice. Under Lenin the Communist Party emerged with its power centered in a small disciplined organization, prepared to subject the means it used to no rigid framework of rules, facing with equanimity the prospect of enclosing on the Russian majority or even on its own narrowing group of adherents an overriding judgment from the top concerning an historically correct line of action.

It was essential to the process which occurred during and after the Russian Revolution, however, that these doctrines were not the only ones which played a part in the thinking of Lenin and the Bolshevik Party. Marxist pre-revolutionary thought contained within it an important element of general democratic conceptions derived from the progressive thinking of the previous two centuries, e.g., the right of free assembly, the notion of free and secret elections, the inviolability of the person and of the home, the freedom of conscience, of speech, of the press, the right to strike—all interwoven in the minds of both the leaders of the revolutionary movement and their followers with a hard core of practical rules for action. The process of removing this "ideological baggage of parliamentary democracy" represents an important part of the evolution of the Soviet state after they had achieved power.

A second piece of Marxist inheritance that had to be abandoned was, as noted above, the Marxist conception that societies must pass from a feudal to a bourgeois- to a proletariat-dominated phase. It was probably not until shortly before Lenin returned in 1917 to a Russia already in revolt that he permitted himself, at last, whole-heartedly to contemplate the possibility of a direct seizure of power by the Bolshevik Party without a preliminary phase of more conventional bourgeois parliamentary government.

It is thus the conclusion at this stage of the argument that even before 1917 the inheritance of an important element in Marx's political theory converged with the bitter and practical experience of conspiracy and with aspects of nineteenth-century Russian political thought. These converging influences gave to Lenin and his colleagues fundamental bias in the following form: when a choice had to be made between a course of action which would enhance the power of their own political group as opposed to its being in conformity with Marxist doctrine, the subsequent goals of revolution, the broad ideological aims and traditions of the progressive movement, or the majority will of the peoples concerned, the choice would lie on the side of short-run political realism and practice. In some instances the ideological inheritance of the revolution converged with the pursuit of power; in many instances there was conflict—consistently resolved and enforced in the interests of short-run power. The evolution of the Soviet regime since 1917 is, in its essence, the dynamic consequence of this persistent, gradually strengthening and ultimately institutionalized bias in the context of Russia and of the world scene.

*   *   *   *   *

Stalin's contribution to communist doctrine can, in one sense, be regarded simply as a sustained effort to supply a more or less consistent rationale to the situation he inherited and exploited after Lenin's death. The revolutionary doctrines of 1917 had incorporated within them the necessity for world revolution to occur concurrently with the revolution in Russia; but at Brest-Litovsk Lenin had decided in fact to proceed with socialism in one country. The revolutionists of 1917 had devoted a good part of their lives to attacking the concept of the state and had looked to a variety of devices under the order which would diminish or eliminate the traditional functions of a national state and its bureaucracy; but, in fact, from 1917 forward, a bureaucratic state of machinery was put into operation and has been consolidated. Lenin's rationale for this violation of the revolutionary doctrines had been *ad hoc* and empirical. He did what he did in order to cope with urgent situations while holding on to precarious power based upon minority support. Stalin took it upon himself to supply the Leninist heritage with a more rigorous theoretical foundation.

*   *   *   *   *

Stalin's two main tasks . . . in terms of Communist theory, were to supply a rationale, apparently consistent with the theoretical writings of Lenin, for the pursuit of socialism within one country as opposed to world revolution; and to explain why it was that the national state not only showed no signs of withering away under Communism but exhibited a remarkable tendency to grow—in scale, authority, and degree of centralization.

The manner in which Stalin resolved his priority for the Soviet Union with his ultimate communist commitments for world revolution is indicated in the following quotations:

> *The goal is to consolidate the dictatorship of the proletariat in one country; using it as a base for the overthrow of imperialism in all countries.* Revolution spreads beyond the limits of one country; the epoch of world revolution has begun.
>
> . . . The very development of world revolution . . . will be more rapid and more thorough, the more thoroughly Socialism fortifies itself in the first victorious country, the faster this country is transformed into a base for the further unfolding of world revolution, into a lever for the further disintegration of imperialism.
>
> While it is true that the *final* victory of Socialism in the first country to emancipate itself is impossible without the combined efforts of the proletarians of several countries, it is equally true that the development of world revolution will be the more rapid and thorough, the more effective the aid rendered by the first Socialist country to the workers . . . of all other countries.

Stalin's theoretical reply to Trotsky and the others, then, was that the world revolution could be achieved only by stages and not in the single way of revolutionary effort. To those Communists abroad or at home who were restless and wished to get on with the task of world revolution, Stalin said, simply: "The time is not ripe; your duty is to strengthen the Soviet Union as the ultimate base for further revolution elsewhere." From 1924 to his death this remained Stalin's position, with the apparent exception of the moves in Eastern Europe after 1945 taken in the shadow of the Red Army, and the assistance to Mao in China from early 1946 forward. But examined closely, these cases disappear as exceptions, for the direct Soviet interest had directed Moscow's interest in both cases.

*   *   *   *   *

While Stalin's communist opponents, both within and without the Soviet Union, could and did argue that his conception violated the aspirations of most Russian Communists and the bulk of the pre-revolutionary writings of Lenin, Stalin's theory was in full harmony with Lenin's practice, and he sought valiantly to make it consistent with selected extracts from Lenin's texts.

Whereas Stalin's views on socialism in one country were expressed firmly and promptly after Lenin's death, his theory of the Party and State underwent some progression over the years. The brute fact of bureaucratic dictatorship was difficult to square with the revolutionary hopes and myths; and, to this day, the method of dictatorship is concealed beneath the elaborate theological and even institutional cover.

To the extent that Stalinist theory has made explicit the emerging role of the Soviet state it has depended heavily on its prior rationale for "socialism in one country." Stalin's progression on this subject closely parallels events within the Soviet Union and his own policies. Like other aspects of Stalin's theories, his views on the state may be legitimately regarded as an ex-post rationale for policy decisions and actions already taken.

During the NEP, Stalin wrote as follows, in the course of an argument urging the Party to bide its time before instituting accelerated programs of collectivization and industrialization:

The concept of dictatorship of the proletariat is a state concept. The dictatorship of the proletariat necessarily includes the concept of force. There is no dictatorship without force, if dictatorship is to be understood in the strict sense of the term. Lenin defines the dictatorship of the proletariat as "state power based directly on *force*." (Lenin, *Collected Works*, Russian edition, Vol. XIX, p. 315.) Hence, to talk about dictatorship of the party *in relation to the proletarian class*, and to identify it with the dictatorship of the proletariat is tantamount to saying that in relation to its own class the Party must not only be a guide, not only a leader and teacher, but also a sort of state power employing force against it. Therefore, whoever identifies "dictatorship of the Party" with the dictatorship of the proletariat tacitly proceeds from the assumption that the prestige of the Party can be built up on force, which is absurd and absolutely incompatible with Leninism. The prestige of the Party is sustained by the confidence of the working class. And the confidence of the working class is gained not by force—force only kills it—but by the Party's correct theory, by the Party's correct policy, by the Party's devotion to the working class, by its contact with the masses of the working class, by its readiness and ability to *convince* the masses of the correctness of its slogans.

By 1930, however, with the First Five-Year Plan and forced collectivization in full cry, Stalin was more nearly prepared to define dictatorship of the proletariat as "state power based directly on force" with somewhat less attention to the requirements of popular persuasion. His pronouncements during the First Five-Year Plan include a positive rationale for the state, and a bold claim that the day when the state could wither away safely was still at some distance. At the Sixteenth Party Congress (1930) he said:

We are for the withering away of the state, while at the same time we stand for strengthening the dictatorship of the proletariat which represents the most potent and mighty of all the state authorities that have existed down to this time. The highest development of state authority to the end of making ready the conditions for the withering away of state authority: there you have the Marxist formula!

With Stalin firmly in control of both Party and State, and with his own canonization as the sole legitimate inheritor of the mantle of Marx, Engels, and Lenin gathering momentum, he moved to a still more explicit rationale for the Soviet State in his report to the Congress of the Communist Party in 1939. Here he links his doctrine of socialism in one country to the rationale for an all-powerful soviet state, displaying an evident confidence in modifying traditional Communist doctrine which in many fields marked the later phase of his rule:

It is sometimes asked: "We have abolished the exploiting classes; there are no longer any hostile classes in the country; there is nobody to

suppress; hence there is no more need for the state; it must die away.
—why then do we not help our Socialistic state to die away? Why do
we not strive to put an end to it? Is it not time to throw out all this
rubbish of a state?"

What could have given rise to this underestimation? . . . It arose
owing to the fact that certain of the general propositions in the Marxist doctrine of the state were incompletely worked out and inadequate. It received currency owing to our unpardonably heedless
attitude to matters pertaining to the theory of the state, in spite of the
fact that we have twenty years of practical experience in matters of
state which provide rich material for theoretical generalizations, and
in spite of the fact that, given the desire, we have every opportunity
of successfully filling this gap in theory. . . .

. . . what if Socialism has been victorious only in one country, taken
singly, and if, in view of this, it is quite impossible to abstract oneself
from international conditions—what then? Engel's formulation [the
withering away of the state] does not furnish an answer to this question. . . .

In order to overthrow capitalism it was not only necessary to remove the bourgeois from power, it was not only necessary to ex-
appropriate the capitalists, but also to smash entirely the bourgeois
state machine and its old army, its bureaucratic officialdom and its
police force, and to substitute for it a new, proletarian form of state,
a new socialist state, and that, as we know, is exactly what the Bolsheviks did. But it does not follow that the new proletarian state may not
preserve certain functions of the old state, changed to suit the requirements of the proletarian state. Still less does it follow that the forms
of our Socialist state must remain unchanged, that all the original functions of our state must be fully preserved in the future. As a matter of
fact, the forms of our state are changing and will continue to change
in line with the development of our country and with the changes in
the international situation. . . . We are going ahead toward Communism. Will our state remain in the period of Communism also?

Yes, it will, unless the capitalist encirclement is liquidated, and unless
the danger of foreign military attack has disappeared. Naturally, of
course, the forms of our state will again change in conformity with
the change in the situation at home and abroad.

No, it will not remain and will atrophy if the capitalist encirclement
is liquidated and a Socialist encirclement takes its place.

Here is where Communist theology left the matter down to
the time of Stalin's death.

Thus German Marxism evolved into Russian Communism. But what agencies and institutions were to be constructed to carry out this "theology" and its imperatives? How was the word to be made flesh? How were faith and doctrine to manifest themselves in national polity?

For answers to these questions we turn to descriptions of Soviet economic and political structures.

III

THE FLESH

CHAPTER 5

Communist Factory and Farm

With the November Revolution of 1917, modified Marxism—Communism—came to Russia. But for three years, 1918–1920, the Bolshevik leaders were too busy putting down White rebellion and foreign intervention to make headway with Socialism. Then, from 1921 to 1928, they followed their New Economic Policy—the famous N.E.P., really state capitalism—because they had no other choice; civil war and internal chaos simply had required it. Thus it was not until the spring of 1929 that the brave Communist words began to take on substance—before the word became deed. In that year the First Five Year Plan was born.

Under it, both industry and agriculture were genuinely collectivized. Out of the travail of this period and the purges which followed, the shape of present-day Communist Russia appeared.

We are here concerned with coming to an understanding of the basic features of the new socialist economy. We shall examine first the new regime in industry, and then turn to its counterpart in agriculture.

The section on Soviet industry is from Professor Barrington Moore's SOVIET POLITICS: THE DILEMMA OF POWER, *one of the most powerful contributions to an understanding of Soviet society that has been offered in recent years. In the preparation of his analysis of the Soviet system, Professor Moore had the assistance and advice of a number of scholars asso-*

ciated with the Russian Research Center located at Harvard University.

"Politbureau," referred to but not defined in this section, is the name given to the top echelon of the Communist Party—the small elite which makes all important decisions. Its official name since 1952 is Presidium. It is taken up in the next chapter in the section on the Party.

The description of Soviet agriculture is from MANAGEMENT IN RUSSIAN INDUSTRY AND AGRICULTURE, *by* G. Bienstock, S. M. Schwarz, *and* A. Yugow. *This able work was published under the auspices of the Institute of World Affairs, established by the New School for Social Research, and offers, in the opinion of this editor, one of the most constructive approaches to an understanding of the Soviet farm economy available to the "beginning student."*

FROM

Barrington Moore, Jr.

SOVIET POLITICS: THE DILEMMA OF POWER

. . . any industrial economic system has to find ways and means for making four groups of decisions. First, it is necessary to decide what to produce, in the second place, decisions have to be made concerning the most efficient way of combining labor and resources in order to produce the guns, butter, and other myriad products of a modern industrial order. Thirdly, it is necessary to provide some means for deciding how much economic effort should go into the building of new plants and the replacement of equipment that has become worn-out or obsolete. Finally, there have to be devices for insuring the orderly distribution of the products of the economy among the population.

*   *   *   *   *

How does the Soviet system provide for reaching decisions on whether to produce guns or butter, machinery or knitting needles?

From the available evidence it is reasonably certain that the major decisions on the general production goals of the Soviet economy, including the types of products and quantities of each, are now reached by the Politbureau and embodied in the various Five Year Plans. This concentration of the decision-making power on matters of national import in the economic field parallels the political concentration of power. The present situation differs markedly from that before Stalin's accession to power. The First Five Year Plan was itself the product of discussions and small-scale trials that lasted from the November revolution until 1929.

The highest planning body on economic affairs is the Gosplan (State Planning Commission). However, as the English economist Maurice A. Dodd, who is not one to emphasize the authoritarian aspects of the Soviet regime, points out, the Gosplan is an advisory body and "not an executive department of state." It is a part of the Council of Ministers, and, according to Soviet sources, receives its directives from them and from the Supreme Soviet.

*   *   *   *   *

The procedure by which the Five Year Plans are actually drawn up is quite complicated and need not be considered in detail here, especially since this aspect of the Soviet system has received considerable attention from Western writers. It is sufficient to point out that in formulating the details of a Plan the Gosplan authorities must take careful account of existing capacities and resources, an operation which requires an accurate knowledge of such capacities and resources of the USSR as a whole. In the second place, the planners have to make sure that the plans for each industry and area match one another. For example, in expanding the amount of electric power, the Gosplan has to be sure that there will be available the necessary steel and other equipment for building the new power plants, and that this power in turn will be in a locality where it will be useful to other factories. Thus, it is quite clear that the planners, including not only the technicians but also the political authorities, do not and cannot have a completely free hand in the choices that they make.

The conclusion that the basic decisions concerning what to

produce and in what quantities are made in their essentials by the Politbureau goes directly counter to the official ideology, according to which the masses participate widely in the planning process and thereby help to control their economic destiny. A recent semipopular Soviet exposition of the planning machinery devotes a whole chapter to the participation of the masses in planning.

An examination of this and other material bearing on the point throws very severe doubts upon the official contention. What happens, apparently, is that, under the stimulus of the Communist Party, the workers, factory directors, and collective farmers produce counterplans, in which they promise to carry out, or often to overfulfill, the official government plans. In 1947 and 1948 these counterplans had taken the form of long letters to Stalin, printed on the front page of the newspapers, in which groups of workers or farmers set themselves specific production goals that they are pledged to fulfill. Other forms of so-called mass participation in planning are the Stakhanovite movement and "socialist competition" in which various groups of workers or factories as well as collective farms vie with one another for prizes awarded to the group with the greatest output. All of these movements are carefully controlled and stimulated by the Party. There is not the slightest evidence that they can in any way affect the fundamental aims of the Plan. They do not affect such basic decisions as whether the economic resources of the country will be directed into heavy industry or light industry, into war goods or peace goods, consumers' goods or producers' goods, which are the essential decisions of the Plan. There are merely additional stimuli to production that, together with the elaborate apparatus of control, help to take the place of the spurs and checks provided by the market in a capitalist economy.

Once the decision has been reached concerning what goods are to be produced, there remains a host of decisions to be made concerning the most efficient combination of raw materials, factory equipment, and labor necessary to produce them. Under a capitalist system, the profit motive provides the major stimulus for the maximization of efficient production, and the bankruptcy court, the chief negative sanction for inefficiency. The capitalist entrepreneur under textbook conditions, is free to obtain his supplies of men and materials where he can find them. Actually, he does a great deal of shopping around for them. Likewise, he makes the decision of whether or not to expand his plant by adding new buildings and machines. In practice, these decisions may be greatly influenced or limited by government authorities. The Soviet manager enjoys only a very limited autonomy in the search for supplies, and on his own initiative can do next to nothing about the major aspects of the size and capacity of the plant intrusted to him by the state. This series of graded distinctions in the power to make important economic decisions, and the motivations behind these decisions, is more important in practice at least than differences in property rights in distinguishing between the Soviet manager and his capitalist counterpart.

As a motivating force to interest the manager in the efficiency of his plant, the Soviets make use of the profit motive in a manner that has certain strong resemblances to familiar capitalist arrangements. The utilization of this device, often regarded as a distinctive feature of capitalism is openly recognized and accepted in current Soviet doctrine. The Five Year Plan adopted in 1946 aims to "increase the importance of the profit motive and economic accounting as an additional stimulus to production." Nevertheless, the operation of the profit motive is hedged in under the Soviet system by limitations of the opportunities to bargain for supplies, the centralization of decisions concerning plant expansion, and taxation policies that return most of the profit to the state. In this manner it is harnessed to the socialist chariot and prevented from becoming a force that might disrupt Soviet institutions.

To understand the operation of the profit motive and the limitations of the managers' power of decision, the Soviet production process at various points may be examined. Beginning at the point of sale, and working back from there, one may note that the products of a plant are sold at prices fixed by the government. Exceeding these prices is punishable by law. But the prices do not represent the money equivalent of the cost of production. The plant is expected to produce its goods at a cost that is less than the price set by the government. A so-called turn-over tax and an amount included as the planned profit are added to the anticipated cost of production. Lowering the quality of the goods to increase the margin between cost of production and selling price is punishable by law. If the manager holds costs below the anticipated amount, the profits of the plant are increased. In 1945 the total profit for the Soviet Union as a whole amounted to 21,051,000,000 rubles.

At earlier stages in the production process, the limitations on the managers' power of decision and the operations of the profit incentive are connected with control over the physical equipment of the plant and over supplies of raw materials. The basic assumption of the Soviet system is, of course, that the manager is not free to buy or sell factories, which are regarded as government property intrusted to him to manage. In the process of spelling this principle out in actual legal and institutional forms, the Soviets have for some time drawn a distinction between what they call basic and circulating resources. Very different possibilities are open to the manager for the utilization of each.

The terms "basic resources" and "circulating resources" derive from the differences Marx believed he saw between the *means* of labor—factory building, machines, etc.—and the *objects* of labor—raw materials, semi-finished products, and the like. These differences would exist in any form of society, Marx declared. In general, the means of labor are regarded as the basic resources and the objects of labor as the circulating ones. The distinction between the two types of resources does not depend upon the nature of the object itself, but the purpose for which it is intended. Thus a linotype machine that is the product of the factory that makes them is part of the circulating resources of this factory. When this same machine is transferred to a printing establishment, it becomes part of the basic resources of this plant. In practice, difficulties soon arose in the application of these distinctions. In 1923 it was decreed that basic resources were those that were not used up or destroyed in a single act of production—buildings, machines, and the like—and that circulating resources were those that could only be used once—fuel, raw materials, and others. In 1936 the definition of circulating resources was broadened to include objects whose useful life was less than a year, independent of their cost, and objects whose cost, independent of their useful life, was less than 200 rubles.

Basic resources cannot be bought or sold again by the individual manager. In other words, the Soviet manager cannot increase or decrease the size and equipment of the plant intrusted to his care through buying and selling operations in the fashion of his capitalist counterpart. However, he does have a voice in the disposal of a small portion of the plant's profits which can be used for expansion. Thus the outlet for the operation of the profit motive is, in this part of the production process, a very small one.

Circulating resources provide the opportunity for the profit motive to serve as a stimulus to production and efficiency. The minimum of supplies necessary for the operation of the plant is determined according to the Plan. The flow of supplies to the plant is controlled in different ways for different types of supplies, depending on the scarcity of the commodity concerned. Some of them may be purchased directly from other producers. The production plan for the individual plant includes a certain profit rate called the planned profit. If the manager makes efficient utilization of his resources, he may exceed the planned rate of profit. Should this take place, the extra profit remains at the disposal of the plant. In 1940, 70% of the cost of production for industry as a whole is reported to have been spent on raw materials, fuel, and other items that come under the definition of circulating resources.

In addition, the manager is permitted to add to his circulating resources through loans from the bank. These loans are supposed to be issued only for strictly defined purposes, though their utilization for purposes other than those defined is deprecated in strong enough terms to suggest that it may occur rather often. Such loans probably increase the leeway available to the manager in the making of production decisions, at the same time providing a further check upon managerial operations in a way that resembles banking control over production decisions in a capitalist society.

The disposition of the profit indicates further its limitations as an incentive. Part of it is tax and part placed in the Industrial Bank (Prombank) for purposes of capital development within the industry. A third part goes into what is called the Director's Fund, a slightly misleading name, since it does not appear that this fund is a direct reward for the manager.

The Director's Fund is primarily a way of rewarding the workers for energy and efficiency. Since the way the fund is expended is left partly to the discretion of the director, it is safe to assume that it represents a series of tempting prizes that the manager may distribute to those he chooses. In 1940 the amount distributed through the Director's Fund was 2,600,000,000 rubles. In some, presumably exceptional plants, individual workers received cash awards of 500 to 1,000 rubles. Though payments into the Director's Fund were replaced by other rewards during the war years, they were revived again in 1946. Under the postwar legislation, only 2 to 10 per cent of the planned profits may be credited to the Director's Fund, the percentage varying with different industries. A much larger proportion, between 25 and 50 per cent, of the profit in excess of the plan may be credited to this fund. This arrangement presumably acts as a stimulus for greater profit on the part of both workers and management. The proceeds of the fund may be spent on improving the housing conditions of the workers and for other amenities, for individual bonuses, trips to rest homes, sanatoria, and the like. While the director has the right to allocate the fund, it does not appear that he may spend any of it upon himself.

On the other hand, salary bonuses for the managers are closely related to profit, though not calculated as a percentage thereof. In coal mining, for each per cent of reduction of real cost of production below planned cost, the manager, chief and assistant engineers obtain a bonus of 15 per cent of their monthly salary. Similar rules prevail in other sectors of heavy industry. On occasion the total bonuses granted to managers and engineers equal or exceed their annual salary.

The Soviets have taken the profit motive of capitalist society and adapted it to the requirements of their own ideology and social system, hedging it in with numerous restrictions, so that it may not act as a socially disruptive force. After 1929 they did much the same thing to the capitalist device of competition, which the Webbs described as being, under socialism, the use "of the sporting instinct to augment the wealth of the nation." Socialist competition, as it is known in the USSR, usually takes the form of a race between two or more factories, or shops within factories, to see who can turn out the maximum output. It is thus closely allied to the Stakhanovite movement. The winners receive group publicity in the Soviet press, banners, and other symbols of achievement. During the war there developed, as part of the system of Socialist competition, the "200 per cent movement," that is, groups of workers who fulfilled double the requirements of the plan. Whether this type of speed-up leads to an efficient utilization of men and machines is open to doubt, since it often leads to a rapid breakdown of both. It should be noted that socialist competition, directed chiefly toward the quantitative maximization of output, differs sharply from competition in capitalist society, which takes the form of competitive bidding for labor and resources on the side of production, and in competition by price, quality, and services on the side of distribution.

In the light of the foregoing it is safe to conclude, as others have done, that non-economic incentives and checks play the more important role in producing the desired behavior on the part of the Soviet manager. Chief among these are the possibilities of advancement to positions of greater and greater responsibility and prestige for those who have learned to combine men, machines, and materials in the most efficient manner, and the probabilities of disgrace, or even active physical suffering, for those who fail to measure up to the assigned task. Economic failure is likely to be identified with sabotage, and hence becomes a "sin" in an even stronger sense than is the case in the United States, with severe penalties meted out in this light.

Though large allowances have to be made for the part played by earlier conditions, and the relative smallness of the managerial group with which the Soviets began, it may also be concluded that the system has not inculcated through its rewards and penalties the habits of prompt decision-making and accurate attention to detail that are desired by the Soviet leaders. At a meeting of the Supreme Soviet in October 1946, the chairman of the budget commission repeated the typical complaint that many factory directors refused to look at a balance sheet, to learn the cost of their products, or to eliminate unproductive expenditures. Likewise, the Party press from time to time slashes away at managers who "look for a quiet life and sit with folded arms," paying no attention to cost and quality. While such criticisms cannot be taken at face value, they may be used as evidence for the hypothesis that, together with the historical factors just mentioned, the system of rewards and penalties that apply to the Soviet manager does not yet lead to an efficient combination of men and resources. Still another element in this complex situation is the fact that the Soviet factory manager is under terrific pressure to turn out the goods and probably knows that the penalties for cutting corners on quality and efficiency are less than those for failure to produce at all.

Throughout a considerable sector of the Soviet economy, that directly controlled by the secret police, the incentives provided by profit and competition appear to be almost totally absent. In this area political motivations, the need to eliminate political enemies, covered by euphemisms about the restoration of deviants to society (concentration camps were called "Corrective Labor Camps"), are combined with economic ones and may overshadow them. The extent of these operations remains a state secret that cannot be reliably penetrated from the available fragmentary information. They may be recalled, however, as a reminder that even in the Soviet Union more than one set of rewards and penalties operates within the economy.

According to classical economic theory the resources needed for the construction of new plants and the replacement of worn-out machinery come from the sacrifice of present consumption. To a considerable extent they are derived in a capitalist economy from individual savings that are loaned to industry through the purchase of securities. Interest payments have been widely regarded as a form of reward for the sacrifice of present consumption, thus permitting the construction or replacement of capital equipment.

To some extent individual savings are a source of plant construction and replacement in the Soviet Union. The virtues of thrift are recognized there, too. As early as 1926 Stalin himself spoke out in favor of interest payments as the normal way of "mobilizing" individual savings. But they play a much smaller role in the Soviet Union than they do under capitalist conditions.

When the Soviets in the thirties started the drive for socialist industrialization, they could not, for a variety of reasons, afford to rely upon individual thrift alone, or upon voluntary abstention from consumption as a source of real capital investment. Perhaps the most important of these considerations was that the sacrifices required were too great for reliance on voluntary means. Nor could the regime permit people to save money with the idea that they would invest it wherever there was the greatest opportunity for profit. Both socialist doctrine and the requirements of the day demanded that decisions concerning real capital investment be centralized.

For these reasons, capital investment has been, and is, financed very heavily out of the national budget. During the period of War Communism, the economy operated for a time as if Soviet industry were one large factory. Assignments from the budget were the only resources of the individual plant, and all of its monetary income returned to the treasury. This extreme centralization was subsequently abandoned and a number of other schemes tried out. During the thirties between three quarters and two thirds of the amounts devoted to capital construction were derived from the budget, the remaining portion being left to the individual enterprise to reinvest in its own operations, in ways apparently left to the managers' discretion. During the war, and subsequently, this amount has become much smaller.

* * * * *

During the period from 1938 to 1940, capital investment constituted nearly one fourth of the budget expenses. This proportion dropped precipitously during the war years, as might be anticipated, and in 1946 formed less than one seventh of the budget. Plans for the current (Fourth) Five Year Plan called for a total capital investment of 150,500,000,000 rubles, according to one calculation, and according to another, based on estimated 1945 prices, a total of 250,300,000,000 rubles. The differences between the two figures may reflect a price inflation, since most Soviet statistical calculations are based on 1926–1927 prices. Presumably, most of this will come from the budget and may constitute a heavier drain on it than pre-war capital investment. . . . the chief source of budget revenue and hence, indirectly, of capital investment is the turnover tax. It constituted 61.1 per cent of government revenues between 1938 and 1940, and 60 per cent in 1946, although the figure dropped to 40.8 per cent in 1945. This tax, with more than 2,500 individual rates, is imposed on almost all consumption goods at the point where they leave the producing plant and enter channels of distribution. It is the major factor in the difference between the cost of production and the selling price of any article. Even plants that fail to operate at a profit must pay this tax.

A second, and far less important, source of state revenue is the tax on profits. It constituted just over one tenth of the state revenues in the period 1938–1940, and under 5 per cent in 1946. Nevertheless, it sops up most of the profits of industry, taking in 1945, for instance, nearly 17 billion rubles out of the total profit of 21 billion rubles. In a sense, this tax is an unnecessary bookkeeping operation, since both the turnover tax and the tax on profits come out of the difference between the cost of production and the selling price. There is, however, a distinction, in that the turnover tax is levied and collected even if the firm fails to make a profit.

Other taxes are relatively unimportant. Before the war direct taxes on the population, including income taxes, provided only about 5 per cent of the total state revenues. During the war the proportion rose to 14 per cent.

In the Soviet system for the distribution of goods to the population at large, one may observe the same mixture of what are commonly considered socialist and capitalist principles as appear in the other aspects of their economic arrangements. The present arrangements for distribution are the product of a long period of trial and error. By the time of the outbreak of the Second World War, the system devised was to sell the products of socialist industry, as well as most of the products of agriculture, through government and cooperative stores at fixed prices. In addition, there is a free market for certain agricultural products. . . . In this system the turnover tax provides the means for matching prices to available supplies. With certain relatively minor changes this is the principal arrangement in effect today. Under this system, incentives produced by inequalities in income, have their full effect. Additional money income means an additinal opportunity to purchase the necessities and good things of life. This situation is in accordance with the socialist maxim, "From each according to his abilities, to each according to his work."

However, at various times and under emergency conditions, the Soviet regime, like its capitalist competitors, has found it expedient to resort to other distributive devices. One of these is, of course, rationing, which has existed from time to time, including the period of the Second World War. Wartime rationing was abolished on December 16, 1947, at the same time that consumer demand was checked by a devaluation of the currency. Special stores, where "members of the intelligentsia and highly skilled workers" could obtain various scarce goods, usually at higher prices than those in the regular distribution channels where the goods were often non-existent, have been another distributive device. Still another has been the organization of special canteens in the factories. During the war the role of these canteens, which often drew their supplies from collective farms that made special agreements with the particular factory, increased sharply. Before the war they accounted for only 4 per cent of the retail turnover in the USSR, while in 1942 they accounted for 28 per cent, and in special areas, such as the Urals, for as much as 45 per cent. Despite these variations, the distribution of consumers' goods has by and large been based on the principle of "come and get it if you can afford it."

Even writers sympathetic to the Soviet Union assert that the system of retail distribution is one of the least successful products of the regime, and the Soviets themselves have denounced it perhaps more frequently than any other feature of their society. Service tends to be disinterested and slow. Little or inadequate attention is paid to local needs and tastes, or to seasonal requirements. "Stores are replenished with merchandise irregularly, and the most necessary goods are lacking." Store staffs are "neither accustomed to nor interested in laying in supplies on time or carefully storing perishable commodities." The Webbs' remark, "There have been not a few occasions when village and even city stores have been clamoring in vain for particular supplies, when these have been lying unopened, and even forgotten, at some intermediate point."

These difficulties may be attributed to both ideological and institutional sources. As Yugow argues, the nationalization and centralization of retail trade was undoubtedly premature in Russia, at least from a strictly limited economic point of view. It created an unwieldy and expensive bureaucratic apparatus that paid little or no attention to the habits, customs, and tastes of the people. Of perhaps even greater importance is the fact that while the reigning ideology romanticized the construction of industry, it did not provide motivations and rewards for the distributive side of the economic machine. Stalin recognized some of these difficulties. He endeavored to use his prestige to correct them and to develop a Bolshevik version of the American ideal of "service" in the course of his report to the Seventeenth Party Congress of 1934. His remarks are worth quoting in full as evidence of the difficulties derived from ideology:

To begin with there is still among a section of Communists a supercilious, contemptuous attitude towards trade in general, and towards Soviet trade in particular. These Communists, save the mark, look upon Soviet trade as a thing of secondary importance, hardly worth bothering about, and regard those engaged in trade as doomed. Evidently these people do not realize that their supercilious attitude towards Soviet trade does not express the Bolshevik point of view, but rather the point of view of shabby noblemen who are full of ambition but lack ammunition. (Applause) These people do not realize that Soviet trade is our own, Bolshevik, work, and that the workers employed in trade, including those behind the counter—if only they work conscientiously—are doing revolutionary, Bolshevik work. (Applause) It goes without saying that the Party had to give these Communists, save the mark, a slight drubbing and throw their aristocratic prejudices on the refuse dump.

In their various attempts to ameliorate this situation, the Soviet leaders have borrowed from the capitalist arsenal and endeavored to introduce the competitive incentive into the retail trade. These efforts parallel, though perhaps less successfully, the Soviet introduction of the profit motive into the production side of the economy. On the same occasion cited above, Stalin reported to the Party Congress that the various commissariats had been ordered by the Party to start trade in the goods manufactured by the industries under their control. This led, he claimed, to an extensive improvement in the "competing" cooperative trade and to a drop in market prices.

As happens in many cases of cultural borrowing, only the superficial aspects of an institution were taken over without the essential supporting arrangements, which in this case would have involved a general abandonment of socialist principles in favor of the free play of market forces. It is not surprising, therefore, that the difficulties have continued. Nor is it altogether surprising that the Soviets have continued to try to meet them in the same way. On November 9, 1946, the Council of Ministers again issued a decree that required the cooperatives to compete with the state monopoly of retail trade. Surplus agricultural products, formerly sold by the peasant on a local open-market basis, under the new arrangement are purchased by consumer cooperatives managed by Party officers. These foodstuffs are supposed to be distributed to the city population at prices not exceeding those charged in the special stores for the intelligentsia mentioned above. Producers' cooperatives likewise receive government assistance in the form of supplies and diminished tax burdens, while the prices of their products are set by government authorities.

Some of the ideas associated with the classical doctrine of consumer sovereignty have even been put forth by the Party press, which has warned the manufacturers of consumers' goods that the population will not take whatever goods the producer wants to turn out. "The consumer is a much stricter controller than the technical control section of some factory or other. Entering a store he puts to one side merchandise of poor quality and expresses his preference for the products of that establishment whose trade mark has earned a good reputation." This emphasis on the consumer as the ultimate arbiter is reminiscent of the American slogan, "The customer is always right." In the same issue cited above, *Pravda* warns the various economic ministries and lesser economic units to pay more attention to quality and variety of choice in their products. Now, it is asserted, they spend more time "on the registration of complaints than on correcting mistakes." It is unlikely that these admonitions will have much effect so long as the underlying conditions of centralized control over the decisions about what products are to be made, which is basically independent of consumer pressures, remain a central aspect of the Soviet system. It also appears that these institutional factors would make it difficult for a system of retail distribution, sensitive to the requirements of the population and supported by an ideology of service along American lines, to take effective root in the USSR. It probably will be a long time before "the customer is always right" becomes an accepted Bolshevik slogan.

In order to make their economic system work, the Soviets have arrived by a trial-and-error process at the stage where they have borrowed a number of the motivations of capitalism: inequality of rewards and incomes, the profit motive, and some of the superficial aspects of competition. These borrowings do not provide a warrant for the viewpoint that regards the Soviet system as closely similar to capitalism. They do provide support for the assertion that a modern industrial society implies certain common problems and even certain common solutions. The extreme claim of universal validity for the principles of classical economics is not warranted according to the Soviet evidence. But neither is the extreme claim of cultural or institutional relativism established according to the same evidence.

The motivations generally lumped under the rubric of personal acquisitiveness, which, as Weber points out, are likely to crop up under widely disparate social situations, do not receive the scope and approbation that they do in the United States. The Soviet economic system is one that keeps them hemmed in at every turn and channeled into what are considered socially useful paths. To take their place other motivations and prestige rewards have been developed. Likewise, other justifications for the Soviet system have received wide dissemination: allegations concerning the greater security of the individual, and the system's claimed freedom from the corrosive effects of crises and unemployment.

In this respect Soviet culture is still a materialist culture. The virtues claimed for the system are material virtues. There is none of the contempt for so-called debilitating material comforts displayed, if not practiced, by the leaders of Nazi Germany or Fascist Italy. The Soviet system of values is much closer to the American system in this respect than it is to Western totalitarian ideologies, or to the ascetic ideologies of the East.

In this system of values the conflict between authoritarian and populist elements finds a reflection in economic institutions. The belief that the masses must be led to their salvation played its role in the programs of forcible industrialization and collectivization. It may also be traced in the creation of a highly centralized system for the making of economic decisions. In its present form this highly centralized system is not yet capable of distributing to the people efficiently and courteously the objects it produces. On the one hand, the system emphasizes the desirability of material goods; on the other hand, it is unable to satisfy this demand. The passage of time will reveal, unless an improbable catastrophe intervenes, whether or not this contradiction can be solved.

In general, however, the Soviets have come closer to achieving their original goals in the area of industrial institutions, regarded by their doctrine as crucial, than in any other. They have succeeded in imposing their ideology to a very great extent, yielding only at certain points and borrowing just enough from the capitalist competitors to make their own system function.

Professor A. Yugow, in the following section, describes how the Communist word was made flesh on the agricultural front.

FROM

G. Bienstock, S. M. Swarz, and A. Yugow

MANAGEMENT IN RUSSIAN INDUSTRY AND AGRICULTURE

THE *kolkhoz*, or collective farm, is a new form of productive organization in agriculture.

*   *   *   *   *

The agrarian revolution of 1917 abolished the privileges of the nobility and the church and gave legal equality to the peasants. But it did not succeed in solving the problem of poor harvests and chronic crop failures. Nor was it able to solve the problem of supplying urban food needs. New radical agrarian reform was imperative if the level of agricultural productivity was to be raised sufficiently to improve the standard of living of both city and village. This could be done only if Russia were to abandon primitive forms of agriculture for modern methods. The antiquated three-field system had to give way to modern crop rotation, the wooden plow and flail to the metal plow and threshing machine, extensive methods to intensive methods. On the other hand, there was required a government policy that would encourage broad economic development in agriculture.

The policy of zigzags and half-hearted concessions pursued by the government during the NEP period affected the economy adversely. It failed to stimulate the development of agriculture sufficiently or to supply the city adequately with the necessary material resources. Developments in the NEP period tended in the direction of solving the agrarian problem by the creation of a limited class of rich and powerful peasants at the expense of the rest of the village. But the Soviet government, ideologically and politically opposed to the creation of a rich peasantry, would not consistently encourage the development of individual farm ownership.

It long vacillated between granting partial privileges to encourage rural development, and such policies as struggling against 'rent abuses and hired labor in the village,' and kulaks, i.e. peasants who owned two or three horses. In 1929, the government decided to industrialize the nation and adopted the first Five Year Plan. This program demanded tremendous investments of capital, which, under Russian conditions, could be obtained only from the villages and only on condition of their rapid economic development. It was imperative to choose a definite economic policy. The encouragement of a 'strong peasantry' implied a corresponding distribution of national income and, consequently, a much slower rate of industrialization than that projected by the authors of the Five Year Plan. It would also confine the Revolution to agrarian reforms and political democratization, while considerably restricting in scope the socializing measures of the government.

In the same year, after some hesitation and internal Party struggle, crowned by a surprising declaration of Stalin, which, in fact, contradicted the Five Year Plan, the victorious faction adopted complete socialization. It was decided to organize agriculture along the lines of highly productive, large-scale collective farming, as well as to establish sovkhozes (government farms), and to abolish individual peasant farming within the shortest possible time. The first Five Year Plan called for the collectivization of only 18 per cent of all land under cultivation. There began, however, particularly after Stalin's pronouncement 'on transition to the policy of liquidating the kulaks as a class' and the subsequent decision of the Central Committee of the Communist Party 'to carry out full collectivization,' such a rapid process of compulsory collectivization that, by the end of the Five Year Plan, more than two-thirds of all land under cultivation had been collectivized.

Both in organizational methods and tempo, compulsory collectivization begun in 1929 was completely unlike the collectivization of the first Soviet years. The new policy, both painful and ruthless, aroused stubborn resistance on the part of broad sections of the peasantry and was carried out at the cost of millions of peasant lives and the destruction of vast national wealth. The government accomplished the task by ruthless coercion. Relying on the poorest strata of the village, the landless, the horseless, the chronically starved; utilizing their hatred of the village 'rich' and their longing for a better life; applying all forms of administrative and economic pressure—it succeeded, in the course of several years, in liquidating individual peasant farming and making the kolkhoz the dominant economic form.

In 1929, 3.9 per cent of former individual peasant farms and 4.9 per cent of cultivated land area were collectivized. By 1931, 52.7 per cent of peasant farms and 67.8 per cent of cultivated area were collectivized. By 1935 the kolkhozes embraced 83.2 per cent of all farms and 94.1 per cent of all cultivated land. In 1940 they embraced 96.9 per cent of all farms and 99.9 of all cultivated land. It may be said that, on the outbreak of the Russo-German war in 1941, collectivization of agriculture had been fully accomplished.

The government aimed not only to raise agricultural productivity, but also to strengthen its own rural economic position. From their inception, kolkhozes required government assistance, both in financing and in obtaining machinery. Government aid was given in the form of loans, seed, and machines. In 1930, a new policy was adopted. Instead of distributing tractors, threshers, and other machines directly to kolkhozes, the government set up Machine-Tractor Stations to service the kolkhozes. At first these were organs of the kolkhozes. In 1931, they became joint enterprises of the kolkhozes and the government. In 1932 they were transformed into purely government organs, servicing collective farms with tractors and combines at fixed fees. When the government decreed that all large machines servicing kolkhozes be concentrated in Machine-Tractor Stations, it became the owner of all the instruments of production, rural as well as urban. In the rural areas it now owned both the land and all large machines. The kolkhozes were thus placed in a position of even greater economic dependence on the government.

In 1930 there were 158 Machine-Tractor Stations in the U.S.S.R., servicing 27.4 per cent of all kolkhozes. In 1940 there were 6,980 stations servicing 94.5 per cent of all kolkhozes.

Kolkhoz land belongs to the government and cannot be alienated by the kolkhozes or their members. It is attached to the kolkhoz for permanent use. Work animals are kolkhoz property. Cattle and poultry belong in part to the kolkhoz, in part to individual members, within limits set by law. Productive machinery, with the exception of small tools, belongs, as already mentioned, to the government, which, by agreement, works the land and harvests for the kolkhozes. Labor is furnished by the kolkhoz, which, in addition, is obliged to assign a specified percentage of its manpower to certain compulsory tasks (road work, transportation, felling timber, etc.) and to work in urban factories.

The product is divided between the kolkhoz, its individual members, and the government. The last-named takes its share in various forms. In addition to compulsory deductions in money and kind, there are fees for the services of Machine-Tractor Stations, and direct and indirect taxes. The kolkhoz receives its share in the form of allocations to compulsory funds and reserves. The individual kolkhoz member receives his share as compensation for labor; the amount of compensation depends on the size and profitableness of the kolkhoz as a whole.

In addition to collective work, there is a field of enterprise in kolkhozes in which private-property factors have a broad opportunity for development. Each household is granted a plot of land for individual cultivation. Generally these small homesteads are cultivated intensively, and all income from their output belongs to their holders. These homesteads do far more than provide for the fuller satisfaction of peasant consumer needs. Within a short time they have become an important part of the national economy, supplying a good deal of the meat and dairy products, vegetables, fruit, poultry, honey, and eggs.

During the first years of compulsory collectivization, kolkhozes varied greatly in size. The majority consisted of five or six households, cultivating fifteen to twenty hectares. There were also giant kolkhozes of thousands of households, with tracts of cultivated land up to 2,000 or 3,000 hectares in area. The size of the kolkhoz depended largely on the speed of and forms assumed by compulsory collectivization in the particular region.

It soon became clear that small kolkhozes were not profitable and that giant kolkhozes did not lend themselves to efficient

management. By 1938 the average kolkhoz comprised 78 households and 484 hectares of land under collective cultivation. Size
varies with region, depending on crops and specialization. Ukrainian kolkhozes, producing mainly grain or cattle, are the largest.
In 1935, 65.2 per cent of all Ukrainian kolkhozes covered more
than 500 hectares; and 1.1 per cent, less than 100 hectares each.
The smallest kolkhozes were found in Georgia (grapes, medic-
inal herbs, tea), where 65.8 per cent of all kolkhozes covered
less than 100 hectares, and only 1.8 per cent more than 500
hectares.

In recent years, kolkhozes have been the chief form of agricultural enterprise in the U.S.S.R. According to data for 1937,
they produced 62.9 per cent of total agricultural output, State
farms 9.3 per cent, homestead plots 21.5 per cent, workers'
suburban plots 4.8 per cent, and individual independent peasants
1.5 per cent. In 1938, kolkhozes produced 86 per cent of all the
grain, 30–35 per cent of all the livestock and animal products,
and 90–95 per cent of all cotton, sugar beet, flax, and oil-yielding
crops.

Despite ruthless and coercive methods of collectivization,
which aroused much bitterness against the kolkhozes, reorganization of the entire agricultural economy along the lines of large
mechanized enterprises using advanced methods has begun to
yield positive results. The agricultural output is rising, land
productivity has improved, livestock breeding has begun to re-
cover, rural production for the market has risen, and extreme
fluctuations of crop yield, formerly habitual in Russian agriculture, have considerably abated. The average annual grain crops
in millions of tons were 67.6 in 1910–14; 73.6 in 1928–32; 94.5 in
1933–7; 95 in 1938; 110.3 in 1939; and 119 in 1940.

The kolkhoz has been economically consolidated; it is the new
and predominating form of the life and work of the Soviet
peasantry, the overwhelming mass of the population of the
U.S.S.R.

To organize kolkhozes and to determine efficient methods of
administration were difficult tasks. Socially and economically,
kolkhozes were so new a form that it was impossible to organize
them on the basis of experience in the administration of in-

dustrial enterprises, of large estates in Russia, or of large-scale farms in the United States. New forms of organization and administration had to be sought empirically. There were groping and serious blunders. Forms developed in the course of several years of practical work.

*   *   *   *   *

In 1930, at the height of the effort toward 'full compulsory collectivization' and the drive against kulaks, the central organs of government developed the first set of statutes for kolkhozes. These did not attempt to regulate internal life, but consisted of instructions on organization; a definition of eligibility for membership; a definition of kulaks (subject to confiscation); a definition of property of members subject to collectivization; and regulations of relations between kolkhozes and government organizations.

These somewhat incomplete statutes, which served neither to regulate administration or to protect members' interests, remained in force until 1932. Then, after a period of sharp compulsory collectivization, a series of new decrees was issued, substantially altering the internal administration of kolkhozes and reducing the arbitrary element in relations between kolkhozes and government.

These decrees were dictated by a desire to consider the mood of the peasants and to strengthen their economic interest in improving kolkhoz work. They legalized the right of kolkhoz members to carry on homestead farming, in addition to participating in the work of the kolkhoz. They abolished collectivization of cows and poultry, permitted kolkhozes to sell 'surplus output' on the market, and established quotas for the compulsory delivery of produce to the government. At the same time, these decrees strengthened political control over the managerial personnel of the kolkhozes, and reduced interference by local Party and State organizations.

In 1935, after the economic consolidation of the collective system, a 'Model Statute for Artels,' proposed by Stalin at the Second Congress of kolkhoz shock brigaders, was adopted and subsequently ratified by the highest Party and government organs. With slight modifications, this is the statute under which kolkhozes operate today.

Changes and fluctuations in government policy toward kolkhozes (the drive against kulaks, the struggle against fictitious collectivization, distrust of the wealthier and reliance on the poorest rural elements, the rule of 'appointees,' direction by political bodies, training of leaders, etc.) have all affected kolkhoz forms and methods of administration. Having survived all these fluctuations, the kolkhozes have, since 1935, begun to function under relatively stable conditions, without sharp changes in organizational structure. Revolutionary conditions of compulsory collectivization have been left behind, giving way to a period of evolution and internal consolidation.

The Model Statute of 1935 defines the legal status of the kolkhoz, the forms of its administration and organization, and its relation to other organizations. It is the 'supreme basic law, stabilizing agricultural production in the U.S.S.R.' In a special decree, the Central Committee of the Communist Party and the Council of People's Commissars instructed Party organs that 'the Statute shall not only formally but in reality have the force of a basic State law. Violations must be severely punished.' And, in fact, the Statute plays a supremely important role in the life of the kolkhoz, regulating all its activities and defining all its rights and obligations.

Its definition of the kolkhoz as an independent, voluntary association of peasants is, however, entirely false. While the Statute provides that the kolkhoz be built on the basis of voluntary membership, the overwhelming majority of kolkhozes were organized through coercion. The government resorted to a variety of methods to achieve full collectivization, but administrative and economic pressures were decisive. The usual method of organizing kolkhozes was as follows:

On the initiative of Communists, the poorer elements of a village adopted a resolution to organize a kolkhoz. The property of the well-to-do was then confiscated and turned over to the kolkhoz. Peasants who actively resisted were arrested and sent into forced labor. Those who, in various ways, tried to avoid joining were deprived of the possibility of buying industrial commodities and were subjected to special taxes. Peasants who joined the kolkhozes received tax exemptions and special privileges in marketing 'surpluses' and purchasing manufactured goods. In the light of these circumstances, kolkhozes can hardly be considered voluntary organizations.

Their operation is also subject to the strictest government control and supervision. The government has not only imposed binding regulations but it also directs, through periodic orders, their plans and operations, and maintains rigid control over their entire administrative apparatus.

The Statute of 1935, which is still in force, decrees the collectivization of all work animals, agricultural machinery, seed stocks, feed for collectivized livestock, and farm buildings needed by the collective. Dwellings, some cattle and poultry, and homestead farm buildings remain in the private ownership of individual kolkhoz households; smaller farm tools needed on the homestead farm are not collectivized. Under certain conditions, a kolkhoz can expropriate a member's homestead farm.

The land belongs to the State, but it is attached to the kolkhoz for permanent joint cultivation. Each member is granted a plot ranging from one-quarter to one-half a hectare in area for homestead and private use in gardening, small-animal and poultry breeding, bee-keeping and dairying. Each household may own a cow, one or two calves of horned cattle, pigs, up to ten sheep and goats, twenty hives, and an unlimited number of poultry and rabbits. In some regions variations are permitted in the area of the homestead farm (up to one hectare) and in the number of privately owned livestock.

The kolkhoz consists of peasants of both sexes, over sixteen years of age, who personally participate in its work. On joining the kolkhoz, each peasant must surrender his large farm implements, stock of seed, and work animals. If he has sold his horses during a period of two years prior to joining, and possesses no seed, he must pledge himself to pay in installments, out of future income, the value of a horse and the required seed. The size of the admission share does not affect the member's income.

A member's existence as an individual farmer is at an end. According to the Statute, he may leave the kolkhoz. In such cases his money share may be refunded and he may be compensated by the People's Commissariat for Agriculture 'out of land reserves only, and without damaging the kolkhozes by land fragmentation.' This means, in fact, that any member who leaves loses his entire land share (including the household plot) and the possibility of farming.

The kolkhoz is now governed by the following bodies or persons: the general membership meeting, the Managing Board, the Chairman, the Control Commission, brigade and squad leaders, managers of livestock farms and other auxiliary enterprises, bookkeepers, and various specialists.

The Statute of 1935 proclaims that the administration of kolkhozes be on the principle of self-government. It defines the general membership meeting as the highest organ of kolkhoz administration. The meeting must be held not less than twice monthly. It elects the Managing Board and Control Commission, ratifies production plans, budget, building plans, instructions to brigade leaders, output quotas, estimates of work days, contracts with the Machine-Tractor Station, allocations to various funds, and internal rules. The general membership meeting also has the power of expulsion of members.

The Managing Board is the kolkhoz executive organ. It is elected by the general membership meeting for two years and consists of from five to nine members, depending on the size of the kolkhoz. The kolkhoz Chairman, elected by the general membership meeting for a term of two years, functions as Chairman of the Managing Board. The latter elects from among its members one or two vice-chairmen. The management is responsible for the accounting of output, labor, and money, according to the rules determined by the local and central organs of the People's Commissariat for Agriculture. The Board assigns to its members various functions of management in the economy and productive work of the kolkhoz. According to the Statute, the Managing Board allocates credits within the limits of the budget ratified by the general membership. The Chairman directs all current work; under the law, he can be removed from his post before the expiration of his term only by a court decree or by decision of the general membership meeting. The Control Commission, consisting of three to five persons, is elected for two years. It audits cash and accounts quarterly and checks on the efficiency and legality of all work of the kolkhoz and its organs. The accountant may be selected by the Managing Board from among the kolkhoz members, or may be hired. Within the limits of the budget, the accountant manages the funds of the kolkhoz, makes deductions for stock reserves, records work days of and advances to members, keeps accounts, statistical records, etc. All expense vouchers must be countersigned by the Chairman or a vice-chairman, and by the accountant.

Thus, the Statute fairly consistently sustains the principle of kolkhoz self-government. It would be incorrect to say that the Statute is entirely disregarded. It is followed rigidly in everything relating to the duties of both the kolkhoz and its members. It closely regulates internal administrative and economic activities. But it is far from the reality of kolkhoz relations with the government. Here the kolkhoz functions along entirely different lines, far removed from the spirit and the principles of the Statute. Here self-government and the right of the general membership meeting to decide basic questions are, to a great extent, quite fictitious. All decisions on important questions are previously determined by State and Party organs. All important matters, such as deductions from kolkhoz funds, decentralization of labor, methods of compensation for work, etc., are decided by organs of the central government without preliminary discussion in the kolkhozes. The general membership meeting is obliged to accept government decisions on all important questions. In the discussion of local and current questions, general membership meetings have a somewhat greater function, but even here the outcome is pre-determined by decisions of the Communist group in the kolkhoz. Only in recent years has the Party group been forced to consider majority opinion to some extent.

The question of self-government in the kolkhoz is decisive. That real conditions fail to conform to the Statute and lack the co-operative elements which Lenin believed would stimulate membership activity are facts which have frequently troubled political leaders. In public speeches (26 March and 25 June 1932;

15 February 1935) Stalin has spoken of the necessity of 'leaving all decisions to the kolkhozes themselves,' 'not to substitute administrative bullying and bossing for guidance,' 'not to impose decisions on the kolkhozes,' etc. But the need to obtain from the kolkhozes foodstuffs for cities and raw materials for factories, the hostility of a considerable part of the collectivized peasantry to government policies (a result of compulsory collectivization), and the early economic weakness of the kolkhozes created a situation in which the very speeches of Stalin and government decrees violated the principle of self-government and prompted local State organs to encroach upon it further, imposing their decisions on the kolkhozes.

In recent years, following the economic consolidation of the kolkhozes, the influence of members' opinions has slowly begun to increase. Self-government has begun to be realized in practice, although still in very incomplete forms.

Compared to the constant struggle between the kolkhoz and the government, relations among the various organs within the kolkhoz are relatively unimportant. The struggle over 'one-man control,' important in the early days of Soviet factories, assumed no sharp character in the kolkhozes. It manifested itself in the struggle for leadership between the general membership meeting and the Chairman or, more often, between the Managing Board and the Chairman. In view of the co-operative theory of the kolkhoz, there could be no dispute in principle regarding the decisive role of the general membership meeting. According to the Statute, the Chairman must carry out both the law and the decisions of the meeting. In practice, however, he directs all work, merely reporting to the Managing Board and the general membership meeting. Friction between the Chairman and the Managing Board over jurisdiction is common. In these conflicts the Chairman usually has the support of government and Party organs.

The Chairman is, in fact, responsible both to government organs and to the members of the collective. He must do much to organize smooth and successful functioning. He must fulfil all government demands with respect to the compulsory delivery of goods, labor duties, 'curbing individualistic tendencies' etc.

He is the first to bear the brunt of dissatisfactions of the mass of peasant members. He is held responsible for grievances and unsatisfactory results. If he yields to the pressure of the peasants among whom he must live and work, he is subject to disciplinary action by the government. If he unquestioningly fulfils all the demands of the District Soviet and of local organs of the People's Commissariat for Agriculture, regardless of the mood of the peasant mass, he provokes sharp resentment among the members and often finds himself in a situation in which productive work is utterly impossible. The Chairman must maneuver more or less successfully between the demands of the government and the needs of the kolkhoz members, in extreme cases indicating to the government the necessity of yielding to urgent peasant demands. Chairmanship is thus an extremely difficult and responsible task. It was not by accident that, in the first period of collectivization, the Chairman, when not a city worker sent by the government, or a local friend of the Party, was sometimes chosen by lot from among the kolkhoz members.

In recent years, as the kolkhozes have become economically stronger and as their relations with the government have been relatively stabilized on the basis of definite if exacting law, kolkhozes have begun to produce personalities capable of leadership. At the same time, the functions of the Chairman have become considerably easier and have begun to resemble the usual ones of a manager of an economic enterprise.

* * * * *

From the start, all kolkhoz work has been conducted under the constant direction and control of government and Party agencies. The question of the 'triangle'—managers, Party, trade union—so acute in the early administration of State factories, assumed a somewhat different character in agriculture. Rural trade unions had always been weak and never claimed a share in the administration of the kolkhozes. Here the triangle was composed of representatives of the government, the Communist Party, and the kolkhoz.

Government organs with which the kolkhoz must deal are the District Soviet Executive Committee (*Raiispolkom*), the local (village) Soviet, agencies of the People's Commissariat for Agriculture, and Machine-Tractor Stations. The highest government agency in a district, the District Soviet Executive Committee, generally directs the entire work of the district's kolkhozes. Such direction has never weakened, although it has changed in form with changes in government policies. In 1929–32 the chief task of the District Executive Committee was the accomplishment of compulsory collectivization and the liquidation of the kulaks. Later it was to organize kolkhoz functioning, to select and train qualified kolkhoz administrators, and to enforce obligations imposed on the kolkhozes by the government. The District Soviet Executive Committee still retains general supervision over the work of kolkhozes. It gives orders regarding policy towards individual peasants applying for membership, fixes quotas for grain collection, ratifies production plans, resolves conflicts between kolkhozes and other local organizations. Generally it enforces policies through the local Soviets, but in such important matters as non-fulfillment of grain collections, violations of sowing plans, epidemics, sharp conflicts, it sends special agents to the kolkhozes.

Direction of current production work is carried out by regional and district offices of the People's Commissariat for Agriculture and by the Machine-Tractor Stations. The former decide questions of general agrarian policy and those affecting kolkhoz cadres. Distinction must be made here between kolkhozes serviced by Machine-Tractor Stations and those that are not; the latter are directed by Commissariat organs. On the other hand, the work of kolkhozes serviced by Machine-Tractor Stations, comprising the vast majority, is directed by the Stations in so far as land cultivation is concerned, and by the Commissariat with respect to other branches (animal husbandry, gardening, bee-keeping, etc.). The role of the Machine-Tractor Stations in the operation of kolkhozes is generally great. Besides their functions in tilling, sowing, and harvesting, they directly supervise all current work of the kolkhozes. Between 1933 and 1935, when every Machine-Tractor Station had its Political Department, the latter was the immediate authority on questions of current operation and carried out its decisions through general membership meetings or orders to Chairmen. The Machine-Tractor Stations were thus the 'chief lever in the reorganization of agriculture along socialist principles.' Since 1935 kolkhoz operations have been freed of direct interference by the Machine-Tractor Stations, but the latter still supervise. 'They help the kolkhozes set up plans of production and finance. They fix the correct crop-rotation system, assist in the organization of work and the allocation of income, the training of leaders, the setting up of accounting systems, the organization of competition, and the struggle to increase soil productivity.'

Economic relations between Stations and kolkhozes are fixed by contracts based on a model approved by the Council of People's Commissars on 17 February 1934. Such contracts must be ratified by the general meeting of the kolkhoz.

The organs of the Communist Party play no less a role in the life of the kolkhoz. They direct every important step in its activities. Between 1929 and 1935 a hidden but stubborn struggle went on between Party and government organs for control of kolkhoz productive activity. Characteristically, the Party organs fought not so much against the District Soviet Executive Committees or the Machine-Tractor Stations, whose chiefs were always Communists, as against the local organs of the Commissariat for Agriculture, where the decisive role was frequently played by agricultural specialists. The Statute of 1935 attempted to establish the organs of the Commissariat and the Machine-Tractor Stations as supervisors of productive activity. But the struggle persists. In 1940 *Pravda* wrote that 'Party District Committees have been transformed into a sort of district agricultural office.' A periodical of the Central Committee of the Communist Party also states that 'Party agencies are still striving to displace the organs of the Commissariat for Agriculture.'

Formally, local and district Party organizations have no right to interfere with production, but, as in all other realms of life, they play the determining role in solving major questions, particularly those connected with Party agrarian policies. The Political Departments (composed of Communists) set up in 1933 in each Machine-Tractor Station to direct kolkhoz activities, were important in the first period of kolkhoz organization. Early in 1935 they were abolished and the direction of political work was taken over by the Vice-Chairman of Machine-Tractor Stations and by special agents of the district and regional Party committees. Despite the strengthening of the regular State organs, the highest Party bodies still consider it necessary to maintain constant and close supervision over kolkhozes. In 1940 the Council of People's Commissars issued a decree placing full responsibility for crop rotation on Party district committees, although this is the function of State agencies, i.e. District Soviet Executive Committees, the Commissariat for Agriculture, and the Machine-Tractor Stations. At the beginning of 1941, almost on the eve of the war, a circular of the Central Committee of the Communist Party instructed Party organizations to 'direct daily the work of enlightenment in the villages, to organize leadership and supervise the execution of instructions of Party and government in the villages.'

Some idea of the enormous number of people in government and Party organs of district and regional centers that are engaged in controlling kolkhoz activities can be gained from the fact that, for the 27,000 kolkhozes of the eastern Ukraine, there were over 29,000 responsible officials in control agencies. Although friction between Party and government organs does not, under Soviet conditions, assume the character of open conflict, the position of the kolkhoz in such an 'interdepartmental struggle' is, nevertheless, quite complicated.

The third member of the 'triangle,' the kolkhoz itself, was at first a helpless object. 'The kolkhoz peasant is completely removed from control in the organization of production.' 'He must play merely the passive role of a labor unit.' 'All kolkhoz affairs are decided by the District Executive Committee and the District Committee.' The representative of the kolkhoz, its Chairman, could only maneuver between the Party organs and those of the Commissariat for Agriculture, 'registering' the discontent of his members and pleading their needs. Any expression of opposition immediately resulted in removal from the chairmanship by joint action of Party and State organs. True, government decrees and Party orders have frequently and categorically forbidden the appointment or removal of kolkhoz chairmen. In reality, even as late as 1941, there were cited many removals.

*   *   *   *   *

Economic power has, however, its own logic. As the economic importance of the kolkhozes grew, as chairmen and Managing Boards ceased to arouse political distrust and gained in skill, the government was obliged, in the interests of production, to refrain from 'direct management,' i.e., interference with current work. Yet, because of the peculiar social structure of the kolkhoz, the emancipation of its elected administration from control by government and Party organs is a far slower process than the comparable one in industrial enterprises. The reality of the process cannot be doubted, however.

All questions of taxes, health, and education are decided jointly by the kolkhoz and the local Soviet. In many regions where kolkhozes are economically strong, they have taken over all communal functions of local Soviets: maintenance of roads, lighting, schools, hospitals, etc. At one time, government organs considered abolishing village Soviets and transferring their functions to the kolkhozes, but the central government decided to preserve them as local government branches for maintaining public safety, collecting taxes, issuing legal documents, recording births, marriages, and deaths, etc.

In addition, the kolkhoz has a close relationship with consumer and sales co-operatives, through which it disposes of a part of its production and purchases consumer goods. Where kolkhozes are located near sovkhozes, a constant relationship is maintained. The sovkhoz assists the kolkhoz in procuring selected seeds and blooded stock, while the kolkhoz performs a variety of work for the sovkhoz at harvest time.

CHAPTER 6

Communist Controls

The instruments of control in Russia are the State, the Party, the bureaucratic Apparatus, the Secret Police, and the Army. For the purposes of our study, probably of least consequence is the machinery of the State. To a large extent it is an elaborate façade. The real ruling force is the Party, or rather the small group of elite which dominates the Party. Most intimately connected and concerned with the execution of Party directives is the Apparatus of the bureaucracy. The Secret Police infiltrate the whole fabric of Soviet society and constitute an essential part of it. Back of all stands the Army, an extension of the Party's will.

Some stress is laid, in the sections below, on the Secret Police and the Army. But indispensible as these are, the Apparatus and the guiding work of the Party are given greatest emphasis, particularly the former since its nature and function are least understood by the average American.

The sections on the State, Party, and Secret Police are from Merle Fainsod's HOW RUSSIA IS RULED. *That on the bureaucratic Apparatus is from the previously cited work of Barrington Moore,* SOVIET POLITICS—THE DILEMMA OF POWER. *The concluding section, on the Army, is from Julian Towster's* POLITICAL POWER IN THE U.S.S.R.

Dr. Fainsod, working with his colleagues at the Russian Research Center at Harvard University, has produced, in HOW RUSSIA IS RULED, *a valuable and extremely detailed analysis of the power structure of the Soviet Union. It is a work which will probably be consulted for many years. Still, the*

124

*editor has mixed feelings in presenting excerpts from it. One
of the basic criteria used in assembling this volume is the
avoidance, as far as possible, of loaded language. Dr. Fainsod,
it is felt, does not escape so freely from such a charge as
could be wished. The reader is urged, therefore, to watch for
the prejudicial adjective, the slanted phrase.*

*Professor Towster is Assistant Professor of Political
Science at the University of Chicago. He brings to his work,
in the words of Professor Quincy Wright, "a broad knowledge of Russian history, detailed examination of Soviet official documents and official pronouncements of the Communist Party, and an understanding of Marxist-Leninist
ideology based upon study of the original sources in the Russian language."*

*Immediately following is Fainsod's description of the
structure of the Soviet State.*

FROM

Merle Fainsod

HOW RUSSIA IS RULED

THE Constitution of 1936, although amended in detail over the
years, remains in effect today. Its plan can be briefly summarized. Chapter One, entitled the Organization of Society, proclaims the USSR as a "socialist state of workers and peasants"
and outlines the role of state, collective farm, and private property. Particularly notable in terms of its intended appeal to the
West is the declaration in Article 10 that "the right of citizens
to personal ownership of their incomes from work and of their
savings, of their dwelling houses and subsidiary household economy, their household furniture and utensils and articles of personal use and convenience, as well as the right of inheritance of
personal property of citizens, is protected by law."

The next eight chapters of the Constitution lay down the
political structure of the state. After reiterating that the USSR
is a federal state and that each union republic reserves the "right
freely to secede," the powers of the central governmental organs

are specified in such all-embracing scope as largely to negate the federal pattern on which the government is allegedly constructed. The highest organ of state authority is declared to be the Supreme Soviet of the USSR. The Supreme Soviet is divided into two chambers: the Soviet of the Union, which is directly elected on the basis of one deputy for every three hundred thousand inhabitants, and the Soviet of Nationalities, which is also directly elected on the basis of twenty-five deputies from each union republic, eleven deputies from each autonomous republic, five deputies from each autonomous region, and one deputy from each national area. Both chambers serve for a term of four years and have equal rights in initiating and enacting legislation. In case they disagree and their disagreements cannot be reconciled (an eventuality that is hardly likely to occur under a system of one-party rule), the Presidium of the Supreme Soviet has the authority to dissolve the Supreme Soviet and order new elections.

The Presidium is elected at a joint session of both chambers. As originally established in 1936, it consisted of a chairman, eleven vice-chairmen, a secretary, and twenty-four members. Its membership has since been reorganized to provide for a chairman, sixteen vice-chairmen, a secretary, and fifteen members. The Presidium functions as a collegial presidency. It performs the ornamental functions of head of state, convenes and dissolves sessions of the Supreme Soviet, and appoints and relieves cabinet ministers on the recommendation of the Council of Ministers and subject to subsequent confirmation by the Supreme Soviet. It has the power to annul decisions of the Council of Ministers (before 1946 called Council of People's Commissars) in case they do not conform to law. It interprets laws of the USSR, issues decrees, exercises the right of pardon, ratifies and denounces treaties, proclaims martial law, issues mobilization orders, is authorized to declare war in the intervals between sessions of the Supreme Soviet, and performs a number of other functions of lesser significance.

Executive and administrative authority is vested in a Council of Ministers whose appointment requires the confirmation of the Supreme Soviet. Theoretically the Council of Ministers is responsible to the Supreme Soviet, and its Presidium: members of the Supreme Soviet may address questions to the ministers who are required to "give a verbal or written reply in the respective chamber within a period not exceeding three days." The stenographic reports of the sessions of the Supreme Soviet give no indication that this "right of interpellation" is exercised.

The 1936 Constitution, like its predecessor, provides for three types of ministries: all-union, union-republic, and republic. Since 1936, there has been a considerable expansion in the number of all-union and union-republic ministries with heavy industry largely reserved for all-union jurisdiction while light industry, agriculture, and trade are entrusted to the union-republic ministries. The decentralization of operative functions in the latter case is combined with continued centralization of planning and direction. Decisions and orders of the Council of Ministers of the USSR are binding on all lower organs.

The government of the union republics consists of a Supreme Soviet of one chamber, its Presidium, and a Council of Ministers composed of union-republic and republic ministries. The union-republic ministries are subordinated to the council of ministries of the union republic and its supreme soviet as well as to their counterpart ministries at the center. The republic ministries are directly subordinate to the union republic's council of ministers and its supreme soviet. Autonomous republics also possess their own supreme soviets, presidiums, and councils of ministers.

The local organs of state authority (territories, regions, districts, cities, rural localities, etc.) include soviets elected for a two-year term and the executive committees or *ispolkoms* which are formally responsible to the soviets and selected by them.

The Constitution also provides for a judicial system consisting of a Supreme Court of the USSR, supreme courts of the union republics, territorial and regional courts, courts of the autonomous republics and autonomous regions, area courts, special courts of the USSR established by the Supreme Soviet, and people's courts. People's courts are popularly elected for three-year terms; the members of other courts are selected by their corresponding soviets for five-year terms. Cases are heard in public "unless otherwise provided by law." The accused "is guaranteed the right to be defended by counsel," a right which many survivors of the Great Purge testify was suspended in their cases despite the explicit phraseology of the Constitution. According to Article 112 of the Constitution, "judges are independent and subject only to the law." A recent commentary by a Soviet jurist, N. N. Polyansky, sheds light on the meaning of this formula.

The independence of the judges referred to in Article 112 of the Stalin Constitution does not and cannot signify their independence of politics. The judges are subject only to the law—this provision expresses the subordination of the judges to the policy of the Soviet regime, which finds its expression in the law.

The demand that the work of the judge be subject to the law and the demand that it be subject to the policy of the Communist Party cannot be in contradiction in our country.

*   *   *   *   *

The utilization of the soviets as an instrument of governance has its own supporting rationalization. In the authoritative words of Stalin, the Soviets are a "transmission belt" linking the Party with the masses, "organizations which rally the labouring masses . . . under the leadership of the Party." They are also, according to Stalin, "the most democratic and therefore the most authoritative organizations of the masses, which facilitate to the utmost their participation in the work of building up the new state and its administration, and which bring into full play the revolutionary energy, initiative and creative abilities of the masses in the struggle for the destruction of the old order, in the struggle for the new, proletarian order."

Stripped of their rhetorical flourishes, these statements point to the important role the soviets play in the Communist system of political controls. The soviets themselves are Party-dominated. Responsibility for selection of the membership of the soviets and for direction of their activity remains with the Party. In each soviet, the inner board of control is invariably the Communist fraction. At the same time, the Party leadership seeks to utilize the mechanism of the soviets to broaden its influence with the masses, to enlist sympathetic non-Party elements in the tasks of administration and government, and to reward outstanding achievement by designating the deserving for membership in the Soviets.

At lower levels of the governmental hierarchy, the soviets discharge an important function in ensuring large-scale participation in community activities. In the winter elections of 1947–48, approximately 1,600,000 deputies were chosen to serve in local soviets. In addition, many soviets follow the practice of organizing groups of *aktivs* who are available to assist the soviet members in carrying out their responsibilities. While actual administrative assignments are reserved for the *ispolkoms* or executive committees of the soviets rather than ordinary soviet deputies or members of the *aktiv*, the latter are drawn into a consideration of communal plans and activities, even if it be only in the form of passive attendance at meetings at which reports are rendered by the chairman and members of the *ispolkom*. Ordinarily, however, both deputies and members of the *aktiv* are expected to take the lead in checking the execution of work assignments by soviet officials, in mobilizing voluntary labor for civic improvements, and in serving as agitators among the masses to spread devotion to soviet goals. Since a substantial part of the work plans of local soviets is concerned with the maintenance and expansion of communal services and involves such everyday needs of the electorate as housing, sanitation, transportation, and recreation, interest in the activities of local soviets is not too difficult to arouse. Party-directed participation at this level of government builds on a genuine concern with common requirements.

By contrast, the role of the Supreme Soviet appears largely ornamental and decorative. The matters which engage its attention are of transcendent importance. They embrace such weighty problems as the Five Year Plans, the enactment of the annual budget, and the organization of the government of the USSR. But the proceedings of the Supreme Soviet convey the impression of a well-rehearsed theatrical spectacle from which almost all elements of conflict have been eliminated. The slight budget modifications which are initiated by the Supreme Soviet and the occasional criticisms of the performance of lagging ministries give every evidence of being part of a prepared script. Like the elections, the meetings of the Supreme Soviet symbolize national unity. The proposals of the government are unanimously hailed and unanimously ratified.

The composition of the Supreme Soviet reflects its character as a rally of the faithful. The deputies consist predominantly of members of the Party and governmental apparatus. Only a small minority are ordinary workers and collective farmers, and most of these are usually Stakhanovites who are being specially honored for their productive achievements. The Supreme Soviet is a mobilization of leading figures of Soviet society, but the forum in which they operate lacks creative significance. All important decisions come ready-made from the Party leadership. The task of the Supreme Soviet is not to question but to execute, to clothe the Party thesis in the garb of constitutional legality. The result is necessarily to minimize the authority of the whole apparatus of soviets. As long as the top Party command remains the real seat of power in Soviet society, the soviets and the constitutional structure built around them remain imposing façades rather than sovereign organs.

The Soviet regime has demonstrated great skill in using the trappings of mass democracy to mask the entrenched position of the dictatorial elite which dominates Soviet society. Constitutional myths and symbols have been ingeniously adapted to contribute to the illusion of mass participation and mass control. But the actual configurations of power in the Soviet system are difficult to conceal. The political realities of Soviet life speak the unmistakable language of a one-party dictatorship in which ultimate power is deposited in a narrow ruling group in the Kremlin.

Now follows Fainsod's description of the functions and structure of the Communist Party.

The prototype of the ideal Bolshevik which the Party leadership seeks to fashion and create is essentially that of a dedicated subordinate who identifies himself with the ruling group as the incarnation of the organizational wisdom of the Party. The stern demands which the Party requires its members to meet are made dramatically manifest in the new Party Rules adopted at the Nineteenth Party Congress in October, 1952. "It is the duty of the Party member," state the rules,

a) To guard the unity of the Party in every way, as the prime condition of the Party's strength and might;

b) to be an active fighter for the fulfillment of Party decisions . . .

c) to be an example at work, to master the technique of his own job, constantly to increase his working skills, and in every way to guard and strengthen public Socialist property, as the sacred and inviolable basis of the Soviet order;

d) constantly to strengthen contact with the masses, to respond promptly to the desires and needs of the working people, and to explain to the non-Party masses the meaning of the Party policy and decisions, remembering that the strength and invincibility of our Party lies in its close inseparable ties with the people;

e) to work at increasing his own political awareness, at mastering the principles of Marxism-Leninism;

f) to observe Party and state discipline, obligatory for all party members alike . . .

g) to develop self-criticism and criticism from below, to expose and to seek to eliminate inadequacies in work and to struggle against ostentacious self-satisfaction and complacency in work . . .

h) to report to leading Party bodies right up to the Party Central Committee, on shortcomings in work, regardless of the persons involved . . .

i) to be truthful and honest before the Party and never permit concealment or distortion of truth . . .

j) to keep Party and State secrets and to display political vigilance, remembering that the vigilance of Communists is necessary on every sector and under all circumstances . . .

k) at any post entrusted to him by the Party to carry out without fail the party directives on the correct selection of cadres on the basis of their political and working qualifications. Violating these directives, selecting workers on the basis of friendship, personal loyalties, local ties, or kinship is incompatible with Party membership.

* * * * *

From the point of view of the leaders of the regime, the Party organization operates essentially as a disciplined phalanx to carry out their will. The Party has its units in every major organization and establishment in Soviet society. The Party leadership holds its local representatives responsible for the fulfillment of plans in all local areas and organizations to which they are assigned. To be sure, day-to-day operating responsibilities are

vested in the governmental hierarchy of managers and administrators. But every level of the governmental hierarchy is both
interpenetrated with, and subject to check by, the corresponding
level of the Party hierarchy. Since the Party leadership is the
incarnation of supreme power in the Soviet state, its local emis-
saries serve not only as the eyes and ears but also the voice of
the Kremlin. As a matter of accepted practice, they are expected
to keep in touch with all the enterprises and activities within
their jurisdiction, to be alert to any failure of performance, to
report constantly to their own higher authorities on the state of
plan-fulfillment, and to take such measures, in collaboration with
local administrators, as will insure the realization of the goals and
tasks which the Party high command has set.

Through the party organization, the leadership seeks to consolidate its dominion over the key positions in Soviet society. It
incorporates and assimilates the growing elite into the Party's
ranks. The road to power and preferment in the Soviet system
lies through affiliation with the Party; important posts in the
Soviet control apparatus are reserved for trusted Party members.
By absorbing the power-seekers in Soviet society and making
access to authority dependent on enrollment in the Party, the
Party leadership endeavors to construct a dependable governing
machine which will be responsive to its commands. At the same
time, it attempts to prevent the emergence of any competing
powers which might challenge its monopoly of political direction. While the ruling group is primarily concerned with the
selection of cadres for governing responsibilities, it also tries to
preserve its link with the masses by recruiting leading workers
and collective farmers as party members. The mass membership
of the Party serves the double purpose of widening its popular
support and of facilitating the acceptance and execution of
policies determined by the high command.

A constant objective of the Party leadership is to transform
the Party organization into a completely trustworthy instrument
of the ruling group. The Bolshevik steeling of the Party is accomplished primarily by indoctrination. Through an elaborate
network of party educational institutions, the Party leadership
seeks to instill *partiinost* (devotion to the party) in every party

member. While conformity is enforced by stringent discipline, the leadership demands more than mere conformity. It strives to convert every member to a responsible agent who is deeply persuaded that the ruling group possesses the keys which will unlock the secrets of the universe. The leadership endeavors in this fashion to breed a conscious acceptance of the necessity of subordination. It seeks to build a disciplined army solidified by a unifying faith.

The Party organization also utilizes its members to expand the influence of the Party among non-Party Soviet citizens. A significant feature of modern totalitarian dictatorship is the careful attention devoted to the manipulation of mass sentiment for the purpose of enrolling support for the regime. The Communist dictatorship, in part because of its own historical rise to power on a tide of exploitation of mass grievances, has always taken this function of mobilizing mass support with high seriousness. Through a complex network of agitational, educational, and propaganda activities, which are largely manned by Party specialists, and through control of the media of mass communication, the Party leadership assiduously pursues its objective of winning doctrinal ascendancy over the mind of Soviet man. Party agitation insinuates itself into every crevice of the Soviet social structure, and no competitors are tolerated. As missionaries to the heathen, the Party member communicates the goals and demands of the ruling group into the farthest reaches of Soviet society. . . .

The structure of the Party is designed to provide a skeletal framework to accomplish these multiform purposes. Under the new rules ratified by the Nineteenth Party Congress (1952), the Presidium stands at the peak of the Party pyramid and replaces the old Politbureau and Orgbureau, both of which were abolished by the Congress.

The Twentieth Congress, meeting in February, 1956, left this unchanged.

As originally established, the Presidium consisted of twenty-five members and eleven alternates. After Stalin's death, it was reduced to ten members and four alternates.

This was changed by the Twentieth Congress to eleven members and six alternates. The number included in the top policy-making body has fluctuated since 1918.

According to the official announcement, the change was made "in order to ensure more operative leadership." The same communique revealed that an inner Bureau existed to guide the work of the old Presidium. Presumably, it is this Bureau which has emerged as the nucleus of the new Presidium. Headed by Malenkov and dominated by eight members who have been carried over from the old Politbureau, the Presidium commands a position of unquestioned ascendancy in the Party.

Early in 1955 Malenkov's dominant Party position was assumed by Khrushchev.

Formally it is chosen by the Central Committee of the Party; in fact, if past practice in connection with the Politbureau and Orgbureau is followed, new members are likely to be coöpted, and the role of the Central Committee of the Party will be limited to ratifying the choices which Stalin's successors approve.

The "new departure" inaugurated by the Twentieth Congress in 1956 is discussed in editorial comment, and by Mikoyan, later.

According to the Party Rules, the "supreme organ" of the Party is the Party Congress which is convened "not less often than once every four years." Under the old Party Rules, the Congress was supposed to meet at least once every three years. Actually, a period of four years elapsed between the meeting of the Sixteenth Party Congress in 1930 and the assembly of the Seventeenth Congress in 1934. The Eighteenth Congress did not meet until 1939, some five years later, and the Nineteenth did not take place until 1952, after an interval of more than thirteen years.

The Eighteenth Congress was probably delayed because Stalin in the period 1936–1938 was engaged in a bloody purge of the Party. After the meeting of the Eighteenth Congress, World War II intervened. As noted above, the latest meeting was held in 1956.

Since the rout of the left- and right-wing oppositions in the late twenties and the consolidation of Stalin's power, the Congresses have lost whatever creative significance they once possessed. All decisions are taken unanimously, and the discussions give every outward evidence of being carefully organized in advance to reach a foreordained result. Essentially, the Congresses have become a rally of Party and state functionaries who assemble to applaud and ratify the policies proclaimed by the ruling group. From the point of view of the leadership, the Congresses are chiefly significant as a convenient platform from which new goals and objectives may be launched, revisions in the Party line announced, and shifts in the top Party command formally approved.

The Party Rules require the Congress to elect a Central Committee and a Central Auditing Commission. The latter body is of minor importance. According to the Rules, it "inspects (a) the speed and correctness of the conduct of affairs in central bodies of the Party and the organizational condition of the apparatus of the Secretariat of the Central Committee; (b) the treasury and the enterprises of the Party Central Committee." The chairman of the Auditing Committee renders a brief report to the Congress in which attention is ordinarily called to instances of lax financial discipline in the affairs of Party organizations and the size and efficiency of the Party apparatus are critically appraised.

The Central Committee is, in theory at least, a far more important institution. According to the Party Rules, "in the intervals between Party Congresses, [it] directs the whole work of the Party; represents the work of the Party in its relation with other parties, organizations, and institutions; organizes various Party institutions and directs their activity; appoints editorial boards of Party publications of large local organizations; organizes and directs undertakings of social significance; directs the manpower and resources of the Party, and administers the central fund." It also "guides the work of the central Soviet and public organizations through the Party groups within them" and "has the right to set up political sections and assign Party organizers . . . to individual sectors of Socialist construction which may assume a special importance for the national economy of the country as a whole. . . ." The Central Committee is required to hold "not less than one plenary session every six months."

According to the decisions of the 1956 Congress, this Committee is composed of 133 members, and over a hundred candidate members.

In recent years, the Central Committee has been consigned to the shadowy limbo of mysterious Soviet institutions whose meetings and activities go largely unreported. The large size of the committee, the character of its membership, and the fact that the Party Rules provide for relatively infrequent meetings suggest that its significance is largely honorific. A host of decrees continues to be issued in the name of the Central Committee, but their frequency and character indicate that they derive from the Secretariat of the Central Committee rather than the committee itself. While paucity of information counsels caution in coming to firm conclusions, the available evidence points to a considerable eclipse in the role of the Central Committee as compared with the situation in the twenties.

At this point it is necessary to call attention to a rather startling turn taken by Soviet leaders. What Fainsod says above was true for the Stalin period and shortly thereafter. However, the leaders at the Twentieth Congress vigorously criticized the "cult of personality"—their euphemism for Stalin's dictatorship—which had developed in the period 1925–1953. This Congress lauded collective leadership, especially mentioning the importance of the work of the Central Committee. Because of the possibly "revolutionary" significance of this decision of the leaders of the 1956 Congress, the editor feels justified in quoting in extenso from a speech by Mikoyan, currently rated number three man in the Soviet Union. This excerpt is taken from a Reuters London dispatch reprinted by the NEW YORK TIMES for February 19, 1956.

The conclusions and theoretical precepts contained in [Communist Party First Secretary Nikita S.] Khrushchev's report say that our Central Committee, as is worthy of an organ of the most experienced

Communist party, does not simply repeat known theoretical precepts of Marxism-Leninism.

Guided by the mighty Marxist method of understanding the laws of social development, the Central Committee clarifies the contemporary events of social development, explains them in a Marxist way and arms the working class with conclusions, which generalize and explain not only the facts and events of the period but also subsequent events both in capitalist and Socialist countries.

. . . The main feature which characterizes the work of the Central Committee and its Presidium during the past three years is the fact that after a long interval collective leadership has been created in our Party.

*   *   *   *   *

The principle of collective leadership is elementary for the proletarian party, for the party of the Lenin type. However, one has to emphasize this old truth, because in the course of about twenty years we, in fact, had no collective leadership. The cult of personality condemned already by Marx and afterwards by Lenin, flourished, and this, of course, could not but exert an extremely negative influence on the situation within the party and on its work.

> *Cautious conclusions are still in order, but it would seem from this evidence that not only the Presidium, but the Central Committee are both very much to be taken into account as to where lies political power in the Soviet Union.*

In addition to the Presidium, the major central organs of the Party are the Secretariat and the Party Control Committee under the Central Committee. The 1952 Party Rules vest the Presidium with the power "to direct the work of the Central Committee between plenary sessions" and to provide that the Secretariat shall "direct current work, chiefly as concerns verification of the fulfillment of Party decisions and selection of cadres."

> *Obviously the First Chairman of the Secretariat is in a position to make and wield considerable power. Stalin's rise to power is commonly credited to his having this position. But it should not be forgotten that Malenkov later was First Chairman, with little effect upon his being able to retain power.*

In accordance with the new rules, the Party Control Committee

a) verifies the observance of Party discipline by Party members and candidates; calls to account Communists guilty of violating the Party program and rules or of breaches of Party and state discipline, as well as violators of Party ethics . . .

b) examines appeals against decisions of the central committees of the Communist Parties of Union republics and of territorial and regional Party committees concerning expulsions from the Party and Party censures;

c) has its representatives, independent of local Party bodies, in the republics, territories, and regions.

Next, Fainsod turns his attention to the Secret Police. This is from a chapter he has entitled "Terror as a System of Power."

The practice of totalitarian terror generates its own underlying theoretical justifications. The role of terror in Communist ideology furnishes a prime example. Violence is accepted as implicit in the class struggle. As Lenin said in defining the dissolution of the Constituent Assembly, "Violence when it is committed by the toiling and exploited masses is the kind of violence of which we approve." This instrumental attitude toward violence prepares the way for its sanctification when employed by the Party in the name of the working class and by the Party leadership in the name of the Party.

The rationalization of terror embraces two central propositions. The first emphasizes the safety of the Revolution as the supreme law. In the words of Lenin, "The Soviet Republic is a fortress besieged by world capital. . . . From this follows our right and our duty to mobilize the whole population to a man for the war." The second emphasizes the intransigence of the enemies of the Revolution, the necessity of crushing them completely if the Revolution itself is not to be destroyed. "What is the 'nutritive medium,' " asks Lenin,

which engenders counterrevolutionary enterprises, outbreaks, conspiracies, and so forth? . . . It is the medium of the bourgeoisie, of the bourgeois intelligentsia, of the kulaks in the countryside, and, everywhere, of the "non-Party" public, as well as of the Socialist-Revolutionaries and the Mensheviks. We must treble our watch over this medium, we must multiply it tenfold. We must multiply our vigilance, because counterrevolutionary attempts from this quarter are absolutely inevitable, precisely at the present moment and in the near future.

In essence, Stalin's defense of terror, delivered in an interview with a visiting Foreign Workers' Delegation on November 5, 1927, covers much the same ground, though with notably less frankness.

The GPU or Cheka is a punitive organ of the Soviet government. It is more or less analogous to the Committee of Public Safety which was formed during the Great French Revolution. . . . It is something in the nature of a military-political tribunal set up for the purpose of protecting the interests of the revolution from attacks on the part of the counterrevolutionary bourgeoisie and their agents. . . .

People advocate a maximum of leniency; they advise the dissolution of the GPU. . . . But can anyone guarantee that the capitalists of all countries will abandon the idea of organizing and financing counterrevolutionary groups of plotters, terrorists, incendiaries, and bombthrowers after the liquidation of the GPU? . . .

We are a country surrounded by capitalist states. The internal enemies of our revolution are the agents of the capitalists of all countries. . . . In fighting against the enemies at home, we fight the counterrevolutionary elements of all countries. . . .

No, Comrades, we do not wish to repeat the mistakes of the Parisian Communards. The GPU is necessary for the Revolution and will continue to exist to the terror of the enemies of the proletariat.

The real significance of Stalin's theory of Soviet terror did not become fully manifest until the period of the Great Purge in the thirties. The liquidation of the Old Bolsheviks made it altogether clear that the salient role of terror in Stalinist ideology was to serve as a bulwark of defense for his own monopoly of Party leadership. Since this involved establishing a regime of terror within the Party, Stalin was faced with the problem of reconciling his innovation with the traditional notion that terror was reserved for the class enemy. The problem was neatly and ruthlessly solved by identifying any form of opposition to Stalin with counter-revolution and foreign espionage. The formula of

capitalist encirclement proved elastic enough to embrace the
enemy inside the Party as well as the enemy outside.

*   *   *   *   *

After the Great Purge, Stalin again faced the problem of reconciling the retention of these strong-arm methods with the claim
that antagonistic classes had ceased to exist in the Soviet Union.
In his report to the Eighteenth Party Congress in 1939, Stalin ad-
dressed himself to the issue. "It is sometimes asked: 'We have
abolished the exploiting classes; there are no longer any hostile
classes in the country; there is nobody to suppress; hence there is
no more need for the state; it must die away— Why then do we
not help our socialist state to die away? . . . Is it not time we
relegated the state to the museum of antiquities?'" Again Stalin
rested his case for the retention of the terror apparatus on the
allegation of capitalist encirclement:

> These questions not only betray an underestimation of the capitalist
> encirclement, but also an underestimation of the role and significance
> of the bourgeois states and their organs, which send spies, assassins and
> wreckers into our country and are waiting for a favourable oppor-
> tunity to attack it by armed force. They likewise betray an under-
> estimation of the role and significance of our socialist state and of its
> military, punitive and intelligence organs, which are essential for the
> defense of the socialist land from foreign attack.

Writing in 1950, after a considerable expansion of Soviet power
as a result of World War II, Stalin remained committed to "the
conclusion that in the face of capitalist encirclement, when the
victory of the socialist revolution has taken place in one country alone while capitalism continues to dominate in all other
countries, the country where the revolution has triumphed must
not weaken but must strengthen in every way its state, state
organs, intelligence agencies, and army if it does not want to be
destroyed by capitalist encirclement." Behind these rationaliza-
tions was the crystallization of a system of government in which
terror had become the essential ingredient. Defended originally
as an expression of the class interests of the proletariat, its edge
was first turned against all opponents of Communist ascendancy

and finally against any appearance of challenge to the domination of the ruling clique.

*   *   *   *   *

Current official material concerning the organization of the police and terror apparatus of the Soviet state is virtually non-existent. The traditional policy of the Soviet regime has been to impose a blanket of secrecy on this phase of its operations. This blanket has been substantially lifted in recent years by the revelations of Soviet escapees who have served in the secret police or whose work brought them into intimate contact with it. Much of the detailed information which has been made available in this fashion dates back to 1941 or even earlier. While some of it has undoubtedly been outdated by subsequent organizational changes, an analysis of the structure of the police apparatus as it prevailed a decade ago may well have continuing significance in indicating the range and character of police responsibilities.

In February 1941 it was announced that the NKVD would be divided into two commissariats, the NKGB or People's Commissariat of State Security and the NKVD or People's Commissariat of Internal Affairs. With the outbreak of war, however, the two commissariats were reunited, and the planned division did not take place until April 1943. In 1946 the commissariats were renamed ministries and became the MGB or Ministry of State Security and the MVD or Ministry of Internal Affairs. The MGB inherited the secret policy functions of the old NKVD; all other functions were relegated to the MVD. In 1949–50 the border guards and troops of internal security were also transferred to MGB jurisdiction. After the death of Stalin in March 1953, the MGB and MVD were again reunited in a new Ministry of Internal Affairs (MVD). . . .

The state security apparatus of the MVD is particularly important in terms of its impact on Soviet life since its agents penetrate every crevice of the social structure. Its responsibilities include the protection of high governmental and Party officials, the enforcement of security regulations, the conduct of espionage abroad, the organization of counterintelligence activity in the Soviet Union and abroad, the censorship of correspondence within the Soviet Union and with foreign countries, the planting of agents in all Soviet organizations, and the supervision of a network of informers to detect disloyalty and to report on the attitude of the Soviet populace toward the regime.

*   *   *   *   *

While no authoritative current information is available on the internal structure of the security apparatus of the MVD, the organization of its predecessor agency in the NKVD in the period 1939–1941 has been extensively described in the reports of escapees. A number of accounts compiled by different informants agree in identifying the same basic subdivisions, usually described in Soviet terminology as Chief Administrations. The First Administration was concerned with the security of high Party and governmental leaders. The Economic Administration (EKU) was responsible for coping with wrecking, sabotage, production failures, and other "counterrevolutionary" activity in Soviet industry and agriculture. All personnel occupying responsible positions in Soviet economic life had to be investigated and cleared by EKU, which operated through special sections located in all industrial enterprises of any importance. EKU was also responsible for the collection of economic information from foreign countries. The Secret Political Administration concentrated its fire against members of the Trotsky-Zinoviev and Right oppositions, former Mensheviks, SR's, and members of other anti-Bolshevik parties, leaders of the church and religious sects, nationality deviationists, and members of the intelligentsia whose devotion to the Soviet regime was in question. The Special Section was concerned with the loyalty of the armed forces. Its representatives were assigned to all military and naval formations and constituted an elaborate special hierarchy with its own independent channel of command responsible directly to the NKVD. The Counterintelligence Administration directed its efforts toward combating foreign intelligence agents operating within the USSR. Its responsibilities included surveillance of foreign visitors and foreign embassies and consulates on Soviet soil. The Transport Administration focused its activities on the protection of goods in transit, the fulfillment of state plans for freight movements, and protection against sabotage or other damage to the transportation network. The Foreign Administration devoted its primary efforts to espionage activity outside the Soviet Union. Its responsibilities included the control of Soviet personnel stationed abroad, the penetration of Russian anti-Soviet émigré organizations, the collection of intelligence of value to the Soviet leadership, and the recruitment of foreign Communists, sympathizers, and others as agents in the Soviet spy network.

* * * * *

The reliance on terror as an instrument of dominion has its elements of danger. It is not easy to control. A secret police develops its own laws of growth. The more discord it discovers or develops, the more indispensable it becomes. Its tendency is always to extend its own sovereignty, to seek to emancipate itself from all external controls, to become a state within a state, and to preserve the conditions of emergency and siege on which an expansion of its own power depends. Once terror becomes an end in itself, there is no easy and natural stopping place. From the viewpoint of the leadership, there is an even greater worry, the fear that as the secret police apparatus emancipates itself from external controls, it becomes a menace to the security of the highest Party leaders themselves. It is a risk of which the Party leadership has been aware and against which it has taken precautions. Every effort is apparently made to ensure the subordination of the MVD to the central Party organization. Employees are required to be Party members. The secretaries of the Party organizations in the MVD are used as the eyes and ears of the Party Central Committee to ensure loyalty to the Party. The Special Section in the secretariat of the Central Committee is presumed to have a particularly close supervisory relationship to the secret police. Special groups of the Party Control Committee are assigned to watch over the MVD. In these and perhaps other ways, the Party leadership seeks to safeguard itself against the possibility that "the avenging sword of the Revolution" may turn against the revolutionary leadership itself.

Thus far, no head of the Soviet secret police has succeeded in using his position as a platform from which to strike out for supreme power. The first director of the Cheka and OGPU was Felix Dzerzhinsky, an Old Bolshevik of unimpeachable idealism whose whole career documented the proposition that there is no fanaticism so terrible as that of the pure idealist. Dzerzhinsky gave no evidence of Napoleonic ambitions and died in 1926 without attaining Politburo status. His successor, Menzhinsky, was a much lesser figure, and though he continued as head of the OGPU until 1934, he never moved beyond the second rank of Party leaders. Yagoda, who came next, was removed from office in 1936 and executed in 1938. His successor, Yezhov, was relieved of his duties in 1938 and disappeared in 1939, presumably a scapegoat for the excesses of the Great Purge. Neither Yagoda nor Yezhov could be counted in the front ranks of Party leaders. Beria, who succeeded Yezhov, was the first head of the NKVD to enter the Politburo where he became an outstanding figure. His rise to power, however, gave every evidence of reflecting Stalin's tutelage rather than any independent leverage which his position as head of the NKVD afforded. Thus far, the vigilance of the ruling group has been proof against all dreams of utilizing the terror apparatus as the road to supremacy. The proposition that Beria may carve a new path has still to be tested.

This was written before Beria was executed shortly after Stalin's death.

Even if the Party leadership is successful in imposing its mastery on the secret police, there are other disadvantages in a regime of terror which are not so amenable to skillful manipulation. A system which relies on a large secret police as a basic core of its power is highly wasteful of manpower. The main occupation of the secret police is that of spying, investigating, examining, guarding, and controlling others. Large numbers of talented people are removed from productive work. There is always the hazard that the secret police will run amok and do serious and perhaps unintended harm to the productive and administrative machinery of the state. The atmosphere of universal suspicion which terror breeds is not ordinarily conducive to creative thinking and displays of individual initiative. If the weight of terror becomes too great and the penalty of any administrative failure or mistake is

MVD detention, it becomes difficult to persuade people to take responsibility. Even those driven by fear of the secret police to work as they have never worked before begin to crack under the strain. It is no easy task to apply terror and at the same time to hold it in leash.

Perhaps the most subtle danger in a police regime of the Soviet type is its impact on the quality of political decisions at the very highest level. The MVD is one of the main pillars that sustains the regime. It is also a primary source of intelligence regarding both domestic and international developments. Since the MVD apparatus lives and grows on emergency and danger, its justification hinges upon the maintenance of a state of siege. Consequently, the intelligence that filters through the MVD to the top political leadership is apt almost unconsciously to emphasize the storms that are brewing, the plots against the regime, and sinister threats at home and abroad. The risk which the Party leadership faces is that it too will become the unconscious victim of the Frankenstein's monster which it has created. The ultimate hazard of terror as a system of power is that it ends by terrorizing the master as well as the slave.

At this point Professor Moore takes up an analysis of the bureaucratic Apparatus.

FROM

Barrington Moore, Jr.
SOVIET POLITICS—THE DILEMMA OF POWER

IN general, the spurs and checks found in a capitalist democracy, which are largely the product of the division of authority and economic competition, are replaced in the Soviet system by pitting the various sections of the bureaucracy against one another. On the whole, the Party acts as a spur or spark plug, while the secret police acts as the main negative check. This description is, however, considerably oversimplified, since both the Party hierarchy and the hierarchy of soviets have developed numerous control organs of their own. For example, the regional units of the Party are supplied with a corps of roving "instructors," who visit the factories and farms in the area under their control in an attempt to learn at first hand the problems faced and the measures taken to cope with them. Good instructors manage to find out what is going on at all levels of the Party and in economic organizations, and to give advice in unraveling knotty problems; poor ones content themselves with superficial conversations with local officials. Thus, in addition to the secret police, the instructors constitute supplementary eyes and ears for the regime.

In this connection there is another dilemma facing the Soviet regime. On the one hand, the system requires for its functioning a definite hierarchy of status positions and an adequate allocation of authority. On the other hand, because of the need for means to check up on the execution of policy decisions, there apparently exists a vested interest in confusion, and particularly confusion in the allocation of authority. This situation may be illustrated in the relationships between Party officers and other foci of authority in the fields of industry, agriculture, and the general administrative services.

In the first two of these fields there are three ladders of authority, the economic ladder, the soviet ladder, and the Party ladder, whose relationship to one another, even on paper, is an extremely tenuous one. Beginning with the situation in industry, the main steps in the economic hierarchy are the Glavk or Ministry (formerly called the People's Commissariat), the factory director, and the worker. The hierarchy of soviets also has vague functions of economic supervision. The soviets were recently advised not to take an overly restricted view of their tasks in the economic sphere, at the same time that the factory managers were told not to be perturbed by what at first glance might seem like interference from these organizations. The third ladder of authority is, of course, the Party. Two levels of the Party hierarchy impinge most frequently upon the activities of the Soviet factory director. The regional Party organization (oblast', krai, city, or rayon) is responsible for nearly everything that takes place within its own area, including the operation of industrial undertakings. In practice, regional Party organizations frequently exert sufficient pressure to be able in effect to discharge and appoint the factory directors, although this task properly belongs to the Ministry. If the regional Party organization is both theoretically and actually superior to the factory director, the primary Party organization, or Party unit within the factory, is supposed to be his helper in raising morale, discipline, and the like.

Conflicts and confusion occur primarily at three points in this set of industrial relationships: between the factory director and the Ministry, between the factory director and the regional Party organization, and between the factory director and the primary Party organization within the factory.

The Ministry supposedly grants to the director a wide degree of autonomy in the making of decisions relating to production. But at the same time it tends frequently to interfere in these decisions by such actions as arbitrarily fixing the plant's manpower and payroll, or by even going so far as to allocate the payroll among the main categories of workers, manual workers, technicians, office workers, and so forth—acts which deprive the director of the necessary flexibility required for maximum productive efficiency.

Likewise the regional Party organizations have of late been accused of interfering unduly in the area of decision-making supposedly left to the director. However, official advice on the question of the Party's task in industry is quite contradictory. *Pravda* on March 18, 1948, declared in its editorial columns that the Party regional organizations must be freed of the economic and administrative functions that do not belong to them in "order to be able to exercise real control over the work of the economic organs." "The Party leader," *Pravda* continued, "who gets stuck in current details, duplicates and copies the work of the directors, necessarily comes to the mistaken mixing of functions, and propagates irresponsibility among the economic and technical leaders." At the same time, the regional organizations are told that their task is "to reduce the cost of production, diminish the amount of labor, materials, fuel, and electrical energy per unit of output," a task that is, of course, the major one of the director. They are further informed that they should not merely listen to periodic reports from the directors of enterprises within their area, but should get down to the details of actual production.

Confusion of counsel and practice also prevails rather widely in the relationships between the primary organization of the Party in the factory and the factory administration. According to section 61 of the Party statutes, the primary organizations are granted what is called the "right of control." A recent definition of this right of control includes the right to hear the reports of the directors, the right to uncover weaknesses within the organization and functioning of the enterprise, and the right to bring forward their own suggestions for the elimination of these weaknesses. At the same time, the primary Party organization is specifically warned not to interfere with the orders issued by the factory director or factory administration, or to annul the orders of the director.

Accounts of the activities of the primary organizations criticize them for attempting to administer on their own account. Nevertheless, they are praised for investigating and making suggestions about the quality of production, the introduction of new technology, the organization of labor, and general matters of efficiency. They are required to work "through the director," though they have the right to demand that the director eliminate any faults that they have uncovered. In a typical case, which took place during the war, a factory director attempted to blame war conditions for his failure to produce up to the plan, pointing to the mountain of telegrams on his desk as proof of his efforts to obtain raw materials. The Party primary organization, with the help of the Party city committee, investigated the situation and found that the supply division was buried in unnecessary paper work, as a result of which forms showing that the materials had already been received lay around for weeks.

A parallel situation exists in agriculture. The chief agricultural unit is the collective farm (*kolkhoz*). The *kolkhoz* is the bottom link in a chain that leads down from the Ministry of Agriculture through the Machine-Tractor Stations. It is also subject to the authority of the District Soviet Executive Committee (*Raiispol-*

kom) and one of its constituent units, the village soviet in both political and economic matters. All of these organizations are in one way or another subject to the authority of various echelons of the Party. In agriculture the function of the primary Party organization is the same as that in industry. However, in relation to the number of collective farms, there are still very few Party primary organizations. Because of this, the Party has organized, alongside the units in the collective farms, what it calls "territorial primary organizations," which bring together Party members working in the village soviet, the cooperative, the school, and *kolkhozy* lacking organized Party units.

In the various government offices, including those of the soviets, a similar system of multiple control exists, though there are important differences to be noted. Each government office is under the supervision of a corresponding echelon of the Party. "Inspection and control over the work of the central, oblast' and rayon (soviet) establishments is carried out by the Party oblast', city, and rayon committees." Party primary organizations in the various administrative and soviet offices (that is, the Party cell in government offices, though the term cell is no longer used) do not have the right of control that the corresponding organizations have in industry and agriculture. In this respect the line of authority would appear to be somewhat clearer. However, in addition to seeing that red tape is kept down and that visitors receive courteous attention, the Party primary organizations are required to "signal the weaknesses of the work of the establishment"—a favorite Soviet phrase—by reporting failures and difficulties to the next higher echelon of the Party, as well as to the administration of the office in which they occur.

The general situation may be summed up by the observation that the Bolsheviks proceed by setting the Party against the soviet and the economic hierarchy, and then setting the secret police to watch over all of them. Clear lines of authority on the whole are lacking. It does not appear that this pattern is in general the product of deliberate creation, although some sophisticated individuals at various levels of the bureaucratic hierarchies are undoubtedly aware of some of the principles by which it operates.

As might be anticipated on the basis of the preceding information, there is a tendency within the bureaucracy for informal groupings to spring up and to serve as a defense against the competitive pressures induced by the system. . . . These protective groupings are called by the picturesque and revealing general term of "familyness" (*semeistvennost'*), which conveys very clearly the conception of protective and friendly relations rather than the system of mutual watchfulness encouraged and approved by the regime.

In industry, for example, there is a tendency for the leadership of the Party primary organization to form a protective alliance with the factory administration. Often this protective alliance is sealed by gifts from the director to the secretary of the primary organization. The formation of these protective groupings need not be attributed solely to the desire to cover up one another's faults. It is also much more efficient, from a purely economic point of view, for the factory director and the head of the Party organization, which is responsible to a large extent for discipline and morale, to have a close working relationship. Furthermore, the factory director nowadays is nearly always a Party member too.

Nevertheless, the Party is well aware that if the primary organization is to serve its purpose of standing watch over the factory administration, it must maintain its independence. The Party does its best, therefore, to discourage the formation of these mutual alliances. Frequent denunciations of the sin of "familyness" are scattered through the daily press, and this problem is attacked in several other ways as well. The recurrence of the problem supports the hypothesis, however, that the periodic growth and destruction of these informal social units are inherent features of the Soviet social order: *Pravda* recently (October 27, 1946) reiterated a 1928 Party decree that attempted to cut the dependence of Party officials on the administrators of economic enterprises.

An almost identical situation is found in agriculture. The Party tries to keep the primary organizations on the collective farms separate from the farm administration, in order that the Party group may act as a stimulant and also as an inspection device in relation to the *kolkhoz* administration. However, it appears that frequently the leadership of the Party primary group and the chairmanship of the collective farm end up in the hands of the same individual. In other words, there is a tendency for status relationships to assume a form that leads to inner group harmony. In part, this may be due to the fact that in many localities there is only one outstandingly energetic and capable person or natural leader. Whatever the causes, the situation reflects the difficulty faced by the Party in its efforts to maintain control by setting one organization to watch another.

For similar reasons, Party members in the administrative services often fail to carry out their obligation to report errors and difficulties. Such a situation arises, it has been said, "because the Party buro or the secretary of the Party organization is afraid to spoil his relationship with the head of the establishment, or doesn't want to 'carry rubbish out of the hut' " (the Russian equivalent of washing dirty linen in public).

There is another reaction to the pressures of the bureaucratic regime, particularly to the pressures of routine and the social demand to "get things done," which affect both the capitalist captain of industry and the Communist administrator. For lack of a better name, this response may be called the affirmation of virtue. Soviet administrative staffs, like their counterparts elsewhere, make "decisions" or adopt resolutions which accomplish nothing, but which may relieve some anxieties about conformance to an expected norm of activity. In this fashion activity becomes an end in itself and a way of avoiding the consideration of serious problems. If a man is able to keep busy enough on inconsequential administrative details, his self-esteem is raised, and there is little danger that he will become depressed by the question of whether this administrative activity is serving its stated purpose or any other. He develops what the Soviets call a blind belief in the effectiveness of directives.

*   *   *   *   *

In itself, the responsibility of the authorities is not significant. What is significant is the typical reaction of the local officials to a form of frustration combined with the pressure for achievement.

The regime opposes the tendency for informal protective

groups and other "distortions" to grow up within the bureaucratic structure by drawing upon the ideological inheritance of
equalitarianism. The argument is put forth, correctly enough,
that the growth of these protective associations, the sin of "familyness," prevents the execution of the Party line. To counteract
such development, self-criticism is encouraged and democratic
procedures are restored in Party and other organizations that
have turned into closed cliques. The resultant situation might
be called an open season on bureaucrats, even though it is
definitely an open season on minor bureaucrats and not on the
top leaders of the regime.

In many cases, the criticism takes the form of scapegoating,
in which one official or group of officials is singled out for blame
because of problems that are either inherent in the Soviet system
as a whole or in other general circumstances. It is a common
practice to blame shortages of consumers' goods on the inefficiency of a particular government department, when in fact
they are the result of wartime conditions or the necessities of
building up heavy industry. A typical example may be cited at
random: shortly after the war *Trud*, the trade-union newspaper,
asserted that it was necessary to "purge the trading organizations and control and ration-card bureaus of all parasites and
doubtful workers who are feathering their nests there," and that
better public control was needed to put the supply stores, dining
rooms, and ration-card bureaus in order. It is not difficult to infer that many exasperated consumers were pleased by such official lashings and relieved by the accompanying promise of an
increase in the availability of scarce consumers' goods.

On other occasions the complaints take the form of letters to
the editor of the daily press, of which the following is a typical
example. A woman architect, who had received authorization to
spend her vacation at a tuberculosis sanatorium, arrived at the
railroad station nearest the hospital. No further transportation
was available, and, despite the heat of the day, she was forced to
walk ten kilometers to her destination. There she found that the
sanatorium was closed, and was told by the director of the
liquidated institution that many other people, evidently less trust-
ing than she had been, had telephoned from the same railroad

station to discover this fact. Returning to Moscow, she received no satisfaction from the trade-union officers who had originally issued the authorization. Since they merely shrugged their shoulders and said they knew nothing about the sanatorium's being closed, she went to an officer of the All-Union Central Council of Trade Unions. The latter refused to issue a permit for another sanatorium and put the blame on the original union officers. By this time the woman's vacation was evidently over.

The outcome of this particular complaint is not known, though it is a safe assumption that several uncooperative bureaucrats got into a good deal of hot water. It is not necessary for such letters to be published to be effective. Many people from all over the Soviet Union continually write to Stalin about their difficulties. Part of the task of Stalin's secretaries is to use these letters as evidence of clogging within the administrative apparatus, particularly in areas and matters that the Politburo considers significant at any given time. This fact is frequently publicized by Soviet leaders, who are fond of asserting that fundamental decisions have been reached on the basis of letters or information from simple peasants or workmen. This device may act as a check on some of the more flagrant forms of obstructionism.

At other times, elected officials may attempt to intervene to straighten out some tangled red tape for their constituents in a manner not unlike that of an American Congressman. *Izvestiya* of May 31, 1947, carried a revealing account of this type of work by a deputy of the Supreme Soviet of the USSR, showing quite clearly the status relationships between members of the Supreme Soviet and more permanent officers of the Soviet bureaucracy. The deputy involved, one I. Panin, reported that he received from his constituents more than a score of letters a day, and that in the course of a year he dealt with the questions and complaints of nearly three thousand constituents. When Deupty Panin tried to reach Soviet officials on the telephone regarding these matters, he found that the secretary usually replied that the official was "in conference." At first he believed the secretaries. Later he learned to give his own name after the secretary had said the official was "out," but before she put the telephone down. The result was that the secretary usually said she would "have a look to see if he had come back," and as a rule the official was located and the business transacted without difficulty. On other occasions, however, Deputy Panin ran into outright and repeated refusals of his requests for an interview, preceded by the secretary's careful ritual of writing down the exact nature of his visit, problems to be discussed, and so forth. Evidently, certain of the business folkways of socialism do not differ significantly from those of capitalism, both being behavior patterns developed in adaptation to similar circumstances.

The consequences of the authoritarian and equalitarian pressures, as they work themselves out in the Soviet bureaucracy, may be described in the following manner. The competitive situation is to a large extent the consequence of the extreme centralization of authority. The competitive situation provides the chief method for checking up on the execution of policy, which is acknowledged by the Soviets themselves to be one of the weaker features of the present regime. Equalitarian doctrines and the tradition of "control from below," even if largely abandoned in the strictly technical sense, continue to play an important political role in that they are utilized by the top leadership to control the bureaucratic servants.

In a defensive reaction against these competitive pressures, protective nuclei and alliances tend to grow up within the bureaucracy. There is also a tendency for status relationships to approach a functional division of power and authority, in which the man who has responsibility also has power. These protective nuclei are continually being destroyed at the instigation of the top Party leadership.

The question may be fairly raised whether this continual growth and destruction, which wastes an incalculable amount of human and material resources, is really an inherent feature of the Soviet social system. Is there anything to prevent the top leaders from taking advantage of the tendency to develop a functional system of status and authority, from reaping the benefits of greater economic efficiency and diminished social friction? Obviously, something of the sort must take place at the lower levels of the general bureaucratic hierarchy, when, let us say, the regional Party secretary looks the other way at the growth of illegal combinations and groupings. Otherwise, the complaints would not be so continuous.

Once again, such a question cannot be answered definitively in the absence of experimental methods. One must also avoid the temptation to argue that because things are so they cannot be otherwise. Yet it seems very likely that under present conditions the top Party leaders cannot afford to let matters take their course, and that what we have called the vested interest in confusion is an inherent feature of the current regime. If the top Party leadership permitted the continuous growth of combinations between the factory director and the Party primary organization, or between larger units, such as the factory director, the heads of the local soviet, the heads of collective farms, and the local Party officials, it would soon find itself deprived of a valuable means of checking up on the execution of its major decisions. It seems, therefore, that there is a real dilemma between short-run and local interests in efficiency, and the overall and long-run interests in both efficiency and the maintenance of power.

The nature and function of the Army are now discussed by Professor Towster.

FROM

Julian Towster
POLITICAL POWER IN THE U.S.S.R.

THE Army is not an independent political force. It was always regarded as an instrument of the dictatorship, with emphasis on national or international aims shifting in accordance with Party policy. For two decades there was a deliberate effort to favor workers in recruitment for certain services and the training of commanding personnel, but in the late 'thirties opportunities were equalized for all social groups. Separate nationality military formations have existed on a small scale from time to time, and some are planned for the future, to be closely integrated, however, within the Union military structure. The conception of an army divorced from the political process has never prevailed in the U.S.S.R., and there are many military men in the Party and soviet bodies. But the monopoly and monolithism principles of the Party have been enforced in the Army just as strictly as in all public organizations, and the Army is watched for possible Bonapartist tendencies and is not expected to 'play politics' as a separate and distinct entity. Through a constant increase of the Party element in the military services, perfection of the special political apparatus in the armed forces, and a number of material-psychological measures, the Party continues to maintain strong control over the military arm of the state. The prestige of the armed services has progressively mounted. While serious disaffection occurred among a considerable part of the commanding personnel in the 'thirties, the Army as a whole has been loyal to the regime and its present leadership, and is not likely to become a spearhead of political opposition to the latter.

On the occasion of the tenth anniversary of the Red Army, in February 1928, Stalin spoke of 'three specific features of the Red Army.' The first and basic one, said he, was that 'it is the army of the emancipated workers and peasants, it is the army of the October Revolution, the army of the dictatorship of the proletariat'; secondly that it is 'the army of fraternity of the peoples' of the U.S.S.R., its whole being and structure resting on the idea of 'protecting the freedom and independence of the Socialist Republics that constitute the Soviet Union'; the third consists of 'the spirit of internationalism, the feelings of internationalism' in which the Red Army was trained from the moment it was born, 'in the spirit of respect for other nations, in the spirit of love and respect toward the workers of all countries, in the spirit of maintaining and confirming peace between countries.' The first feature, Stalin went on to say, means that the Red Army would have back of it a strong home front; the second, that in a critical moment, it would be supported by all the Soviet nationalities; while the third feature makes it the army of the workers of all countries, and in case of attack on the

Soviet Union, it would have friends and allies in all parts of the world.

There are, thus, two aspects, a national and international one, in the accepted conception of the Red Army. The international aspect was predominant during the first half of the regime; the national has been almost exclusively emphasized ever since, especially during the recent war. In line with this emphasis, the name of the Red Army was changed to 'Soviet Army' in the summer of 1946. But both aspects are components of the conception of the armed forces.

Soviet political theory and fear of serious repercussions in a largely peasant army, once collectivization of argiculture got under way, dictated a policy of 'proletarianizing' the armed forces. Consequently, for nearly two decades every effort was made by the Party to increase the number of workers in the rank and file and commanding personnel of the Army, and to allocate large proportions of worker-recruits to the more crucial arms. But no substantial increase in the workers' percentage in the army was possible until the industrialization program of the first Five-Year Plan, initiated in 1927–8, began to take effect.

* * * * *

Despite the increase of the 'proletarian kernel' in the army since the late 'twenties, it is obvious that the peasant-derived serviceman remained equally strong in numbers. At least until the 'thirties, they constituted a surprisingly strong element even in such specially watched parts of the service as the Navy, the military schools, and the Party organizations of the armed forces. But as a result of collectivization, the nature of the peasant component of the Army changed radically in the 'thirties. Official figures indicate that whereas in January 1930 only 5.3 per cent of the peasant-soldiers came from the collectivized peasantry, this percentage reached 76.7 in January 1934, and by 1937 non-collectivized peasants constituted no more than 2.3 per cent in the Army.

The principle of social selectivity in the composition of the armed forces affected, however, the size of the Army's potential reserve. With the changes in the social structure detailed earlier, and the emergence of the Nazi threat, this principle was abandoned and the concept of 'class' gave place to the concept of 'the people' in the recruitment of the armed forces. The Constitution of 1936 (articles 132, 133) made universal military service the law of the land, and declared defense to be 'the sacred duty of every citizen of the U.S.S.R.' These principles were embedded in the universal military service law adopted 1 September 1939, and the military schools were thrown wide open to the citizenry without regard to social origin.

*   *   *   *   *

Currently, the Soviet Army consists primarily of young people, drawn from all social strata, and far better educated than their predecessors in the Tsarist Army or the Red Army of civil-war days. Former Tsarist officers, numerically strong in the Red Army during the civil war, and still constituting 10.6 per cent of the Soviet commanders in 1930, are now reduced to a fraction of the officers corps. Likewise, Soviet commanders who won their spurs in the civil war, and formed the overwhelming majority of the highest and middle commanding personnel in 1934, have been greatly reduced in proportion by the purges of 1937–8, and by the influx of younger officers who have matured in the recent conflict. The average age of the present marshals and generals at the beginning of the War was about 42. As regards social origin, the honors seem to be about equally divided between workers and peasants in the ranks of the two dozen or more marshals. Among the hundreds of generals, there are probably more who derive from the peasantry than from the working class, and a smaller proportion from the intelligentsia; while in the ranks below the proportions may be more equalized, but there are no specific data on these points.

*   *   *   *   *

Even more compelling than the former policy of 'proletarianization,' in the eyes of the Party leaders, was the need to increase the strength of the Party element in the armed forces. Not until the early 'thirties, however, did the Party succeed in outbalancing the non-Party element among the rank and file of the Army.

* * * * *

Among the commanding personnel, the percentage of those with Party affiliations increased more rapidly, and even by 1927 Party members constituted a majority of the commanders in the Red Army. . . . At the beginning of 1930 the percentage was 52.5, and in July 1934 it reached 67.8; these figures together with 4 per cent Komsomol [young people's auxiliary to the Communist Party] members among the commanders make the percentages of Party-affiliated in the command 56.6 and 71.8, respectively, in the two years. . . . Despite the extensive purges of the preceding years, Voroshilov told the Party congress in 1939 that more than half of the Army consisted of Party and Komsomol members, and the rest of the servicemen, he added, were also 'genuine non-Party Bolsheviks whose lives belong entirely to the Red Army and their socialist Fatherland.' The top level of the command was almost certainly 100 per cent Communist at the outbreak of the War.

In the course of the War, the Party sustained tremendous membership losses, owing to the high casualty rate among its members in uniform. It lowered its admission requirements and carried out several intensive membership drives, concentrating on the armed forces. Long regarded by the Party leaders as a school of political indoctrination, for the peasant boys in particular, the Army now became the largest recruiting ground for Party membership as well. The pressure was particularly great to enroll decorated men and officers winning rapid promotions. Thus, by the end of the War, a majority of the Party's own membership consisted of members recruited during the War from the ranks of the armed forces.

The conception that an army's business is to fight and that it need have no share in politics has never taken root in the Soviet Union. The constitution (article 138) specifically provides that citizens serving in the armed forces have the right to elect and be elected on equal terms with all other citizens. Many Red

Army men have in fact been elected to soviets, and citizens holding public office have been frequently enabled to continue to discharge their public duties, as far as possible, even after they have been called to the colors.

Generally, the Army is less represented in the Party than in the soviets, and military men have been less in evidence in the high Party councils since the second decade of the regime, especially since the late 'thirties. Outside of General Bulganin, who is a political appointee of recent years, Marshal Voroshilov is the only real military man in the Politbureau. A relatively small number of marshals and generals are members or candidates of the Party Central Committee. A much larger number of military men are elected to the Party congress. On the other hand, there is a conscious attempt to honor deserving higher officers with election to the Supreme Soviet, and at the same time publicly associate them with the decisions enacted. There are 155 Army officers in the Supreme Soviet elected in 1946, comprising 11.5 per cent of the deputies. The military in the Supreme Soviet include almost all the marshals—20 in number—11 army generals, 5 admirals, and dozens of generals of lower ranks, colonels, and majors. The Presidium of the Supreme Soviet contains one Army man at present, Marshal Budenny, and there are less than a dozen military men among the ministers, half of them former civilians put in uniform during the War.

High-ranking generals have participated at diplomatic receptions. They have been called in to take part in international military consultations, and several have acted as chairmen of Allied Control Commissions. But generally they are expected to concentrate their attention on their own tasks, and participate in political administration and consultation only within bounds requested and delimited by the Party. The rules on factionalism, discussions, and other forms of political activeness apply to the military perhaps even more strictly than to other groups. Army men are taught to understand that the Army is the offspring of the Party, living and operating by the rules and laws laid down for it by the Party and the government. And the Army is carefully watched not only against mass disaffection, but against any trait of Bonapartism in its officer cadres and any suggestion of an attempt to raise it into an autonomous entity, free from Party control.

Party control over the Army is maintained by an elaborate system of material and psychological arrangements, designed to keep the entire personnel loyal and satisfied, to prevent any political opposition or moods of exclusiveness from developing in the Army, and to check such tendencies if they do develop.

For the rank and file, food, quarters, clothing, pay, cultural outlets, and training for useful trades while in service have constantly improved in the past twenty-five years. With the progressive professionalization of the service, the material rewards and status of the commanding personnel have also been made more and more attractive. In the ten-year period between 22 September 1935 (when military ranks up to grade of general were established) and the end of 1945, personal ranks—including the ranks of marshal, general, and admiral—special decorations and uniforms, obligatory saluting, epaulettes, orderlies, and other forms of distinction between officers and men were progressively introduced, and with the avowed purpose of strengthening discipline in the Army and adding to the military dignity and authority of the commanding personnel.

These material conditions of army life are co-ordinated with a most extensive system of political indoctrination, permeating all levels of the services. In charge of this work is the Political Administration of the Army, a branch of the Ministry of the Armed Forces, which has for a long time held simultaneously the status of a department of the Central Committee of the Party. The Political Administration operates through political officers—formerly known as political commissars and military commissars—who have the status of deputy commanders in every unit, from front or army group down to regiment and battalion; it carries on its work through the commanders themselves in company units.

The system of political commissars has had quite a checkered career. Originally the institution of political commissar, then known as military commissar (*Voenkom*), was established early in 1918 to watch over, and also to protect, Tsarist officers serving the Red Army, or as the official order put it 'to see to it that the

Army does not become a thing apart from the entire Soviet system and that the various military establishments do not become foci of conspiracies or instruments against workers and peasants.' The commissar was the official alter ego of the commander in each unit, and his signature and assent were required for the validity of military orders. This system lasted until 1924, when the urge of the commanders to take full control of their units was recognized by a declaration of the Central Committee, admitting the 'one-man management' principle (*edinonachalie*) for the structure of the Red Army. In practice a majority of the commanders became single managers of their units during the period of 1924–37, with a subordinate assistant on political matters conducting the actual political work of the unit. The rest of the commanders had commissars functioning side by side with them in their units. In connection with the purges of 1937–8, military commissars were reinstated (in 1937) in all the units as the 'eyes and ears of the Party and the government in the Army,' operating on a complete footing of equality with the commanders. This new duality of control has apparently led to extensive friction between commanders and commissars, and the commissars were abolished on 12 August 1940, only to be reintroduced again on 16 July 1941, when tens of thousands of new, non-Party officers were enrolled in the Army on the outbreak of war. Finally, on 9 October 1942, the military commissars were again abolished and the principle of unity of command was re-established. The explanation offered is that the new commanders have proved 'quite mature both politically and militarily' and that it was best 'to place full responsibility for all the activities of his unit upon the commander.'

The vast political apparatus in the Army was not disbanded with the new reform. Former military commissars and other political workers in the Army, many of whom have acquired regular military skills following repeated urgings by the Party since 1934, were given military ranks and status, and, as deputies to the commanders, they carry on as before the work of building the morale and guarding the loyalty of the armed forces. This apparatus is carefully chosen for proved devotion to the Party leadership. In case of a serious threat to the regime developing in the midst of the Army, it would have the backing of the troops of the Ministry of Internal Affairs, which—though now integrated in standing, uniform, and ranks with the regular Army machine—are composed 100 per cent of Party members, specially recruited on the basis of absolute loyalty to the existing leadership. In the past, this leadership has proved capable of executing transfers, removals, and other redispositions in the Army, including changes in the highest command, and there is no reason to doubt that it would be able to do so in the future. Relinquishment of Party control over the Army is most unlikely. But the forms of the exercise of this control, a repeated source of friction in the past, will probably undergo further changes to meet the inherently difficult problem of maintaining Party control and at the same time preventing it from acting as a fetter on the initiative and skill of the military commanders.

Lastly, we may note a number of measures adopted during and since the War, which tend to assert further the Party's supremacy and counteract any excessive sense of exclusiveness on the part of the professional élite of the Army. In the autumn of 1943, several civilian services were given the prestige of rank and uniform; the employees of the railroad network, the procurators, members of the Foreign Affairs Ministry and the foreign service. In addition to Stalin, a number of top Party officials were endowed with high military ranks. Zhdanov, Kaganovich, Khrushchev, Shcherbakov, and later Bulganin of the Politbureau and many close associates of Stalin in the Central Committee were made generals. In July 1945, Beria, a member of the Politbureau and then head of the Ministry of Internal Affairs, was made a marshal, while other ranks, orders, and medals were conferred on his aides in the ministry. The most significant item in this group of measures is the singular emphasis given in the press and public statements since the latter part of 1943 to the role of the Party in the War and of Stalin as embodiment of the supreme military leadership. While the military leaders who emerged during the War are praised as a group—very rarely as individuals—it is Stalin's role in bringing them out and co-ordinating their strategy and operations that is given the highest emphasis.

Basically, the Army as a group has remained loyal to the regime in crises. Few troops joined the enemy camp in the War, and the misbehavior of some units in occupied countries was more a front-line phenomenon than an expression of political disaffection. Discipline, moreover, has been tightened more and more in the ranks of the Army, as in all organized groups. In the light of all that has been detailed above, it does not seem likely that the Army would become a focus of serious political opposition in the near future, unless unity were broken within the ranks of the highest Party leadership itself.

CHAPTER 7

Communist Problems

The Soviet Union is approaching its fortieth anniversary. What started out as a radical experiment has become, while still radical, a seeming fixture in the contemporary world. For better or worse it has steadily grown in strength and stability. De Tocqueville's prophecy has come true. The twentieth century witnesses the rival maneuverings of two new powers, the United States and Russia.

But if the Soviet Union has grown in power and influence it has nonetheless continued to be beset by problems of large proportions, problems the resolution of which may spell its end, or mark its serious modification—or confirm its growing strength.

The most serious of these problems can be simply stated:

1. Is there an internal opposition which is destined to force a return to capitalism?

2. Can a Communist colossus coexist with non-Communist powers?

3. Will satellite countries allow themselves to remain satellites?

During World War II a Russian general, Vlasov, was captured by the Germans and shortly thereafter formed a "Liberation Committee." Its aim was the overthrow of the Stalinist regime. Some observers saw in this the opening move in a grand design to marshal opposition forces in Russia. With Germany's defeat, this Nazi-sponsored committee obviously was doomed. Vlasov himself was executed by the Soviet government, and his following melted away. But the "Vlasov Movement" was not forgotten by foreign students

165

of the Soviet scene. Perhaps, it was thought, its study would yield some clues in considering the question, does a substantial mass opposition to the regime exist in Russia?

Outstanding is the work of Professor George Fischer in this study. Under the imprint of Harvard University, Professor Fischer published, in 1952, his conclusions after an exhaustive analysis of the available evidence. From this study, entitled SOVIET OPPOSITION TO STALIN, *the following section is taken.*

"While," says Fischer, "the Vlasov Movement differs in a number of ways from anti-Stalin opposition within the USSR itself, it is richly suggestive for this endlessly complex topic."

For this reason, and because Fischer's work represents the most meaningful of any dealing with this subject, the editor presents pertinent portions of it for the reader's consideration.

FROM

George Fischer

SOVIET OPPOSITION TO STALIN

IN the USSR, Inertness, the exclusion of individual initiative in anything in the least related to politics, has become the central feature in the political behavior of the individual.

A major explanation for this trademark of Soviet individuals is, of course, the impact of the totalitarian regime in the USSR. A system in which modern technology is combined with a wholly authoritarian leadership and ideology will inevitably lead to such a reaction.

* * * * *

Inertness, as pictured here, leads to an unmistakable conclusion regarding the likelihood of Soviet opposition. This conclusion is that Inertness makes such native opposition considerably less probable than is widely believed outside the USSR. But this is far from meaning that the picture is one of black and white simplicity.

For instance, neither Inertness nor its opposite (spontaneity and independent thinking on all matters affecting political behavior) can by any means be considered absolutes. This is certainly true of the USSR, where much deviation from Inertness may be discovered either in individual exceptions to the prevailing pattern or in areas of activity furthest removed from politics. Even more importantly, Inertness is certainly never wholly absent from even the freest Western societies. This is borne out, for one example, in the increasing conformism in the American counterpart to Soviet officialdom, the "new middle classes" of professionals and office workers in and out of government, as has been stressed recently in David Riesman's *The Lonely Crowd*, C. Wright Mill's *White Collar* and the much-discussed *Fortune* studies of "corporation wives" and American business. Nor can it be claimed, by any means, that the average person in the United States does much independent thinking in the realm of politics, ideology, or fundamental social issues.

Just how ill-informed on major political matters the average American is in the midst of the most extensive and opulent network of mass communications the world has ever seen is underestimated in the United States itself. This paradox may augur Inertness, for the complexity of these political questions combines here with the increasing unlikelihood of an individual's affecting them one way or the other even in as relatively vigorous a political democracy as the United States. Together, this combination encourages the average person to turn away from independent thinking and action. Although Samuel Lubell's *The Future of American Politics* bespeaks vigor and gusto on election day, a competing trend is thus what Erich Fromm has described as a mass "escape from freedom." The concomitant of this has been the "welfare state." As Isaiah Berlin, the Oxford historian and philosopher, has portrayed it, "today the very virtues of the paternalistic state, its genuine anxiety to reduce destitution and disease and inequality, to penetrate all the neglected nooks and crannies of life which may stand in need of its justice and its bounty—its very success in those beneficent activities—has narrowed the area within which the individual may commit blunders, has curtailed his liberties in the interest (the very real interest) of his welfare or his sanity, his health, his security, his freedom from want and fear."

Much as the Cold War may obscure this, the fundamental trends of the twentieth century are common to the USSR and the West. The ever important differences are emphasized by past history, by ideology and folkways, by the resulting national character and institutional structures. But it is the similarity in human and social relations which is furthered by the dominant features of the current technological stage of the Industrial Revolution: urbanization, mass communication, occupational specialization, and, above all, standardization in production, in management, in consumption, in culture. Therefore elements of Inertness are certainly present, although not as prevalent or as unrivaled, in nontotalitarian contemporary societies. This is as plausible as the reverse of Inertness is in some individuals and in some activities within the USSR.

*   *   *   *   *

Inertness, then, is a highly complex factor in estimating the likelihood of Soviet opposition. Although it is presented here as the decisive factor, neither its complexity nor its various shadings can be overlooked. As specific illustrations of how Inertness exerts its decisive influence—and of its vast complexity—but evolution of the Soviet individual outside of his native habitat and the Soviet response in 1941 to the German invasion may be cited.

It is only *after* the average Soviet national finds himself outside the confines of Soviet power that he tends to reflect systematically upon the innumerable injustices, cruelties, offenses, discomforts that his native regime had brought upon him and his dear ones. It is only at this point, after the break is made, that the Soviet citizen changes radically. Now an exile, he develops an active and also violent, bitter, implacable opposition both to the regime itself and to practically all of its characteristic features. It is at this point, too, that he insists categorically that both his own active opposition and that of a majority of the Soviet population were operative all along. It is essential to recognize this. Together with our insistence that Soviet society, like all others, does possess elements of integration, loyalty, progress, this brings out a cardinal point. The exile's rejection, total and strident, is far rarer within the USSR—not because there is less cause for it inside the country, but because all the immense factors causing Inertness work against its development.

Unless the outside world clearly perceives this postbreak origin of the Soviet exile's clear-cut, black-and-white rejection of the USSR, it may greatly, and fatefully, misjudge the nature and the extent of the undoubtedly important potential of disaffection within the USSR. While Soviet exiles are of the greatest significance in a number of ways, they reflect only partially the mood within their native land.

*   *   *   *   *

The foremost role of Inertness in shaping the political behavior of the Soviet population leads to a rather definite conclusion. Although this conclusion is subject to a variety of qualifications, it is strongly confirmed by Soviet actions in 1941. This conclusion is that effective Soviet opposition to Stalin is rather unlikely. The conclusion is valid as long as Inertness, and the contributing factors both of terror and of social and emotional accomodation, remain nearly universal.

The small likelihood at present of effective Soviet opposition . . . does not in any way obviate a parallel fact. Even if it is not apt to be effective in the foreseeable future, native opposition to the Soviet regime has been present uninterruptedly since 1917. Past opposition, and also any occurring in the future, may be divided into three different forms:

1. Passive disaffection;
2. Individual defection;
3. Organized opposition.

By far the largest part of Soviet opposition so far falls into the first category. Beginning with the Civil War, passive disaffection has been continuous. As has been emphasized throughout this study, it is quite widespread within the restrictive, paralyzing confines of mass political inertness. Precisely what the content and the manifestations of passive disaffection are cannot be judged adequately from the outside. But all of Soviet policy, the content of its pronouncements, the pleading and threatening tenor of its propaganda, the extent and intensity of its terror—all these are aimed in large measure at the widespread passive disaffection of the Soviet population.

Individual defection, the second form of opposition, is manifested most visibly by Soviet citizens who become "nonreturners," who sever their ties with the USSR once they find themselves outside of its borders.

* * * * *

It is our contention that in a large fraction of instances the first step of the Soviet defector-collaborators was motivated by the most elementary and essentially apolitical desire imaginable, that for sheer physical survival. As usual, such a statement needs qualification. Clearly, other motives played a role, a different one in each instance. But with many, and most likely a majority, of the Soviet defector-collaborators involved, survival was the motivation that decided them to take the first step.

This contention is based on the descriptions . . . of the murderous policy of starvation and neglect that was adopted by the German authorities with respect to hundreds of thousands of Soviet soldiers captured during the first year of Wehrmacht triumphs. These Soviet prisoners of war were massed together in vast concentrations, often in the open air, and malnutrition, disease, and total exhaustion rivaled each other in the death toll of these camps. Is it any wonder then—or an act that an outsider can blithely condemn—that many thousands of Soviet prisoners of war chose collaboration in preference to such miserable and seemingly certain death? And how many outsiders can affirm—from the bottom of their hearts and not in polemic or casual judgment—that they would have lived up to the proud injunction uttered by the Communist woman leader, La Passionaria (Dolores Ibaruri), during the Civil War in Spain: "It is better to die on your feet than to live on your knees"? Some can truly answer that they would have followed La Passionaria's injunction, and not a few of these Soviet prisoners of war indeed did. But it is important to raise this profoundly human problem of civic courage. It stands out as a key problem not only of this study but in general of our time—a time of increasing crisis, when civic courage is, alas, a standard intensely difficult to act by.

It should thus be kept ever in view that everywhere in the world man in the vast majority of cases is a creature neither heroic nor addicted to martyrdom. It is of such "average" men, then, that we speak when explaining the first step by the elemental instinct for sheer physical survival.

* * * * *

What, then, of the third major form of native anti-Stalinism, organized opposition?

In terms of the world's preoccupation with the Soviet regime, and particularly with its strength and its future, few topics can be of more immediate interest than organized opposition to Stalin. What are the sources of such Soviet opposition?

Aside from speculation, our sole clue lies in the past record of opposition. This is one of the most secret and least studied phases of Soviet history. Our knowledge of it is severely limited. The two major sources are official Soviet material and the testimony and activities outside the USSR of key figures such as Trotsky, General Krivitsky, and Vlasov.

If all thirty-five years of the Soviet regime are surveyed, the following major sources of organized opposition may be surmised. First, there are those whose opposition was of pre-Soviet origin. In addition to the "White" partisans of the Tsarist regime, this includes the partisans of the February Revolution, the active adherents to the Russian Orthodox Church, the pre-Soviet intelligentsia, and those individuals whose social and economic origins were suspect in the eyes of the Soviets. Pre-Soviet opposition has declined progressively, especially after the Bolshevik victory in the Civil War.

Far more pertinent is the opposition that has arisen since the Soviet regime came to power. Here one can specifically identify two groups. One of these came from within the government. Such leading Communist Party figures as Trotsky, Kamenev, Zinoviev, and Bukharin clashed with Stalin on ideological grounds. An indeterminate number of lesser party members opposed the regime for ideological reasons or because of intraparty rivalries and power struggles. Outstanding figures like the suddenly executed Marshal Tukhachevsky suggest the Red Army as a source of opposition. The second post-1917 group is that outside the government. Dissent arose within the ranks of the technical and professional intelligentsia trained after 1917. Some national minority groupings are clearly an opposition source, as is the peasantry. So in general is that body of persecutees, Communist and non-Communist alike, who were arrested or otherwise repressed without prior participation in any opposition alignments.

But beyond such general observations, the whole subject remains shrouded in mystery. Whatever unrest or uprisings have taken place, the Soviet government has been highly successful at keeping the facts from the outside world. The exceptions, including the famous sailors' uprising at Kronstadt and the wave of unrest which in the 1930's accompanied rural collectivization, merely serve to underscore how little is known. And these known instances are pathetically few and pathetically unsuccessful. It is important to add that to date all available evidence speaks against widespread organization among the groups affected by the Great Purges of the late 1930's. Passive disaffection there was. Individual defection occurred. And unquestionably groups within the Communist Party and also within the Red Army and the nationality sphere considered organized opposition. But such consideration evidently did not pass the initial stage of discussion and tentative planning. If in some instances organized opposition reached a more advanced stage, these instances must have been tragically few and tragically unsuccessful. Neither the Soviet trial proceedings nor the testimony of Soviet "non-returners" offers evidence to the contrary.

This means that organized opposition did exist, to the extent both of local unrest—notably during collectivization and in nationality areas—and of informal preliminary discussion among high and middling party, military, and nationality leaders. But in neither instance did organized opposition reach any significant proportions before being wiped out by the Soviet government.

*   *   *   *   *

The waning of the earlier post-1917 zeal, the savage and extensive purges, the increasing monolithic routinization of life, the ever more blatantly propagandistic nature of Communist party doctrine—all these have made it increasingly difficult in recent years for many Soviet citizens to feel a positive political enthusiasm for their regime. In the Soviet defectors, these factors furthered a violent repudiation of the entire regime. Yet the system had a most profound political impact upon the populace. The ideology of the Vlasov Movement was a striking reflection of the generation within the USSR that the Soviet defectors represented. It also illustrates the remarkable extent to which the Soviet heritage is present in the Vlasov Movement.

What, specifically, are the elements in Vlasovite political thinking that might represent thinking within the USSR, and in particular the aspirations of Soviet opposition?

First of all, there is an increasing tendency abroad to disassociate progressive and libertarian inclinations in the Soviet population from the Soviet system. In doing this, some writers emphasize instead the continuing appeal of the February Revolution of 1917, which used Western democratic methods and slogans. Others concentrate on the powerful appeal to Soviet citizens of current Western ideas, material welfare, policies. Still others point to unique religious or sociological features in the Russian past. The ideology of the Vlasov Movement indicates that although all of this may have played a role, it is the decades under the Soviet regime that were decisive.

At a time when the USSR has surpassed all known forms of despotism, mass murder, and universal oppression, it may appear macabre and ludicrous to contend that its political system could be the source of genuine progressive and libertarian impulses within native opposition. And yet the Vlasov Movement suggests precisely that. How can this be explained?

To begin with, the Bolshevik revolution in 1917 let loose a driving surge of emotion toward liberty, equality, and fraternity. Although subsequent governmental actions and governmental propaganda have done much to negate and blunt its impact, the emotional surge itself has left a deep imprint on most adult Soviet citizens. Even if to a Westerner the passions of 1917 in retrospect may seem laden with the seeds of present-day totalitarianism, to a Soviet citizen it strongly nourishes his yearning for precisely the utopian New Society—with liberty, equality, and fraternity for all—that the early Bolshevik slogans managed so well to dramatize and popularize.

Another basic consideration is that there was one period of Soviet history which in the minds of Soviet citizens embodied much of their image of the 1917 slogans. This is the period of NEP, Lenin's New Economic Policy of the early 1920's. At that time, governmental restraints in economic life were minimized, and private activities were given considerable independence. To a populace which, as already noted, had largely accepted the Bolshevik revolution itself, it is this post-1917 "liberal" period that stands out rather than either the Tsarist era or the confused and unsuccessful tenure of the Provisional Government.

While the NEP period embodies the antistatist, laissez-faire aspirations of many a Soviet citizen, all of Soviet history has contributed another basic tenet. This is a belief in the fundamental Soviet social changes. Included here are state initiative in industrializing and controlling the nation's economy, its large-scale extension of education, and above all its dominant role in social security, health, and welfare—social changes which to millions even today, despite increasing stratification and favoritism, imply an exciting upward social mobility, a "career open to talent." This acceptance even by Soviet opposition of the regime's basic social changes is accompanied by rejection of the cruelties and shortcomings involved and by the desire to make a number of alterations. Nevertheless, this particular aspiration of opposition elements could conceivably facilitate post-Stalin statism. At the same time, however, it champions, at least in part, the kind of progressive social and humanitarian institutions that are also a central goal of contemporary Western democracy.

Many a Soviet citizen, accepting both the Bolshevik revolution and basic social reforms, has been either introduced by the regime to the anti-authoritarian classics of nineteenth-century Russian literature or confirmed in his interest in them. For it is one of the most striking phenomena of present-day Soviet life that, in the midst of extreme totalitarianism, the government has continued to pay homage to the great and freedom-minded works of Pushkin, Lermantov, Gogol, Turgenev,

Chekhov, Tolstoy, as well as Herzen, Belinsky, even Bakunin. In doing so, the Soviet government is motivated by its propaganda considerations. It believes that the harnessing of these nineteenth-century giants of Russian culture for Soviet didactic purposes is both feasible and preferable to attempting their total prohibition. Nevertheless, the continued great popularity and accessibility of pre-Soviet Russian culture means that distinctly nonauthoritarian notions and ideals filter into the minds and hearts of millions of Soviet citizens.

Paradoxical though this may appear, it is thus the Soviet regime itself that provides Soviet opposition with its libertarian impulses and slogans.

*   *   *   *   *

What emerges in the Vlasov Movement's ideology is a mixture. Taking our definitions from the *Oxford English Dictionary*, democracy, "a social state in which all have equal rights," is here combined with authoritarianism, or being "favorable to the principle of authority."

A heady mixture this, and perhaps seemingly nonsensical. And yet it is an all-important mixture, not only for the present analysis of Vlasovite ideology but for many areas of the world today. Everywhere, one great question hangs over the immediate future. Which element will prevail in the inevitable mixture between traditional parliamentary democracy and the welfare state: authoritarianism or democracy?

The Vlasov Movement reflects the Soviet-bred predilection for a non-Western form of the welfare state. From this fact, and from parallel manifestations of intolerance, dependence on authority, and chauvinism, a conclusion is warranted. The Vlasov Movement's welfare-state blueprints showed a greater authoritarian than libertarian tendency.

Whether a similar authoritarian tendency will prevail in future opposition movements cannot be hazarded. The common Soviet heritage, the decades of Soviet totalitarianism favor such a conclusion. This heritage may be at least partially reversed if anti-Stalin currents within the USSR are accompanied by vigorous, and yet understanding, libertarianism in the outside world. To what extent such a libertarianism will exist (or how successfully it will have adjusted to the apparently unavoidable spread of the welfare state), and what effect it will have on a Soviet-bred generation of anti-Stalinists, must remain a subject for prayerful hope and speculation. But the Vlasov Movement suggests that future opposition ideology will continue to combine libertarian aspirations with authoritarian impulses, both focused on the welfare state. In this combination, the ideology of opposition reflects almost completely the values and experience of Soviet life.

But internal opposition to the Communist regime is not, of course, the only problem facing the Soviet leadership. There is the very serious current "iron curtain" problem. Also, there are new worries regarding the proper relationship that should exist between the U.S.S.R. and its satellites.

Mr. Isaac Deutscher, who would not like to be called an "expert on Russian affairs" but who is, presents these two problems in the section below. The first account, dealing with the problem of the iron curtain, is from Mr. Deutscher's STALIN: A POLITICAL BIOGRAPHY; *the second is his "The New Soviet Policy Toward the Satellites" which appeared in the December 2, 1954, issue of* THE REPORTER.

FROM

Isaac Deutscher

STALIN: A POLITICAL BIOGRAPHY

ANOTHER 'dialectical contradiction' in victorious Stalinism relates to the 'iron curtain,' that is the extremely rigid isolation from the outside world in which Stalin brought up a whole Soviet generation. That isolation has in fact been essential to the political and cultural climate of Stalinist Russia, and Stalin may be described as the chief architect of the 'iron curtain.' Yet the reasons for the isolation and the elements that went into its making were diverse and manifold; and it was their combination that made the 'iron curtain' so solid, so thick, so impenetrable.

The first of those elements was the self-defensive attitude of Bolshevism after the frustration of its hopes for world revolution. Bolshevik Russia shut herself off from a hostile world. In this respect she was not very different from Cromwellian England or Jacobin France. Puritan England lived in suspicion and fear of 'French intrigue' and 'French gold' working against her. The spectres of 'English intrigue' and 'English gold' haunted Jacobin France. In each case the revolutionary nation had real reasons for suspicion—the hostile 'intrigue' and 'gold' had not been just figments of its imagination. All the same, in each case the suspicion of and the reaction against the outside world assumed that extraordinary intensity which is characteristic of popular feeling in any revolutionary epoch.

This frame of mind in Bolshevik Russia was tremendously enhanced by native Russian tradition. As in so many other respects, so in this the national custom and habit reasserted themselves the more easily and the more potently, because they harmonized with the real and the apparent needs of the revolution. Russia's age-old seclusion from the west had been dictated by military considerations—the Russian plain had no natural barriers to stop invaders—by the hostility of Greek Orthodoxy to Roman Catholicism and, in later times, by the anxiety of autocratic Tsardom to defend itself against the infiltration of Liberal and Socialist ideas from the west. It is true that in the nineteenth century the Russian intelligentsia partly succeeded in breaching the wall; but even this success, achieved not without a bitter struggle, underlined the basic fact of isolation. Breached, the wall was still there. Russia's Bolshevik rulers tried at first to pull it down; then they found it useful not merely to let it stand, but even to close its breaches.

Seen from another angle, the 'iron curtain' has been a variety of economic protectionism. No great modern nation, with the peculiar exception of the British, has developed its industry without defending itself by high tariff walls and a variety of other prohibitive measures against the competition of older in-

dustrial nations. Shielded by protectionism, the United States and
Germany grew to their industrial maturity. Socialism in one
country could not but resort to the same method. Other nations
had in their industrial development been favoured by the assistance of foreign capital or, in the case of the United States, by
the geographic 'protectionism' of two oceans. Bolshevik Russia
had no comparable advantages. Foreign capital did not help her
to develop her wealth. She had hardly started her industrialization in real earnest before she was confronted with the threat
of new, total war and was compelled to divert much of her
wealth to armament. This made her industrial revolution infi-
nitely more painful than it might otherwise have been; and this
invested her protectionism with extraordinary severity and harshness.

That severity, that harshness, was felt in the first instance by
the ordinary working man. The Government and the planning
authorities had to allocate the national resources to the development of industry and transport, the mechanization of agriculture,
armaments, and private consumption. The larger the resources
allocated to industry and armament, the less, relatively or even
absolutely, was left over for private consumption. This was the
plain economic logic of the situation, a logic which all belligerent
nations were to learn or re-learn, in different degrees, in the
years of the Second World War, but with which Russia had been
uncomfortably familiar many years before. The standard of living of the mass of the people, traditionally very low, was sacri-
ficed to higher purposes of national policy. In spite of all that,
it began appreciably to rise in the late thirties. But the rise was
ephemeral. War once again depressed the standard of living to a
terribly low level.

The mass of the Russian people saw how rapidly the nation
grew wealthier and wealthier, while the overwhelming majority
of its members remained individually poor or even grew poorer
and poorer. True enough, the economists knew that this had
been roughly the position of almost every nation engaged in an
industrial revolution. The essence of protectionism in the nineteenth century was that it withheld cheap foreign goods from
the mass of consumers in order to shield and stimulate the growth

of the nation's industrial strength. But in no other country had the contrast between the accumulation of national wealth and individual poverty been as sharp as in Russia under Stalin; and, what is perhaps more important, in no other country had that contrast been identified with socialism and a classless society. Stalin asked the working classes not only to make the effort they were making and bear the sacrifices they were bearing, but also to believe that they had an easier and better life than the peoples of the capitalist countries. This was not and could not have been true; and this was not the fault of socialism. Nor was it, by and large, the fault of Stalin or of his Government, although some of their mistakes aggravated the situation. But it was Stalin's fault, if this be the right word, that he presented to the Russian people their miserable standard of living as the height of Socialist achievement.

This misrepresentation was the source of an astounding system of hypocritical deception. Its first consequence was that the mass of the people was not to be allowed to make real comparisons between the Russian and the foreign standards of living. The second was that over many years the propagandists not only gilded the conditions of life at home, but persistently set up an absurdly exaggerated picture of the misery of the working classes abroad. The third was that as few Soviet citizens as possible were allowed to study social life in foreign countries either through personal observation or through reading foreign books and news-papers. To maintain the 'iron curtain' became Stalin's major eco-nomic and political interest.

Russia's isolation from the world became hermetic, and turned into a morose psychosis during the great purges. The picture of a sinister, all-pervading foreign conspiracy, which Vyshinsky, the general prosecutor, drew, and which the defendants through their confessions made even blacker, the fact that the conspiracy was alleged to have had its agents in almost every cell of the body politic, the terrible punishment inflicted upon the 'con-spirators'—all that spread a neurotic horror of all things foreign. Every contact, be it ever so casual, with foreigners and foreign affairs was deemed contaminating. Old people suspected, of course, that it was all a frame up; and, from fear, they accepted the isolation. But the young took things at their face value. Their horror of foreign vice coupled with domestic heresy was genuine. It was part of their normal state of mind, part of their character. They had almost from the cradle been moulded by the monolithic state; they had been indoctrinated not with Marxism indeed, but with one crude Byzantinesque version of it. They had not been allowed to acquire the habit of questioning accepted truth; they had not been afforded the experience of any real clash of conflicting views and principles, the experience of independent formation of opinion. The purges finally insulated the mind of the young generation from any disturbing outside influence.

Made up of so many diverse elements, the 'iron curtain' performed in effect a dual function, 'progressive' and 'reactionary.' Behind that curtain the revolution found a degree of safety and the Government could go ahead with the job of industrialization and modernization. (The strictly military value of the 'iron curtain' was up to a point demonstrated in the war, when Hitler's generals, on invading Russia, found that what they had known about their enemy was next to nothing.) At the same time, the 'iron curtain' shielded Stalin's autocracy, his uncanny despotism, his legends and deceptions. In both its functions the 'iron curtain' had become to Stalinism the indispensable condition for its very existence.

It was of that condition, of that sine qua non of its self-perpetuation, that victory now threatened to rob Stalinism. Russia suddenly found herself involved in a thousand ways in the life and the affairs of the outside world. Millions of Russian soldiers marched into a dozen foreign lands. They were, in more than one sense, *l'etat en voyage*, as Napoleon had called an army marching into a foreign country. Millions of former forced labourers returned home from a long sojourn in Germany. Multitudes of Russian officers sat on inter-allied commissions, in daily contact with an alien world. The 'iron curtain' was pierced, breached, almost shattered.

The impression that the capitalist west made on the Russians was by no means as uniformly favourable as some people in the west, given to self-flattery, were inclined to think. The Russians saw Europe in ruin. Millions of their men and women had lived for years behind the barbed wire of German concentration camps or in the shadow of gas-chambers. They saw the hideous diseased rump of European civilization, not its old noble face. To many of them the picture of the outside world must have looked even blacker than the propagandists at home had painted it. Even those who had been spared such gloomy experiences were by no means converted to the capitalist way of life. To most of them any society in which the means of production were not publicly owned was social injustice itself, a baffling or ridiculous anachronism. Nevertheless, in this contact with the outside world, habits of thought, formed in the years of isolation, began to weaken, if not to crumble. Russians noticed that, even amid the ravages of war, foreigners had a higher standard of living than they themselves. They were dazzled by the amenities of life which even the vanquished still enjoyed. They observed, not without envy, that Poles, Hungarians, Czechs, and Yugoslavs were less constrained than they themselves, that they were suffering from fewer inhibitions in speaking their minds; in a word, that they were enjoying a measure of freedom.

The contact with foreign countries generated moral ferment. The scope of that ferment can be gauged from the fact that it affected millions of people who, on their return home, could not be prevented from conveying something of their experience to their relatives and friends. No sensational political developments could immediately result from this. Nor could the ferment crystallize into any definite political ideas—no independent groups or organizations capable of formulating such ideas, had been left in being. The nation could not quickly re-learn those habits of forming its own opinion, from which it had been so forcibly dissuaded. What had begun in its mind, so it seems, was an imperceptible process of transvaluation of values, the duration and ultimate outcome of which nobody could prophesy. The recent experience gave new urgency to the nation's desire for a betterment in the material conditions of its life, a desire which Stalin's Government probably met half-way by levying reparations from the vanquished and by an energetic rehabilitation of the domestic economy. Beyond the sphere of material interest a new vague yearning for freedom and a novel curiosity about the outside world made itself felt; a yearning and a curiosity which the Government was ill equipped to satisfy. Victory could not but impart to the nation, at least to its intelligent, forward-looking elements, the feeling that it had stood its supreme test, that it had attained maturity and outgrown the tutelage to which it had owed and from which it had suffered so much. While it is true that in the mood of victory the nation was willing to forgive Stalin his past misdeeds, it is probably even truer that it was not willing to see a repetition of those misdeeds.

We have said that no groups or organizations existed to translate the new ferment into political ideas. This statement needs to be qualified. Towards the end of the war the officers' corps represented the germ of such an organization. . . . It had a leader to look up to in Marshal Zhukov, the defender of Moscow and the conqueror of Berlin, whose popularity was second only to Stalin's. It may have been by one shade more genuine, because it had owed less to official publicity. This is not to say that Stalin's personal position was in any danger or that Zhukov could have assumed the role of his rival. Much time was probably needed before any political opposition could evolve; and it was highly doubtful whether it could do so while Stalin was alive. But although his own position was not imperilled, Stalin was only too anxious, just as he had been in the thirties, to suppress once more, though in much milder fashion, the potentiality of an alternative government, or rather of a successor to his government whom he himself had not designated. He may have recalled the sequel to the ferment which arose in the army of Alexander I from its contact with Europe. Barely a few years after the victory over Napoleon the Tsar's officers' corps was riddled with secret societies, formed by men whom the observations of life abroad had induced to fight for reform at home. After Alexander's death those secret societies prepared and staged the Decembrist rising of 1825, the forerunner of a long series of revolutionary convulsions.

Stalin's main endeavour was therefore to lift the party back to its old exalted status, which it was to share with no other body. The celebrated marshals and generals suffered eclipse. A few months after the cease fire their names and deeds were hardly ever mentioned by the propagandists. It might be said that this was normal and sound and that it would have happened in any nation which was not under the thumb of a military dictator. Yet there was more to it than that. The eclipse of the officers' corps had its political significance. It was staged with deliberation and consistency. This became clear when in 1946 Marshal Zhukov completely disappeared from the public eye. From then on his role in the defense of Stalingrad and even Moscow was gradually blurred in the official accounts of the war, until, on the third anniversary of the battle of Berlin, *Pravda* managed to commemorate the event without mentioning Zhukov even once. His name was being deleted from the annals of the war, as so many names had been deleted from the annals of the revolution.

Stalin's effort to restore the moral supremacy of the party was coupled with his endeavour to re-establish the party outlook as against the nationalist mood of the preceding years. In the tug-of-war between Revolution and Tradition, the former was strikingly reasserting itself, though it did not completely suppress or eliminate the latter. Peace, like the war before it, entailed many ideological adjustments in every sphere of public life, in politics, in economics, in the writing of philosophy and history, in fiction, and in the arts. From everywhere, the household deities of Mother Russia, only recently re-installed with so much unction, were quietly removed to the lumber rooms, if not cast out altogether. It was no longer good patriotic style to evoke the names of Kutuzov, Suvorov, Minin, and Pozharsky. It was no longer fashionable to glorify the great Tsars, Ivan the Terrible and Peter the Great, whom historians and writers had just treated with more reverence than discretion as Stalin's spiritual forebears. Even Slavophil propaganda was damped down. It was, generally speaking, no longer regarded as desirable that the mind of the people should be turned too much towards its past. The new task was to revive 'Bolshevik consciousness.' The young were now to be taught to value the things in which modern Russia differed from the old, rather than those in which she resembled her. They were to be made aware how much the Soviet Union owed to socialism, to class struggle, and to Marxism-

Leninism as interpreted by Stalin. Something like a Leninist revivalism was now sponsored and encouraged.

In part, the new turn was probably a genuine reaction from the surfeit of wartime nationalism. In part, it may have been dictated by Stalin's personal considerations. In 1941–3 he could still be flattered by comparisons between himself and Peter the Great and take pride in analogies drawn between the two Fatherland wars of 1812 and 1941. Mounted on ancestral shoulders he gained in stature. As victor he had no need for all that. The Peters, the Kutuzovs, the Alexanders looked like pygmies in comparison with him. It was a different thing for him to present himself once again as Lenin's successor, for Lenin's stature had, after all, remained what it had been. But apart from such considerations, about which one can only speculate, Stalin had a broader motive in fostering the Leninist revivalism. Through it he hoped to counter the new impact of the capitalist west upon Russia. Nationalist propaganda had been good enough to arouse the people to its bitter struggle for survival. But it was not good enough when the people had to be braced against the 'corrupting' influence of the outside world and given new hope. Only in the light of the Bolshevik doctrine, which preached that capitalism was bound to disintegrate and socialism to triumph, could the people be made to see that the things by which the west had impressed them were so many pleasant appearances, concealing incurable decay. Stalin tried to stir the old half-extinct ideological zeal and fervour of communism in order to hold his ground against the west, not only outside but even inside Russia. By appealing to that zeal and fervour he hoped, in particular, to restore the morale of the intelligentsia and to re-reconcile it to the rigours of his rule. By one of history's many ironies Leninism was now called upon to stop the breaches in Stalin's 'iron curtain.'

There was a Sisyphean touch about these labours, which was due to an obvious contradiction between Stalin's foreign and domestic policies. His foreign policy was to keep Russia in Europe. His domestic policy was to keep her mind out of Europe. His purpose was to re-isolate Russia not only from that part of the Continent that was under American and British influence, but even from that portion of it that had come under Russian influence, for the way of life and the spiritual climate of the 'people's democracies' was very different from the Russian. In part this was due to the dissimilarity of the national traditions of Russians, Poles, Czechs, Hungarians, Serbs. Even in Russia the formative processes of Stalinism had lasted many years and had necessitated many economic upheavals, political shocks, and slow changes. The end product of that long painful evolution could not be exported ready made to the countries in the Russian orbit. Meanwhile, their economic systems, with private ownership still predominating in farming, with diverse methods of industrial work and varying degrees of efficiency, would be different from the Russian. The standards of living of the Czechs or Poles, traditionally higher than those of the Russians, could not be so depressed for the sake of industrialization as they had been in Russia. All this was likely to produce 'deviations' from orthodoxy. Genuine contact between Russia and the 'people's democracies' —free travel and free exchange of ideas—could easily have become another source of ferment inside Russia. Stalin had therefore to keep in being two 'iron curtains,' one separating Russia from her own zone of influence, the other separating that zone from the west. Public opinion in the west was more preoccupied with the latter, but it was the former that was the more impenetrable of the two. Yet it is questionable whether even this double wall can effectively serve a policy that aspires to keep Russia in and out of Europe at the same time.

The chief drama of victorious Stalinism lies, however, in a wider and much more dangerous dilemma. Stalin has staked everything on revolutionizing the whole of the Russian zone of influence. He apparently believed that, having achieved this, he would be able to secure the great truce, the 'peaceful coexistence,' to use his own term, between the capitalist west and the communist east. These two objectives, revolution within the Russian orbit and the peaceful coexistence of the two systems, have tended to militate against each other. The truce between capitalism and communism, which lasted through the twenties and thirties, was based on a precarious balance of power, which can hardly be restored. Among its essential elements were Russian weakness and American isolationism. Both belong to the past. Any new balance would require that the United States should reconcile itself to Russian ascendancy in the east and Russia to American ascendancy in the west. It would require that the powers should perpetuate the division of the world into zones of influence. Even if they could bring themselves to do that, the new balance would still be highly unstable, because of the extreme polarization of power in the world and the friction on the borderlines of the two systems. More important still, the outcome of the Second World War has posed the question whether the world, on the threshold of the atomic age, has not become too small for the two antagonistic systems. This is not an entirely new question. The advance of industrial technique has long since tended to render nation-states and empires obsolete. But the sudden expansion of both the American influence and the Soviet system, coinciding with the new revolution in industrial technique, has re-posed the question with baffling insistence and unendurable acuteness. Before that question victorious Stalinism, like the rest of the world, seems to stand defeated.

FROM

Isaac Deutscher
"THE NEW SOVIET POLICY TOWARD THE SATELITES"

SOVIET policy toward China and the Communist regimes of eastern Europe has entered a new and significant phase. In this field, as in others, Stalin's successors have been reviewing their legacy critically to see whether and how they can free it of its worst liabilities.

Broadly speaking, their new course aims at lifting from the other Communist governments the odium of puppetry and some of the burdens of vassalage that Stalin's heavy hand had laid on them. The peoples of Communist Asia and eastern Europe are to be reassured that they will no longer be treated as Russia's subjects and that the new government in Moscow shows respect

ISAAC DEUTSCHER 187

for their national aspirations and renounces those quasi-imperialist privileges which Stalin had acquired for Russia. It goes without saying that the Soviet leaders expect that this new policy will eventually strengthen their position within the Soviet bloc.

The new policy is being carried out simultaneously from the various angles of strategy, economy, and politics, from the China Sea to the Elbe. There are broadly three major motives behind it. There is first Moscow's apparent desire to avoid a dissipation of Soviet strength and to cut Russia's strategic commitments.

There is further a new confidence, springing from the recent tremendous growth of the Russian economy, which enables Russia to give up the economic advantages that Stalin had so ruthlessly extracted from the satellites.

The most significant application of the new policy can be seen in the Russo-Chinese agreements that were signed in Peking on October 11, during the celebration of the first five years of Mao's regime, in the presence of a large and important Soviet delegation headed by Nikita Khrushchev, the General Secretary of the Soviet Communist Party. The Soviet leaders chose that solemn occasion to announce that Russia would evacuate the naval base of Port Arthur, Manchuria, by May 31, 1955. Moscow had promised to give up Port Arthur in the Russo-Chinese pact of 1950, but until recently it looked as if that promise would never be honored. At first Stalin delayed evacuation on the ground that the Russian garrison must remain at Port Arthur as long as Russia and Red China had not concluded a peace treaty with Japan—it was as a reinsurance against Japan that Russia had acquired the Manchurian naval base in the first place. Then during the Korean War, which the Chinese feared might spread to Manchuria, it was they who asked the Russians to hold Port Arthur as a deterrent. The imminent evacuation indicates, therefore, a new Russo-Chinese confidence in the maintenance of peace in that part of the world.

But whatever the broader international context, the move will soothe Chinese patriotic feelings, which have always been offended by the presence of foreign garrisons. And the Russian gesture is sure to be acclaimed throughout the rest of Asia, for Asians recall very few instances, if any, in which a great power has given up a first-rate strategic base on foreign territory except under direct hostile pressure from another power or under the immediate threat of revolt in the occupied country. Throughout Asia, Chinese and Soviet propagandists are contrasting the Russian evacuation of Port Arthur with the establishment of new American bases under the Southeast Asian Treaty Organization. Moscow has chosen this moment to emphasize that it sees the rivalry between East and West in terms of economic and political competition rather than of military action. From this point of view, the Soviet Union's spectacular abandonment of one great naval base may be a more profitable operation than the acquisition by the United States of a score of new bases: It helps to make all China a single, solid base of Communism.

Less conspicuously, Russia is also withdrawing from the long-lasting, silent rivalry with China in Sinkiang, Mongolia, and Manchuria. In all those provinces, Stalin's agents had worked hard to establish Russian influence by economic penetration and direct and indirect control. The results of their work are now being scrapped, and Peking's sovereignty is being restored all across China's northern boundary.

The most important single act of this second strategic withdrawal is the disbandment of the mixed Russo-Chinese joint-stock companies, also announced in the October agreements. These companies exploited the gold mines, the oil wells, and possibly also the uranium deposits of Sinkiang. They controlled shipyards in Manchuria, and they managed the whole of China's civil aviation. Moscow is now giving up the assets it held in those companies on a fifty-fifty basis and is withdrawing its general managers. Last but not least, it is giving up some of the facilities that enabled the agents of its intelligence services to obtain access to every corner of China and to every aspect of Chinese life, facilities to which Stalin attached very great importance.

Unlike the evacuation of Port Arthur, the disbandment of the mixed companies had not been promised in any previous Russo-Chinese agreement. But the companies naturally reminded the Chinese of the old concessions, with extraterritorial privileges, formerly maintained by the western powers. Therefore the disbandment removes a grievance. It dispels lingering suspicions of Russia's intentions, and it is being hailed as proof of Russia's "socialist generosity and disinterestedness."

This instance of the reversal of Stalin's policy is not, however, so sweeping as are some others. The attitude of the Peking government toward Moscow has never been that of a vassal. Even Stalin was anxious to spare Chinese susceptibilities and to make the Chinese Communists feel that they were treated like respected allies. But the habit of ordering his satellites about was so deeply ingrained in Stalin that he could not rid himself of it entirely even when he tried to humor Mao Tse-tung. And so only Stalin's successors have been free to renounce the assets and advantages for which Stalin had bargained so hard—and thus to base the Russo-Chinese alliance on a more solid foundation.

The new course is not designed merely to placate Russia's only great and important ally. This can be seen from the fact that it has been extended to Russia's less independently powerful satellites of eastern Europe. There also the mixed companies have been disbanded at a stroke—in Hungary, Romania, Bulgaria, and East Germany.

It will be remembered that these companies figured largely in the conflict between Stalin and Tito; the Yugoslav Communists viewed them as instruments of their economic subjection by Russia. Through these companies Russia controlled the entire navigation of the Danube and all civil aviation in the Balkan countries. The companies operated such essential parts of the Balkan economy as Romanian oil and Hungarian bauxite and aluminum. Even the National Bank of Romania was under the management of a mixed Soviet-Romanian company.

The companies enjoyed extraordinary privileges: Their profits were exempt from taxation; they were free to import and export goods without observing the restrictions to which local concerns, even those owned by the state, were subject; the general managers of the companies, usually Soviet citizens, fixed prices, freight rates, and tariffs, and thereby exercised a powerful influence over the whole economic life of the area.

But the Yugoslav charges that the companies were instruments of Russian "state-capitalist exploitation" were only partially justified. It was mainly during the first postwar years—roughly up to 1950, while the Soviet economy still labored under the aftereffects of war—that Stalin was bent on speeding up Russia's economic recovery at the expense of the satellites. In those years he did use the mixed companies for transferring wealth from central and eastern Europe to the Soviet Union. Later, after the Soviet Union had recovered somewhat economically, a two-way traffic developed, and then eastern Europe began to benefit from Soviet investment and technological assistance. But Moscow still saw that it got its share of the profits made by the companies, and it still held many "commanding heights" in the eastern European economy.

Now this whole chapter of direct Russian control over that economy is being closed. The Danube may soon cease to be a Russian river. Control of its navigation may soon be back in Yugoslav, Hungarian, Bulgarian, and Romanian hands. This is not to say that Russia's economic influence will decline. But Russia will now exercise its influence indirectly, by the sheer weight of economic preponderance, geographic proximity, and ideological affinity rather than through menace and political pressure.

The end of direct Russian economic control may foreshadow moves of even broader international significance. The ending of that control may be part of a scheme for the reorganization of eastern Europe in case of a withdrawal of Soviet occupation armies and of a consequent windup of Soviet communication lines in the Balkans. But it is difficult to see how such a withdrawal can take place before East and West reach settlements on Germany and Austria.

It is only natural that at this stage, when so many of the original causes of the break between Moscow and Belgrade are vanishing, Moscow should initiate a rehabilitation of Tito.

Some time ago, the virulent campaign against Titoism was quietly called off throughout the Soviet bloc. Normal relations between Yugoslavia and all eastern European governments have been re-established. The Yugoslavs have regained their influence on the Danube Commission, from which Stalin had unceremoniously ousted them. The Soviet economic boycott of Tito's government has ceased. Bulgarian and Hungarian troops have been withdrawn from the Yugoslav frontiers, and Tito has cut armament expenditures and decreed partial demobilization. Finally, Russia has acknowledged the settlement over Trieste even though it had not been consulted on it and had had no say in it.

This ideological and political truce, ordered in Moscow, induced a lot of soulsearching in the Yugoslav Communist Party. Even before that, its leaders had not seen eye to eye on the prospects of their conflict with Russia. A group headed by former Vice-President Milovan Djilas reckoned with an indefinite prolongation and aggravation of the conflict and favored closer links between Yugoslavia and the West than those to which Tito had consented. Another group, headed by Vice-President Edvard Kardelj, hopefully expected that after Stalin's death changes would occur in the Soviet Union that might make reconciliation possible. Tito himself tried to keep balance between the conflicting views until, last January, he disavowed Djilas and his theories and cautiously placed his authority behind Kardelj's views.

Until the last few weeks, however, neither Moscow nor Belgrade was prepared to go beyond an ideological cease-fire. Tito was, and probably still is, afraid of being caught in the shifting crosscurrents of Soviet policy. If he were to take a few steps in the direction of a return to the Soviet bloc, he would cut himself off from the West. But if as a result of factional struggle a group hostile to Titoism were to gain the upper hand in Moscow, he might find himself dangerously isolated from both East and West, distrusted and perhaps attacked by both. Tito therefore trod cautiously, equally anxious to encourage the new conciliatory attitude in the East and to avoid arousing suspicion in the West. On the other hand, Stalin's successors wondered how far Tito had gone in his commitments toward the West and whether it was too late for them to try and conciliate him.

But Moscow has now decided to allay Tito's fears. Of its own accord it has initiated his rehabilitation. The occasion chosen was the tenth anniversary of the Red Army's entry into Belgrade, which was celebrated in both Moscow and Belgrade on October 20. On that day, for the first time since 1948, *Pravda* and other Soviet newspapers mentioned Tito's name without the customary abuse. Moreover, they underlined the "heroic role" Tito and his Partisans had played.

It will be remembered that Stalin consistently played down that role and that shortly before the schism he rudely told the Yugoslavs that the Red Army had liberated them from German occupation. According to the new version of history produced in a letter from Stalin to Tito on May 4, 1948, Tito's Partisans were incapable of effective action against the Germans because of Tito's failure as a leader. From then till the end of the Stalin era, Soviet writers repeated that version, which accorded so well with the then fashionable glorification of all things Russian.

Since October 20 Moscow has made amends for the insults Stalin had heaped on Tito and the Partisans. Its writers now almost lean over backward to pay tributes to Tito. Here is *Pravda* now saying:

"We had to act in close co-operation with the National Liberation Army of allied Yugoslavia . . . which has made a serious contribution to the common struggle for emancipation of the peoples of Europe. . . . We knew how much courage and steadfastness Yugoslav Partisan detachments had shown . . . they took a most active part in our battles . . . they were everywhere with us . . . and not rarely it was they who secured the outcome of a battle. This happened many times."

Acknowledging explicitly Tito's role as Commander in Chief, *Pravda* now disposes of Stalin's myth that the Red army had to fight single-handedly for Yugoslavia's liberation.

Stalin's successors are evidently ready for a full, explicit, and a spectacular rehabilitation of Tito as a good Communist. But it is not sure that Tito is prepared to accept the rehabilitation; and one may guess that this is now the chief topic of discussions between Moscow and Belgrade. It is quite likely that Moscow does not even demand from Tito that as the price of rehabilitation he should dramatically renounce Yugoslav's commitments toward the West or the pacts with Greece and Turkey. In their present

mood, Moscow's rulers are inclined to admit that Stalin, not
Tito, must be blamed for Yugoslavia's defection to the western
camp. And on November 7, during the celebration of the thirty-
seventh anniversary of the October Revolution, they repeated
their overtures to Tito before the whole diplomatic corps as-
sembled in the Kremlin.

The beginning of this rehabilitation poses a number of absorbing problems to the leaders of other Communist parties. If
Tito is no longer a "traitor" and a "fascist," should those Communist leaders who have been tried and executed in eastern
Europe as his associates and agents continue to be branded as
traitors? Tito's vindication may be the beginning of a post-
humous rehabilitation of Laszlo Rajk, Rudolf Slansky, Vladimir
Clementis, and others. A hint to this effect has already been
thrown out in Budapest where the Central Committee of the
Hungarian Communist Party has declared that there were "many
innocent comrades" among the victims of governmental terror in
recent years. Rajk's adherents have already been released from
prison and reinstated as party members; and the reinstatement
of one leading Hungarian "Titoist," former Foreign Minister
Gyula Kallai, was carried out at a solemn party meeting by
Matyas Rakosi himself.

The wider issue of the inner regime of the Communist Parties
looms behind this pardon extended to Titoism. Reluctantly and
hesitantly, Stalin's successors are abandoning the hallowed principle of the infallibility of Communist leadership. If a dissenter
like Tito was right against the Soviet Central Committee, then
dissent is no longer a crime. The "monolithic" outlook of the
Communist Parties thus comes into question.

Since Stalin's death the Communist Parties have certainly
borne far less dictation from Moscow than they did in Stalin's
days. The Russian party now seems to exercise its influence
primarily through example. It favors in any case the substitution
of "collective leadership" or of government by committee for
the party regime controlled by a single leader.

Inevitably, the transition from the one regime to the other is
causing friction and dissension. Here and there the single leader

of the Stalin era attempts to defend his prerogatives and privileges. This has been the case with Rakosi in Hungary, whom the Central Committee put in his place at its October session although he still holds the office of its First Secretary. In Poland President Boleslaw Bierut seems to have reconciled himself to collective leadership. In the Czechoslovak party the problem solved itself with the death of Klement Gottwald, the single leader of the Stalin era. In Romania the party is still in the throes of a crisis: The fate of Ana Pauker is still in the balance, and though they are less savage than they were under Stalin, the purges continue.

What is obstructing and confusing the evolution of the eastern European Communist Parties is that the Governments they control are far less stable than the post-Stalin regime in the U.S.S.R. itself. The peasant smallholder still dominates the rural life of eastern Europe. The old bourgeois parties still have a potential following. A Social Democratic tradition is still alive in the working class. Relaxation of discipline in the ruling Communist Parties may be taken as a sign of their weakness, may encourage opposition, and may lead to political convulsions. Therefore, the Communist rulers view with mixed feelings the infectious reformist ferment from Moscow.

This accounts for the paradox that at times the east European Communist Parties cling to Stalinist orthodoxy much more obstinately than does Stalin's own party. On the other hand, they cannot go on clinging to that orthodoxy when it is manifestly crumbling in its own homeland. Tito's rehabilitation throws the dilemma into even sharper relief and is sure to entail new ferments and new shifts throughout the Communist world.

Whatever new twists Russia's old problems may develop, one facet of Soviet effort remains unchanged—its attempt to see clearly and denounce unremittingly the non-Communist shape of things beyond its borders. In the following chapter, what the Communist sees when he looks abroad and what he thinks when he sees it are set forth by Russian and non-Russian observers. To see ourselves as others see us is as important in the international dimension as it is at the personal level. While the reflection may not please, it may still instruct.

The following chapter will probably make the average American reader see red; it would be rather surprising if it didn't. It is to be hoped, however, that red irritation will not obscure a clearer picture of Red Russia.

CHAPTER 8

The Communist View of the Non-Communist World

Probably the average American views the Russians as frightened slaves of a brutal and aggressive totalitarian regime. In its official and unofficial pronouncements the United States government has done little to encourage another concept. Right or wrong, this seems to be the prevailing American view of the U.S.S.R.

What do the Russians see from the other end of the glass? How does America look from Moscow? A working understanding of the government and people of the Soviet Union requires some study of this question.

The following accounts are from the works of persons trained to observe, and skilled in reporting their observations. It is too much to ask that they be free entirely from bias; indeed, it is doubtful their work would be as valid without it.

The first selection was written in the 1930's by Ilya Ilf and Eugene Petrov, two well-known Soviet writers of that period. They toured America and compared it with their own land. The product of their observation and comparison has since become the most famous of its kind. Originally it was published as ONE STORIED AMERICA; *translated into English from the Russian it appeared as* LITTLE GOLDEN AMERICA. *The portion presented here is made up of two chapters bearing the titles "American Democracy" and "They and We."*

The second excerpt is by Michel Gordey, Russian born

196

correspondent of the French newspaper, FRANCE-SOIR. *In 1950
he toured Russia and published his findings under the title,*
VISA TO MOSCOW. *"I did not," he says, "go to the U.S.S.R. ex-
pecting to find a heaven or a hell. I went with an open eye,
consciously seeking to wipe the slate clear of my previously
acquired conceptions. I was possessed by an immense curiosity. I wanted most of all to understand, to feel human beings."*

The third section is from THE SOVIET IMAGE OF THE UNITED
STATES, *by Professor Frederick C. Barghoorn. Published
under the auspices of the Yale Institute of International
Studies, it is the only work of its kind so far to appear.*

*Ilya Ilf and Eugene Petrov picture the America of depres-
sion days, of the unemployed and the bread lines, of the
programs of the radicals and panaceas of the demagogues, of
racketeers and Congressional investigations of the rich, of
the Lindbergh kidnaping and of bloody strikes, of Franklin
D. Roosevelt, John P. Morgan, Huey Long, Dr. Townsend,
and Senator Nye. But to these visiting Russians even depres-
sion America was a land of the fabulously rich—and the
fabulously corrupt.*

FROM

Ilya Ilf and Eugene Petrov
LITTLE GOLDEN AMERICA

ON a rainy winter day a small freight boat came to the shores
of England. A hatless man came down the wet gangplank to the
pier. With one hand he held his wife and with the other he
pressed his child to him. He was attacked from all sides by
photographers, motion-picture operators, and journalists. The
man walked right through, paying no heed to anyone. Only
after he took his place in a taxi did he turn to look back at the
crowd that followed him, and in his look was reflected hatred
and fear.

That man had fled from America. He abandoned America at
night, when the country was asleep, after eluding the vigilance

of New York's fleetest reporters. In order to avoid persecution, he departed not on a comfortable passenger ship, but on an old shabby freighter, where there was not even a convenient cabin. And this man who had abandoned his native land was happy to be on a foreign shore.

That was Charles Lindbergh, one of the most famous men in the world, and his native land was the United States of America, the country of the greatest democracy, as Americans firmly believe.

All know, of course, the reasons that drove Lindbergh to the necessity of undertaking the most serious step in the life of any man—to abandon his native land. America was not able to protect the inviolability of personality of its national hero. It was unable to defend his domicile from the intrusion of bandits. It was unable to protect his family.

There is no doubt that Lindbergh loves America and that Americans adore Lindbergh. And if one will read carefully the text of the American Constitution, it is easy to discover there grandiose and equitable sections which would seem to guarantee the general welfare. Nevertheless, Lindbergh fled, while the Constitution in the capitalist country is merely a bronze tablet or a no less beautiful parchment preserved in the vault of a lawmaking institution.

From the story of the famous man let us pass to the story of an ordinary woman for whom as much as for Lindbergh were written the sonorous words of the Constitution of the United States.

That American woman had a seventeen-year-old daughter and a grown-up son. On one occasion the daughter did not return home. She did not come back all through the night, nor did she return the next day. The girl disappeared. The police looked for her and did not find her. The mother regarded her daughter as lost. A year passed. Then, in one way or another, a friend of her son's told him a horrible bit of news. He had seen the girl whom they all regarded as lost in a secret brothel. (Officially, there is no prostitution in America. As a matter of fact, there are any number of secret brothels there.) At once the brother, pretending to be a client, went to this den of iniquity.

There he actually saw his sister. He recognized her with difficulty, so frightfully had the young girl changed. What she told
him was even more horrible. She had been kidnaped and sold.

"I'm lost," said the girl, "and don't try to save me. The people
who abducted me are so powerful that nobody can fight them.
They will not hesitate to kill you or mother."

Nevertheless, the fight began. The mother went to the police.
But nothing came of it. Behind the backs of the bandits stood
some unknown but extraordinarily powerful people. The mother
appealed to the courts. The lawyer of the bandits proved that
the girl was an old prostitute, and the menace to society were
not the bandits who had abducted her but she herself. The superior court of the state likewise decided the case in favor of the
bandits. A trip to Washington did not help the mother. Washington simply has no power over the court of the state. That's all
there was to it. The girl remained in the brothel.

This happened in a country which has freedom of the press.
The girl's mother had complete freedom, not only to speak but
even to shout. She shouted, but no one heard her.

This happened in a country where freedom of the press has
been declared. Yet not a single newspaper wrote a thing about
this case. Where were all the resourceful, tireless, fleet-footed
reporters from whose penetrating gaze not a single robbery can
escape, or a single wealthy wedding, or a single step of a motion-
picture star of even the fourth magnitude?

This happened in a country where inviolability of person
exists. But a poor person sat in a brothel, and no power could
free her from it. It seems to us that if Abraham Lincoln himself
were able to rise from his grave, even he could not do anything
about it. Not even the cannons of General Grant could help
him!

For some reason, every time one begins to sift in his memory
the elements of which American life is composed one recalls
bandits and if not bandits, then racketeers, and if not racketeers,
then bankers, which as a matter of fact is one and the same
thing. One recalls all this human garbage which has polluted an
excellent, freedom-loving, and industrious country.

What could be gladder tidings than free elections in a democratic country whose citizens according to the Constitution are guaranteed all the rights to "liberty and the pursuit of happiness"? In their Sunday best the electors go to the ballot boxes and gently drop into them ballots with the names of their favorite candidates.

As a matter of fact, what happens was what our Chicago doctor told us—racketeer politicians come and by means of blackmail or threats force a good man to vote for some crook.

And so, the right to liberty and to the pursuit of happiness is undoubtedly there, but the possibility of actually enjoying that right is exceedingly dubious. This right is in too dangerous proximity with the money vaults of Wall Street.

But, to make up for that, the outer forms of democracy are preserved by Americans with extraordinary meticulousness. And that, one must say in truth, is rather impressive.

Henry Ford, by virtue of his position in American society, is a figure almost unapproachable. Yet on one occasion he walked into one of the buildings of his plant where several engineers happened to be, shook hands with all of them, and began to talk about the business on which he came. Throughout the conversation old Henry looked very worried. A certain thought tormented him. He stopped several times in the middle of a word, evidently trying to recall something. Finally, he excused himself, interrupted the conversation, and walked up to a young engineer who was sitting in a far corner of the room.

"I am very sorry, Mr. Smith," said Mr. Ford, "but I think I forgot to say hello to you."

An extra handshake will not lie as a heavy burden on the balance sheet of the Ford automobile plants, while the impression produced was tremendous. Ford will never invite that young engineer to his home, but they are equals on the job, they make automobiles together. Ford knows many old workers in his plant and calls them by their first names—"Hello, Mike!" or "Hello, John!" And Mike and John address him: "Hello, Henry!" Here they seem to be equals; they make automobiles together. But old Henry alone will be selling them. And old Mike or old John, after they've worked themselves out, will be thrown out into the street, just as worn-out bearings are thrown out.

And so, after making ten thousand miles, we found ourselves in the capital of the United States.

Washington, with its comparatively low government buildings, its gardens, its monuments, its broad streets, looks somewhat like Vienna, somewhat like Berlin, somewhat like Warsaw, somewhat like all the capitals. And only automobiles remind one that this city is located in America. Here there is an automobile for every two persons, but there is not a single permanent theater for the entire population of five hundred thousand. Having looked over George Washington's house in Mount Vernon, having visited sessions of Congress, and having been at the grave of the Unknown Soldier, we discovered that there was really nothing else to see. Only the President remained to be seen. In America that is not so difficult.

Democratism in relations between people, the democratism of daily intercourse, is quite strongly developed in America and reaches quite far at times.

Twice a week, at ten o'clock in the morning, the President of the United States receives journalists. We managed to come to such a reception. It takes place in the White House. We walked into the reception room. There stood a large round table made of sequoia wood. It was a gift made to one of the former presidents. There was no cloakroom, so the incoming journalists laid their overcoats on that table, and when there was no more room on the table, they began laying them on the floor. Gradually about a hundred people gathered. They smoked, talked aloud, and looked impatiently at the small white door, behind which, apparently, the President of the United States was sequestered.

We were advised to stand as close as possible to the door, so that as people were being admitted to the President we would find ourselves in front; otherwise, it might so happen that behind the backs of the journalists we would not see anything. With the skill of experienced streetcar fighters, we pushed ahead. Before us were only three men. They were grayish and quite respectable gentlemen.

The reception hour struck, but the journalists were not yet admitted. Then the grayish gentlemen, at first quietly but then louder, began to rap on the door. They were knocking to be admitted to the President of the United States, just as some assistant director might rap on the door of an actor to remind him of his entrance cue. They knocked laughingly, but still they knocked.

Finally, the door opened and the journalists, crowding each other, rushed ahead. We ran with the rest of them. The cavalcade raced across the corridor, then passed through a large empty room. In that room we easily outstripped the panting gray-haired gentlemen and were the first to run into the next room.

Before us in the depths of a circular private study—on the walls of which hung old lithographs depicting Mississippi steamers, and in the small niches of which stood models of frigates— at a medium-sized writing desk, a smoking cigarette in his hand, and Chekhovian pince-nez on his large handsome nose, sat Franklin D. Roosevelt, President of the United States. Behind his back twinkled the stars and stripes of two national flags.

Questions began. The correspondents asked them, the President answered.

All of this ritual was, of course, somewhat conditional. Everybody knows that the President will not disclose any particular secrets to the journalists. Certain questions the President answered seriously and quite extensively, parried some with a jest (it is not so easy, of course, twice a week to get off with a joke against a hundred pushing journalists), to still others he replied that he would discuss them the next time.

Roosevelt's large handsome face looked tired. Only the day before the Supreme Court had vetoed the AAA, Roosevelt's law regulating farmers' sowing of crops, one of the pivots of his program.

The questions and answers took up half an hour. When a pause came, the President looked quizzically at the people gathered there. This was understood to be a signal for a general retreat. There resounded a helter-skelter "Good-bye, Mr. President!" and everyone departed. And Mr. President remained alone in his circular study among the frigates and the star-spangled banners.

Millions of people, old and young, who compose the great American nation, an honest, boisterous, talented people, who have a somewhat too great respect for money but who are hard-working, can do anything they like according to the Constitution, for they are the masters of the country. They can even take Morgan himself, John Pierpont Morgan himself, and call him out for questioning in a senatorial commission and ask him severely:

"Mr. Morgan, didn't you pull the United States into the World War because of the mundane interests of your personal enrichment?"

The people can ask that. But this is how Mr. Morgan answers—we heard him ourselves.

And on that occasion, too, everything was very democratic.

The entrance to the hall where the Senate Commission was sitting was free. Again you were free to do with your overcoat what you liked—put it on the floor, or shove it under the chair on which you were sitting.

At one end of a small hall were chairs for the public; at the other end, a table at which the questioning was proceeding. The table was covered with neither red nor green cloth. It was a long polished table. Everything was very simple. Right beside the billionaire on the floor lay his thick and no longer new brief case. Morgan was surrounded by his lawyers and advisers. They were numerous. Gray and pink-cheeked, fat and bald-headed, or young with piercing eyes—they were all armed with facts, information, documents, folios, and folders. All this band of Morgan's braves felt quite unconstrained.

In the chair was Senator Nye, his face thin, inspired, almost Russian. (A Russian shirt would suit him very well.) The interrogation was carried on by Senator Clark, round-faced and gay. It was at once evident that he enjoyed questioning John Pierpont Morgan, Jr.

"Junior" was almost seventy years old. He was a huge and obese old man in a long dark coat. On the back of Morgan's apoplectic head was visible the gray fuzz of a chick. He was calm. He knew that nothing untoward would happen to him.

He would be asked a question, he would look at his lawyers, the latter would begin to dig frantically in their books and would prompt the answer to him.

It was an amazing spectacle. Several score of advisers whispered something into Morgan's ear, shoved little papers to him, prompted him, helped him. It was not Morgan speaking, it was his billions speaking. And when money talks in America, it always talks authoritatively. After all, America's favorite saying is: "He looks like a million dollars."

Indeed, a million dollars looks very good.

And Morgan, in his long dark coat resembling an old fat hawk, looked like several billions.

For being summoned to the Senate Commission, the person subpoenaed is entitled to daily pay, the normal government daily pay for expenses. John Pierpont Morgan, Jr., took that money. He took advantage of all the rights which a democratic constitution gave him.

Morgan received everything he was entitled to under the Constitution—even a little more. But what did the people get?

On the territory of the United States live more than a hundred and twenty million people.

Thirteen million of them have not had work for several years. Together with their families they make up one-fourth of the population of the entire country. Yet economists insist that on the territory of the United States right now, even today, it would be possible to feed a billion people.

Our journey came to an end. Within two months we had been in twenty-five states and several hundred towns, we had breathed the dry air of deserts and prairies, had crossed the Rocky Mountains, had seen Indians, had talked with the young unemployed, with the old capitalists, with radical intellectuals, with revolutionary workers, with poets, with writers, with engineers. We had examined factories and parks, had admired roads and bridges, had climbed up the Sierra Nevadas and descended into the Carlsbad Caves. We had traveled ten thousand miles.

And throughout that entire journey we never once stopped thinking of the Soviet Union.

We had traveled over American highways but in our thoughts were Soviet highways. We spent nights in American hotels, but we thought about Soviet hotels. We examined Ford's factories, but in our thoughts we saw ourselves in our own automobile factories, and while conversing with Indians we thought of Kazakstan.

Through the tremendous distance that separated us from Soviet soil we envisioned it with especial incisiveness. It is necessary to see the capitalist world in order to appreciate in a new way the world of socialism. All the attributes of the socialist arrangement of our life, which man ceases to notice because of daily contact with them, seem especially significant at a distance. We understood the mood of Maxim Gorky when upon his return to the Union after many years of life abroad, tirelessly, day in and day out, he repeated one and the same thing: "It's a remarkable thing you are doing, comrades! A great thing!"

We talked constantly about the Soviet Union, drew parallels, made comparisons. We noticed that the Soviet people whom we frequently met in America were possessed of the same emotions. There was not a single conversation which in the end would not end up with a reference to the Soviet Union: "But at home it is like this," "but at home it is like that," "it would be well to introduce it at home," "we don't know how to do that yet," "that we have already adopted." Soviet people abroad were not mere travelers, not merely engineers or diplomats on a mission. All of them were lovers who had been torn away from the object of their affection and who remembered it every minute. It is a unique patriotism that cannot be understood, let us say, by an American. In all probability the American is a good patriot. If he were asked he would sincerely say that he loves his country; but at the same time it will be found out that he does not love Morgan, that he does not know and does not care to know the names of the people who planned the suspension bridges in San Francisco, that he is not interested to know why in America drought increases every year, who built Boulder Dam and why, why Negroes are lynched in the Southern states, or why he must eat frozen meat. He will say that he loves his country—yet he is profoundly indifferent to questions of agriculture, since he is not an agriculturist; to questions of industry, since he is not an industrialist; to finances, since he is not a financier; to art, since he is not an artist; and to military problems, since he is not a military man. He is a hard-working man who receives his hundred and thirty dollars a month, so he sneers at Washington with all its laws, at Chicago with all its bandits, and at New York with its Wall Street. He asks only one thing of his country—to let him alone, and not to interfere with his listening to his radio or going to the movies. Of course, when he becomes unemployed, then it's a different matter. Then he will begin to think about everything. No, he will not understand the patriotism of a Soviet man, who loves not his juridical native land which gives him merely the rights of citizenship, but a native land which is tangible, where to him belong the soil, the factories, the stores, the banks, the dreadnoughts, the airplanes, the theaters, and the books, where he himself is the politician and the master of all.

The average American cannot endure abstract conversations nor does he touch upon themes too far removed from him. He is interested only in what is directly connected with his house, his automobile, or his nearest neighbors. He shows an interest in the life of the country once in four years, at the time of the presidential election.

We do not at all insist that this absence of spirituality is an organic attribute of the American people. There was a time, after all, when the Northern armies marched off to liberate the Negroes from slavery! It is capitalism that has made these people thus, and in every way it nurtures in them this spiritual lassitude. Terrible are the crimes of American capitalism, which with amazing trickiness has palmed off on the people the most trivial of motion pictures, radio, and weekly journalistic tosh, while reserving for itself Tolstoy, Van Gogh, and Einstein, but remaining profoundly indifferent to them.

Essentially there is in the world only one noble striving of the human mind—to vanquish spiritual and material poverty, to make people happy. Yet those people in America who have made it their goal to attain that—the advanced workers, the radical intellectuals—are at best regarded as dangerous cranks, and in the worst case as the enemies of society. The result is that even indirect fighters for human happiness—men of learning, inventors, builders—are not popular in America. They and their works, inventions, and wonderful constructions, remain in the shadows, while all of fame goes to boxers, bandits, and motion-picture stars. While among the people themselves—who see that with the increase in the number of machines, life becomes not better but worse—prevails even hatred of technical progress. There are people who are ready to break up machines, just like the drowning man who, in desperation to get out of the water, seizes his savior by the neck and drags him down to the bottom.

We have already said that the American, in spite of his busi-nesslike activity, has a passive nature. Some Hearst or some Hollywood shyster can manage to drag millions of good, honest, hard-working average Americans down to the spiritual level of a savage. But even these all-powerful men cannot divest the people of the notion that life must be improved. That notion is very widespread in America. But when it finally finds its expression in the form of political ideas, their level does not exceed the level of the average Hollywood picture. And such ideas have a colossal success.

All the political ideas which tend to the improvement of the welfare of the American people are inevitably presented in the form of easy arithmetic problems for students of the third grade. In order to understand the idea, the voter need merely take a sheet of paper, a pencil, make a quick calculation, and it's done. As a matter of fact, all of them are not really ideas but tricks, suitable for advertising purposes only. They would hardly bear mentioning, if scores of millions of Americans were not carried away by them.

How to save America and improve its life?

Huey Long advises division of wealth. A sheet of paper and a pencil appear on the scene. The voter, puffing, adds, multi-plies, subtracts, and divides. This is a terribly interesting occupa-tion. What a smart fellow this Huey Long is! Everyone will get a large sum of money! People are so carried away by this impudent arithmetic that it does not even occur to them to think about where these millions will come from.

How to improve life? How to save America?

There arises a new titan of thought, another Socrates or Confucius, the physician Townsend. The thought which has entered the thinking head of this respectable practicing physician could have been born in any small European country only in a psychiatric hospital in a ward for the tranquil, quiet, polite, and utterly hopeless madmen. But in America it has a dizzying success. Here it isn't even necessary to bother with subtraction and multiplication. Here everything is quite simple. Every old man and every old woman in the United States upon attaining the age of sixty will receive two hundred dollars a month under obligation to spend these dollars. Then trade will increase automatically and automatically unemployment will disappear. Everything takes place automatically.

We saw a sound newsreel of a meeting of the Townsend Committee under the management of the thinker himself. The meeting began with Dr. Townsend, a haggard old man with a freckled face, in spectacles and an old-fashioned coat, delivering a short speech on his plan.

"Ladies and gentlemen," he began, clearing his throat, "I spent many sleepless nights before I thought up my plan."

If Mark Twain could only take a look at this freckled old man, so methodical, so neat, and undoubtedly Godfearing! There is no doubt that it is precisely such an old man, coming out of Sister McPherson's ecclesiastical musical hall, weighs himself and weighs his entire family, in order to calculate how many pennies of live weight he must pay for, through the intercession of the esteemed sister, to the Lord God.

After Dr. Townsend spoke the old men and women who filled the hall. They came out on the stage and asked questions, to which the thinker replied.

"In other words, I will receive two hundred dollars?" an old man asked.

"Yes, if my plan goes through," the thinker answered firmly.

"Every month?"

"Every month."

"Well, thank you," the old man said.

And he vacated the place for the old woman who followed him.

"Listen, Dr. Townsend," she asked excitedly. "We are two old people—my husband and I. Will both of us really receive two hundred dollars each?"

"Yes, both of you," the thinker replied importantly.

"That is, all told, we will get four hundred dollars?"

"Quite right—four hundred dollars."

"I also receive a pension of seventeen dollars. They won't take that away from me?"

"No, you will likewise receive your pension."

The old woman bowed low and went away.

When we were leaving America the number of Townsend's followers was increasing at a frightful rate. Not a single politician dared to speak against this doctor of genius on the eve of elections.

But American capitalists understand that motion pictures, a radio broadcast, stories in weeklies, billboards about revolution "which can never happen in America," churches, and arithmetical plans may not prove sufficient, so there are already growing "American Legions" and "Liberty Leagues," and little by little fascist forces are trained, so that at the necessary moment they may be turned into the most genuine kind of storm troops, which will be ordered to stifle the revolutionary movement by force.

America is rich. But it is not merely rich. It is phenomenally rich. It has everything—oil, grain, coal, gold, cotton—everything that can only lie beneath the earth or grow upon the earth. It has people—the best workers in the world—capable, neat, efficient, honest, hard-working. America marched toward its enrichment at a quick rate of speed. The country reminds one of a man who has made a rapid career, who at first sells suspenders from a pushcart on the East Side, then opens his own store of ready-made clothes and moves to Brooklyn. Then he opens a department store, begins to play the stock market and moves to the Bronx. And finally he buys a railroad, hundreds of steamships, two motion-picture factories, builds a skyscraper, opens a bank, joins a golf club, and moves to Park Avenue. He is a billionaire. He had striven for that goal all his life. He bought and sold everything in any old way. He dispossessed people, speculated, sat at the stock exchange from morning until night, he toiled sixteen hours a day, he awoke with the thought of money, he fell asleep with the same thought, and now he is monstrously wealthy. Now he may rest. He has villas by the ocean, he has yachts and castles, but he becomes ill with an incurable disease. He is dying, and no billions can save him.

The stimulus of American life has been and is money. Contemporary American technique grew up and developed so that money might be made faster. Everything that brings in money develops, and everything that does not bring money degenerates and wilts away. Gas, electricity, construction, and automobile companies, in their chase for money, have created a high standard of living. America has raised itself to a high degree of welfare, having left Europe far behind. But precisely at this point it has become clear that America is seriously and dangerously ill. The country is now facing its own reductio ad absurdum. It is capable now, today, of feeding a billion people, and yet it cannot feed its own hundred and twenty millions. It has everything needed to create a peaceful life for its people, yet it has come to such a pass that the entire population is in a state of unrest: the unemployed fears that he will never again find a job; the employed fears that he will lose his job; the farmer fears a crop failure, because then prices will increase and it will cost him more to buy bread, but he also fears a good crop, because then prices will fall and he will have to sell his produce for a pittance. The rich fear that bandits will kidnap their children, bandits fear that they will be placed in the electric chair. Immigrants fear that they will be deported from America; Negroes fear that they will be lynched; politicians fear elections; the average man fears illness, because then doctors will take everything he owns; the merchant fears that racketeers will come and riddle his store counters with a machine-gun fusillade.

At the foundation of life of the Soviet Union lies the communist idea. We have a definite goal, toward which the country advances. The slogan that technique decides everything was given by Stalin after that idea triumphed. That is why we, the people, by comparison with Americans of the average kind are now already much calmer and happier than they, in the land of Morgan and Ford, of twenty-five million automobiles, of a million miles of ideal roads, the land of cold and hot water, of bathrooms, and service. That is why technique does not seem to us an evil spirit sprung from a bottle. On the contrary, we want to catch up with technical America and to outstrip it.

America does not know what will happen with it tomorrow. We know, and we can tell with definite accuracy, what will happen with us fifty years from now.

Nevertheless, we can still learn much from America. We are doing that. But the lessons which we learn from America are episodic and too specialized.

To catch up with America! That task which Stalin set before our people is immense, but in order to carry out this task we must first of all study America, study not only its automobiles, its turbine generators and radio apparatuses (we are doing that), but likewise the very character of the work of American workers, engineers, business people, especially the business people, because if our stakhanovists sometimes outstrip the norms of American workers, while the engineers are no worse at times than the American engineers (about that we heard frequently from Americans themselves), still, our business people or economists are considerably behind American business people and cannot compete with them in any way.

We will not discuss now the attributes of our economists, their loyalty to ideas, their devotion, their efficiency. These are the attributes of the Communist party, which brought them up. Nor will we touch upon the deficiencies of American business people, their lack of loyalty to ideas, their lack of principle, their chase after the dollar. These are the defects of the capitalism which brought them up. It is important for us right now to study their attributes and our defects, because it is necessary for us to learn from them. Not only engineers but also economists, our business people, must learn from them.

The American businessman always finds time for a business conversation. The American sits in his office with his coat off and works. He works quietly, unobtrusively, without making any fuss. He is never late anywhere. He never hurries anywhere. He has only one telephone. No one waits for him in his reception room, because an appointment is usually made with absolute accuracy, and not a single extra minute is wasted during the interview. He is occupied only with his business, exclusively with his business. When he holds conferences nobody knows. In all likelihood, he holds conferences rarely.

Should an American say in the course of a conversation, even incidentally, "I'll do that," it is not necessary to remind him of anything at all in the future. Everything will be done. The ability to keep his word, to keep it firmly, accurately, to burst, but keep his word—this is the most important thing which our Soviet business people must learn from American business people.

We wrote about American democracy, which in fact does not give man freedom and only masks the exploitation of man by man. But in American life there is a phenomenon which should interest us no less than a new machine model. That phenomenon is democracy in intercourse between people, albeit that democracy, too, covers social inequality and is a purely outward form. The outward forms of such a democratism are splendid. They help a lot in work, deliver a blow to bureaucratism, and enhance human dignity.

We drove out of Washington to New York. In a few hours, and our journey over the American land would come to an end. We thought about America during those final hours. We think that in our book we have told everything that we have thought.

Americans are very angry with Europeans who come to America, enjoy its hospitality, and later scold it. Americans often told us about this with annoyance. But we do not understand such posing of the question: to scold or to praise. America is not the first night of a new play, and we are not theater critics. We transmit to paper our impressions about that country and our thoughts about it.

What can be said about America, which simultaneously horrifies, delights, calls forth pity, and sets examples worthy of emulation, about a land which is rich, poor, talented, and ungifted?

We can say honestly, with hand on heart, that we would not like to live in America. It is interesting to observe this country, but one does not care to live in it.

Sixteen years later, years of inflation and hot and cold wars, Michel Gordey reports his view of the Russian view of America.

FROM

Michel Gordey
VISA TO MOSCOW

FOUR years of "cold war" have given rise in the Soviet Union to a whole anti-American literature, the most striking expression of which is probably to be found in the theater. Anti-imperialist or anti-capitalist plays are no novelty in the USSR: the Soviet playwrights had produced a certain number of them before the Second World War. These older plays, however, used to refer for the most part to the history of the Revolution, and more particularly to the foreign intervention during the Civil War. At the present time the anti-American theater chooses strictly contemporaneous subjects. With the encouragement of the party, twenty-eight anti-American plays were written and presented from the end of the war up into 1950. The subjects of these plays have to do with American life or with the Soviet-American struggle in Europe. This new theatrical genre is an instrument of domestic propaganda to combat the sympathetic feeling for the United States engendered by the Russian-American war alliance, and to put the Soviet public on guard against the "perfidy" and the hostility of that country, which is represented (not only in the theater, but also in the press, in films, on the radio, and in books) as the worst enemy of the Soviet Union and of peace in general.

I saw six of these plays. It would have been possible to see a score of them. The content of the piece interested me, every time, in an equal measure with the public reaction. These evenings in the theater revealed to me many things concerning the essential problem of the world today: relations between Russia and America. It would be a mistake to think that the authors of the twenty-eight anti-American plays represent Soviet public opinion; but in carrying out the wishes of the regime, these authors disclose a certain attitude, fix certain directives, and seek to create in the public certain reactions desired by the party. The quality of their productions depends, obviously, on their respective talents. For a spectator who knows America, some of these works would be seen to be filled with monstrosities, monumental psychological and political errors. The majority of the supposedly American characters represented in these tragedies or comedies have no relation whatever to reality in America. But what proportion of the Soviet playgoers has even the slightest acquaintance with the United States? Surely not more than one in ten thousand. The Soviet dramatists are thus quite free to create totally artificial American types and invent situations and predicaments that could never have occurred in America. The fact is that the Americans exhibited in the Soviet theater greatly resemble most Soviet cartoons, from which ferocity has erased —at least for a Western eye—every trace of humor. Will the tricks and lying of the anti-American propaganda that abounded in the Soviet theater in 1950 be able to bring about important results? Certain small signs I observed do not allow me to think it is doing so yet. But a continuous barrage of fire directed always toward the same target must in the long run produce effects.

Among the anti-American plays I saw in Moscow, the one that seemed to me the least artificial, the nearest to a certain semblance of reality, was *The Voice of America,* by Boris Lavrenev. This piece also reveals, perhaps more clearly than the others, the objective pursued by the ideological directors of the Soviet theater in their anti-American propaganda.

I saw this production at the Red Army Theater, the newest and handsomest theater in the capital. Built in amphitheater form, all in white and red, with a huge revolving stage (which makes it possible to bring on horses and even tanks for the military spectacles), this theater has stately foyers and assembly rooms, monumental staircases, and, of course, an abundance of the stucco columns that in the USSR are indispensable to architectural dignity.

The audience included a larger proportion of soldiers than I was used to. It was a matinee performance, however, which may account for the imbalance. As children under sixteen are not admitted to evening performances in Russia, the matinees are especially picked out for young spectators; and that afternoon there were many children, accompanied by their parents, in the crowd. It was considered, then, that a play like *The Voice of America* ought to be shown to the future Soviet citizens.

This drama has as hero an American army officer, who fights against the Germans on the Elbe, is decorated for his bravery by both Americans and Russians, and returns to the United States dreaming of living in peace for the rest of his life. Through a whole series of intrigues, in which a brutal-visaged Senator (with the inevitable cigar) cuts a prominent figure, the officer comes to be accused of wanting to betray his country, simply because he keeps his wartime admiration for the Russians and, also, does not believe in the "inevitable conflict" between the United States and the USSR. He is summoned to Washington to appear before the Committee on Un-American Activities, where it is proposed that he make a speech on the radio against the Soviet Union. When he refuses, he is dismissed from his post and reduced in rank. He then returns his American decoration, but keeps the one that was given him by the Red Army. He wishes to counter-attack and disclose the underhand dealings of his enemy, the "warmongering" Senator. But the latter has a long arm: he tries to have the honest officer assassinated by a gangster who haunts the corridors of Congress, offering his services to members who are having difficulty squaring themselves with their opponents. The officer barely escapes being murdered, but in self-defense kills the man who was trying to strike him down. When a charge of murder is brought against this good officer, his eyes begin to open (up to this point he has still believed in the valid functioning of American democracy).

His former sergeant, a Communist and militant labor-union man, finally convinces the persecuted hero, and demonstrates to him the rottenness of the system under which he lives. The officer and his wife make up their minds to join the forces of peace, and to strive, "clandestinely if need be," for the triumph of democracy and peace in the United States under the aegis of the Communists.

The play has in it several minor characters who demonstrate the primitive brutality of the American businessman, the immorality of young American women, the political opportunism of American soldiers. As in all the other anti-American plays shown in the USSR, one or two characters always symbolize the "good American," who stands out against the despicable background of a country militarized, degenerate, and perverted by alcohol, gangsterism, and capitalism.

I observe the reactions of the audience. The veterans, like the children and their parents, are opening wide eyes before the horrors of this terrible country which, by all evidence, is preparing for war against the Soviet Union. The hero and his friend, the Red sergeant, on the other hand, have all the sympathy of the spectators, who express their approbation by prolonged applause at the places provided for this purpose by the author. The moral of the drama is that salvation for America lies in following the American Communist Party, which gathers into its fold the only honest and peace-loving men in the United States. Assuming that the Soviet public accept this thesis (on looking around I see not the slightest indication to the contrary), they must then conclude that the triumph of the American Communist Party offers the only means of keeping the peace. Yet the directors of Soviet policy know (quite as well as their American opposites) that in a country of 150,000,000 inhabitants this party numbers some fifty thousand members, whose advent to power is, to say the least, unlikely. What point does this convention serve? What is the function of the "good American" in the anti-American plays produced in Moscow?

I put this question to a Soviet journalist. He replied: "We Soviet citizens hate no one. We should not be Marxists if it were possible for us to hate a whole people. We do not assume that the American people as a whole is made up of gangsters and warmongers. It is just to keep our public from having reactions of nationalistic hatred that our playwrights always insist on the fact that there are also good Americans."

The other plays of the same kind that I saw or read during my stay in the USSR usually presented the good Americans under a much more sorry aspect than does *The Voice of America*. In these plays corruption, degeneracy, and the machinations of the "henchmen of Wall Street" are shown in a still cruder light, with exaggerations that prove at any rate that the authors have never met an American or sojourned in the United States. Most of these plays also set out to prove that every American (indeed, every Westerner) in the USSR, whatever his declared purpose, does nothing but busy himself with espionage, sabotage, and anti-Soviet activities. The personages thus represented may be diplomats, journalists, or scholars; underneath their masks, they are all spies, and sworn enemies of the Soviet Union. Usually, just as these villains are on the point of succeeding with their sinister designs, the MVD intervenes and saves the situation. Often the MVD only wins out because of the spontaneous co-operation of some simple Soviet citizen who denounces the suspicious goings-on of the traitor-spy-malefactor-imperialist Americans to the authorities. As for the good Americans whose presence is deemed indispensable, they are sometimes honest but a little stupid, and sometimes idealistic to the verge of stupidity, but for them the only means of becoming active and efficient is generally indicated at the denouement: they are going to enroll in the American Communist Party or, more vaguely, to "swell the ranks of those who are fighting for peace."

From this stylized picture of America what idea can the Soviet spectator form of a country that is unknown to him? The United States must appear to his vision as a nation implacably hostile to the Soviet Union, ruled by fascists and gangsters who are making ready for anti-Soviet war and who do not recoil from the most sordid crimes that may help them carry out their plans. The American people are thus divided into criminals, imbeciles, and dollar-chasers, who make up the majority, and a small minority of Communist-oriented citizens (pursued, persecuted, and oppressed) who are struggling "to save the peace." Even in its exaggeration of the importance of this latter group the picture of the whole is disquieting if not portentous. An average spectator, who in one year will have seen a dozen plays and films of this type, is not likely to be reassured about the future. There is nothing for him to do but behave like a good Soviet patriot and approve the policy of his government, which is resisting the "implacable enemy" by every means in its power. He will demonstrate his patriotism by being—more than ever—suspicious of the several Westerners whom he may run into in the streets of Moscow. After all, how can he know—he, the ordinary citizen —whether these Westerners are good or bad? If he judges by his last visit to the theater, there is a big chance that the Westerner he sees before him may be an enemy of his country: a spy, a potential saboteur, a man who wants to make war against him. If the Soviet citizen were Latin in temperament, a creature of impulse, he would spit in this foreigner's face. Being what he is, having the national character that he has, he prefers to keep silence and to treat the infrequent foreigners he encounters with the hostility and distrust instilled in him by official propaganda.

Professor Barghoorn, in this final section, elaborates upon what official Russia thinks of capitalist America.

FROM

Frederick C. Barghoorn
THE SOVIET IMAGE OF THE UNITED STATES

LIKE its interpretation of American foreign policy, Moscow's picture of life in America exemplifies basic tenets of Soviet Marxism and aims at both Soviet and foreign propaganda targets. The Kremlin's version of American institutions and culture is a multi-purpose political weapon. It seeks to assure the Soviet elite of ultimate victory over American "bourgeois" democracy. It consoles the Soviet masses by trying to demonstrate to them that the lot of their brothers in even the greatest and richest capitalist country is far worse than their own. It seeks to persuade the peoples of Europe and Asia that America is the heart of a dying world from which can emanate no hope or promise for the future and to which it is futile and dangerous to turn. Finally, to all in America who will listen, it sets forth as the model for the future the Soviet way of life, which Moscow professes to believe will some day be installed in America as well as the rest of the world.

It is logical in terms of Marxism-Leninism and faithful to the spirit and emphasis of Soviet propaganda to discuss the Kremlin's presentation of the American scene under four main rubrics. A mighty stream of communications conveying each of these four basic themes has radiated from Moscow throughout the postwar period. The first deals with the fatal ills of the American capitalist economic system. The second describes the social problems of the United States in somber colors. The third draws the inevitable political conclusion from these economic and social fundamentals. Finally, to use a classic Marxist term, the cultural and spiritual "super-structure" of American capitalism is presented as a complex of devices by which the ruling class poisons and perverts the mind of the masses.

*   *   *   *   *

Molotov in his November 6, 1948, speech referred to the "obsolescent capitalist system, with its private ownership and anarchy of production and the social and political antagonism and crises which rend it." Capitalist countries are doomed, he said, to "periodic shocks and revolutionary upheavals."

With the increase in unemployment in the United States in the early months of 1949 the Soviet press stepped up its news coverage of American economic conditions. Items appeared frequently under such headings as "The sharpening of the economic situation in the United States." *New Times* for June 15, 1949, suggested that millions of unemployed Americans and Western Europeans could be put to work for orders for the Soviet Union and Eastern European countries. This editorial was only one of many items which related the question of the supposedly deepening economic crisis in the United States to one of the Soviet Union major foreign policies, namely, the apparent desire to increase East-West trade, on Soviet terms. This campaign had been proceeding in the U.N. economic commission for Europe since the summer of 1948 and had been publicized in many ways, including statements by the Soviet ambassador to the United States and Soviet representatives in U.N. General Assembly meetings. The prominence of this theme of East-West trade, which apparently was one of the Soviet concerns in connection with the Paris Conference of Foreign Ministers in June, 1949, is indicated by the fact that, according to Joseph B. Phillips, writing in *Newsweek* for June 20, 1949, *Pravda* or *Izvestiya* on five of the seven days of the week ending June 4 carried news stories on this subject.

Thus 1949 found Soviet propaganda regarding the American economic situation reverting to the thesis of the beneficial effects for American labor and industry of trade with Russia and the "new democracies." This theme was set against the background of doctrinaire Marxist-Leninist predictions of the catastrophic consequences for America of a new economic crisis.

*   *   *   *   *

Soviet propaganda regarding social conditions in the United States is a logical corollary to the Kremlin's above diagnosis of the maladies of American capitalism.

*   *   *   *   *

A very large part of the Soviet propaganda material dealing with American social problems consists of statements or alleged factual accounts of the pathetic lot of various social groups in the United States. The *Agitator's Notebook* (*Bloknot Agitatora*), for January, 1949, quoted an agitator's speech to factory workers as follows:

"Not long ago I read several articles on the life of American workers. Gloomy pictures of capitalist realities appear before one's eyes. Unemployment is increasing constantly in the U.S.A. Wages are being cut and prices are rising and the standard of living of the toilers is deteriorating. It is a calamity if a worker becomes ill. He loses all possibility of receiving any means of existence, for there is no social insurance in the United States." This *Notebook* was published in an edition of 171,000 copies, for distribution among professional Communist Party agitators.

Another issue of the same publication contained an item entitled "How the Workers Live in the U.S.A.," in which a Bronx truckdriver describes the unbearable hardships of the life of a worker in the United States. His wife states that obtaining food and clothing for her family is an almost impossible task. Both of these items were somewhat inconsistent, as they harped simultaneously on the evils of inflation and deflation. They are typical of a vast mass of material published in the Soviet press, the thesis of which is that although dreadful poverty prevailed among American workers before the Second World War, this poverty since the war has become still worse. The American worker is pictured as undernourished when employed and subjected to humiliation and degradation when unemployed.

The Soviet armed service radio broadcast on July 14, 1948, that the American worker's wages did not suffice for the purchase of an overcoat once in six years. On December 3, 1947, the trade union newspaper *Trud* published a dispatch entitled "In New York" by its correspondent Lapitski, containing the statement that more than one-third of Americans live in condemned houses. Lapitski's article gave the impression that the majority of the inhabitants of New York City live in frightful slums. In this connection, it may be recalled that Stalin in September, 1947, on the occasion of the 800th anniversary celebration of the founding of Moscow, contrasted the absence of slums in the Soviet capital with the existence of slums in capitalist countries, which doomed the majority of the toiling masses to slow death. The ridiculousness of Stalin's statement is obvious to all who have seen Moscow, which by New York or Chicago standards consists of a few islands of relative splendor such as the Kremlin, a city within a city, set in an ocean of slums.

The plight of American miners and farmers is painted in as black colors as that of factory workers and city dwellers. The magazine *Slavyane* (*Slavs*), September, 1948, alleged that the average American mining family hardly had a toothbrush to its name. It described as typical a mining family which possessed four beds for ten members of the family, no running water, and one towel. With regard to the plight of American farmers the Moscow radio on the eve of Thanksgiving, in 1948, broadcast a grim picture of the life of these American peasants, the majority of whom did not have enough food to live on. This was also true, according to the Soviet radio, of the majority of the American people in general.

*   *   *   *   *

As is well known, one of the chief targets of Soviet propaganda has always been the evils of racialism in the United States. A great volume of virulent propaganda regarding the situation of Negroes in America has been appearing in the Soviet press since 1945. Like the general anti-American line, the attitude on this question has grown sharper since 1946. Items which appeared on racial questions in 1945 and 1946 were unfair, one-sided, and created the impression of discrimination without presenting positive facts regarding Negroes and other minorities in America. Those which have been published in 1947, 1948, and 1949 have been not only unfair but lurid and fantastic. The tone of Soviet comment on the Negro question in the United States in the past two years is represented by an article by David Zaslavski in *Pravda*, December 8, 1948, entitled "The America of Lincoln Before the Court of Lynch." Zaslavski took the case of a lynched American Negro named Mallard as the text for his excoriation of American racialism and the American system in general. "If Lincoln had fallen into the hands of Lynch," Zaslavski said, "he would have been hanged, beaten, and burned alive. The morality of Lynch is the morality of the real rulers of America." A fine example of the way in which Soviet propagandists utilize isolated facts to draw general conclusions which may be employed in their ruthless ideological war against American democracy is afforded by the following quotation from the Zaslavski article: "You say that in the United States there exists freedom of the person? Answer: 'Mallard.' You say that in the United States there exists culture and law? Answer: 'Mallard.' You say that in the United States there exists freedom of the press? Answer: 'Mallard.' "

The Soviet propaganda machine grasps eagerly at all examples of discriminations against Negroes and utilizes them in this manner. Extreme prominence was given in the Soviet press to American newspaper articles suggesting that Mr. Ralph Bunche declined an appointment as Assistant Secretary of State because of discrimination against Negroes in the city of Washington. The Soviet youth newspaper *Komsomol Pravda* gave much publicity in 1949 to a series of articles by Paul Robeson entitled "Two Worlds."

It should also be mentioned that Soviet propaganda devotes a great deal of attention to the plight, both past and present, of the American Indian. Nor does it neglect real or fancied discrimination against Jews, Armenians, Chinese and other peoples. Even the relatively mild Ehrenburg articles referred to above charged that the United States had created a "racial hierarchy" in which the aristocracy were the English, Scotch and Irish, followed by the Scandinavians and Germans, the French and Slavs, the Italians, the Jews, the Chinese, and lower still the Puerto Ricans, and finally at the bottom of the scale, the Negroes.

Another favorite thesis of Soviet propaganda is the alleged extreme discrimination against women in the United States. This is a constant refrain given special emphasis every year in connection with International Women's Day, which is celebrated in the U.S.S.R. on March 8. A resolution of the Central Committee of the Communist Party on International Women's Day published in *Pravda*, March 6, 1948, contained the characteristic assertion that "in the bourgeois world working women continue to remain the most oppressed of all the oppressed strata of society." *Komsomol Pravda* for October 25, 1947, contained an item typical of Soviet propaganda treatment of this subject. It referred to an earlier article published on December 27, 1945, written by one of the top officials of the Communist youth league, Olga Mishakova, asserting that as a result of loss of wartime employment American women were being forced to return to the hardships of housework and that many of them had been forced to engage in prostitution in order to make a living.

* * * * *

Soviet criticism of American bourgeois democracy follows well-known conventional Leninist lines. It is, however, important to emphasize the enormous volume of material devoted by the Soviet press and on the Soviet radio to this question. Literally millions of words were poured out by the Soviet press in connection with the elections to the U.S.S.R. Supreme Soviet in 1946 and 1950, and the republic and local Soviet elections of 1947 and 1948, regarding the superior merits of Soviet political institutions. Similar material was produced in staggering abundance for the election of judges to the "people's courts" which took place in 1948. Ironically enough, these were the first elections of the lower Soviet judiciary, although the Stalin constitution of 1936 prescribed the election of judges and Soviet statesmen and propagandists had frequently and unfavorably contrasted the appointment of judges in capitalist Britain, for example, to the election of the judiciary in the U.S.S.R. prescribed by the Stalin constitution.

The propaganda regarding democracy has followed Lenin's line that proletarian democracy is a million times more democratic than bourgeois democracy. It maintains that only in the U.S.S.R have class antagonisms been eliminated, and that only where the people own the means of production can there be true democracy. It contrasts this happy situation with the dictatorship of the bourgeoisie in capitalist countries like America. According to this Soviet propaganda, American democracy is merely "formal" democracy. Since the bourgeoisie control the means of production, they have the real power, including political power. Moreover, according to the Soviet line, even formal political rights are limited in America. Discrimination against Negroes and devices like the poll tax exclude considerable segments of the population from enjoying even the limited political rights available under American democracy. In the field of civil liberties, in which actually the Soviet Union has the worst record of any modern state, the Soviet propagandists maintain that

Soviet citizens are better off than those of America. They harp constantly on the police terror under which Americans are said to live.

But let us now turn to the postwar Soviet line regarding the course of postwar American politics. This line, staying always within the framework sketched above, maintains that the major American political parties are instruments of Wall Street. The Kremlin must have faced some embarrassment in reintroducing this traditional Soviet view of American politics. For, after all, during the war Stalin himself had favorably contrasted Anglo-Saxon democracy with German fascism. It is true, of course, that he had expressed, even then, certain reservations regarding British and American democracy. The death of President Roosevelt must have been a stroke of luck for the Soviet propagandists. It enabled them to suggest that with this great progressive figure removed, American capitalist politics moved naturally to the right. That this hypothesis is correct is suggested by the astute way in which Soviet propaganda handled Roosevelt's death. It treated it as "a great divide" in American history. Roosevelt was acclaimed as a world "town crier" of democracy and international collaboration, two concepts which had been intertwined in both wartime and postwar Soviet propaganda. At the same time, it was suggested that the future would show whether or not Roosevelt's successor would continue his policy.

As is well known, the postwar Soviet line has been that President Truman rejected the Roosevelt policy. This is tersely summarized in the following quotation from a Soviet handbook:

"Under the pressure and in the interests of monopoly groups, the composition of the government was changed; ministers of the Roosevelt cabinet were gradually replaced by conservative figures. Reactionary forces took measures against the vital interests and democratic achievements of the working class. . . ."

There were further charges that not only the wealthy but the military were taking over the American government. The Soviet press pounded away at the theme that the appointment of General Marshall as Secretary of State, of General Smith as Ambassador to Moscow, and similar postwar developments, indicated that a coalition of the military and Wall Street was directing the post-war policies of the U. S. The new forces in charge of American politics have throughout the postwar period been accused of basing their policy on repression and terror against labor and progressive elements. Such charges have been accompanied by allegations that the American ruling classes, intoxicated by "atomic diplomacy" and a new Anglo-Saxon version of Hitler's philosophy of a master race, have been seeking to transform the United States into the base for a policy of world domination.

IV

PROSPECT

CHAPTER 9

The Shape of Communist Things Today and To Come

The year 1952–1953 opened a new phase in Soviet history. Enough is known by Western observers to say this, but scarcely more. In the several years in which this phase has developed some changes in personnel have been announced and certain modifications of policy have been noted. But time is needed to focus the full and the true picture. At this point it is worthwhile to summarize these changes and modifications.

But it is profitable, too, to reflect on certain overall evaluations of the impact of Communism on Russia and the world, and cautiously to conjecture the shape of things to come.

For a full generation now, the "question of Russia" has been discussed or, more accurately, argued. Almost every conceivable answer has been advanced, but still the debate goes on. The books on Russia seem to number as the sands of the sea; probably most will be no more lasting. But the writers who passionately defend or denounce have not pre-empted the field, though it may sometimes seem that they have. The selections offered below were written by men whose works are marked by a balance of thought and feeling, by a sensitive treatment of imponderables limited and conditioned by a judicious consideration of the "facts."

By deliberate intention the selections given here do not, in the main, agree with each other. In an effort to give to the American reader some of the best thought on the whole

229

*question, both "sides" are presented. Whatever the final judg-
ment, it will be better for having weighed these evaluations.*

*The author of the following summary, Professor Philip E.
Mosely, is one of the best known authorities on Soviet history and contemporary developments in this country. He
lived for a number of years in the Soviet Union, and from
1943 to 1946 "took an active part in wartime and postwar
negotiations with the Soviet government on problems concerning Germany, Austria and the countries of Eastern Europe." He is Professor of International Relations at Columbia
University where he serves as director of the University's
Russian Institute. The summary is from his* RUSSIA AFTER
STALIN, *published in 1955 by the Foreign Policy Association.
In it he discusses personnel changes after the death of Stalin
in March, 1953, the strong and weak points of the Soviet's
most prominent figures, the possible place of the Secret
Police and Army in the new regime, and the question of
whether that regime may henceforth be directed by a "col-
lective leadership" or by a new Stalin.*

FROM

Philip E. Mosely
RUSSIA AFTER STALIN

TO a degree unrivaled by autocrats of the past, Stalin brought
all levers of power into his hands. His nod raised party officials,
engineers and generals to positions of great authority and gave
official monopoly to artistic, musical and scientific views which
he favored. His disfavor meant obscurity and frequently annihilation. Stalin commanded the actions of a powerful state. He
was also the fountainhead of dogma, strategy and tactics for a
powerful worldwide movement.

Stalin's disappearance from the scene was in itself a new fact
of great importance. But what next? Would Stalin be succeeded
by "a new Stalin," a similarly absolute dictator or would the
power he had wielded be exercised collectively by a small group

of leaders, would the struggle for power weaken the dictatorship, make it more attentive to the needs and aspirations of his
own people and less hostile toward the non-Soviet world? Would
the Soviet government turn inward, to raise the standard of living
at home, or would it continue to subordinate the well-being of
its people to the aim of maximizing its power and expanding the
area of Communistic control? What did the new leadership mean
when it proclaimed unceasingly its desire for "coexistence" and
"peace"? And what do these changes, since March, 1953, spell
for the hopes and fears of the non-Soviet two-thirds of the
world?

Whether or not Stalin intended to pave the way for an orderly
transfer of power to a single chosen successor remains a matter
of doubt. At any event, his long rule has shaped the main instruments of control; the dictatorial party, the all-knowing secret-
police apparatus, the governmental administration, the armed
forces, the huge state-operated or state-controlled economic system. Has a one-man supremacy re-emerged, or is the Soviet
Union ruled by a "collective leadership"?

Immediately upon Stalin's demise supreme control passed to
three powerful subordinates: Malenkov, Molotov, and Beria.
Georgi M. Malenkov had risen through service in the Moscow
party organization and in Stalin's personal secretariat to become
in March, 1939, one of the secretaries of the party's Central
Committee and a member of its Organizational Bureau, which
controlled a wide range of appointments in all parts of the
Soviet machinery of rule. During World War II he was a member of the extremely important State Committee on Defense,
which ran the entire civilian and industrial side of the huge war
effort.

In February, 1941, Malenkov became an alternate member of
the Politburo, the driving-wheel of Soviet policy, and a full-
fledged member in March, 1946. The sudden death of Andrei
Zhdanov in August, 1948, seemed to have removed from the
scene his principal competitor for Stalin's favor. At the long-
deferred Nineteenth Party Congress held in October, 1952, Malenkov delivered the major address, obviously at Stalin's direc-

tion, and thus seemed to most observers, and probably to the Soviet party apparatus, to be marked as Stalin's intended successor.

Vyacheslav Molotov, long associated with the conduct of foreign affairs, is the last of the "Old Bolsheviks" the early supporters of Lenin, still in high place. A close associate and follower of Stalin from 1917, he has held great responsibilities for more than twenty-five years and has had a major place in the making of foreign policy since May, 1939, and perhaps, through his role in the Politburo, for several years before that. However, the nature of his role since the War does not give him direct authority over any of the principal power instruments of authority, and this factor, combined with his acknowledged diplomatic and administrative experience, may actually have made him something of an arbiter among rivals for power in the post-Stalin period.

Upon the announcement of Stalin's death the Supreme Soviet, the hand-picked "legislature" of the Soviet Union, was called into session to ratify a realignment of the leading posts. On Beria's nomination Malenkov was unanimously elected chairman of the Council of Ministers, the highest administrative body. At the same time Beria resumed direct control of the secret police, which he had run since 1938, and Molotov again took official charge of the Ministry of Foreign Affairs.

The Presidium of the party, which had been enlarged to 36 members at the October Party Congress, was again reduced to 10 members and thus took the place of the former Politburo as the central policy-making organ of the entire regime. Beria, along with Malenkov and Molotov, remained a member of the Presidium.

In mid-July 1953 the world was startled to learn that Beria had been deposed from power some three weeks before, on a motion presented by Malenkov to the Central Committee and had been placed at once under arrest and "investigation" for various alleged crimes against the Soviet regime. After a secret trial Beria, together with several of his henchmen, was summarily executed, in December 1953. Rumors of a large-scale curtailment of the numbers and powers of the secret police began to circulate. There were well-substantiated accounts of strikes and riots in some of the forced-labor camps. What was Beria accused of? Under a dictatorship, published accusations have a symbolic and political rather than a literal meaning. Beria was accused, somewhat obscurely, of obstructing the government's agricultural policy. Perhaps he had been skeptical of the program of concessions to the collectivised peasants or perhaps this was a device for strengthening among the peasants their confidence in the new leadership intention to make life a little easier for them. He was accused of sowing dissension among the various nationalities. Perhaps this reflected a feeling on the part of Beria, as a Georgian, that Stalin's constant harping on the "superiority" of the Great Russians over the "lesser nationalities" might in the case of a new crisis, prove a real weakness for the regime. After Stalin's death Beria's name was also associated with the reversal of the "Doctor's case," which, in Stalin's last months, had given ominous indications of an official flare-up of anti-Semitism.

What was doubtless genuine in the bill of indictment against Beria was the charge that he had attempted to put the political police above the Communist party. As long as all Communists except the handful at the top could be arrested by the secret police, forced to confess, and then tried, sentenced and executed in secret, there was always a danger that, by determining who was or was not a loyal Communist, the police would dominate and decimate the ranks of the party, as it had under Beria's predecessor, Yezhov, in the great purges of 1936–1938. At the same time, because of the secret nature of the task assigned to it by the dictator, the political police can resist penetration of its thoughts and actions by the "ordinary" party mechanisms of control. Added to this is the strong probability that Beria had been, after the elimination of Zhdanov in 1948, Malenkov's strongest rival for power and for the succession. Whether or not Beria was actively striving to seize power between Stalin's death and June 21, 1953, Malenkov and the top party apparatus had every reason to remember old fears and to insist upon bringing the machinery of repression under their own control.

The elimination of Beria and the purging of the secret police, accompanied apparently by some scaling down of its size, powers and privileges, were followed by two significant structural changes. First, the two police ministries—State Security, and Internal Affairs—reunited under Beria's control in March 1953, were again separated. This reduced somewhat the concentration of powers which can arise through combining them. Presumably, it also assured the top leadership of two networks, rather than one, for reporting on the moods and morale of the population. Second, whereas Beria had long sat in the top policy-making body—in the Politburo, and after October 1952 in the Presidium of the party—since his downfall the secret police is no longer represented directly in this all-powerful party. On the contrary, the Presidium appeared to control the police collectively, through a newly created Committee on State Security. This makes the police apparatus more an instrument for executing policy and less a factor in shaping it.

Two years later, on February 8, 1955, an astonished Supreme Soviet listened to the reading of an abject letter signed by Malenkov, by which he resigned as head of the government. "I see clearly," he wrote, "that the carrying out of the complicated and responsible duties of chairman of the Council of Ministers is affected negatively by my insufficient experience in local and (administrative) work and also by the fact that I have not had occasion, in a ministry or economic organ, to exercise direct administration of individual branches of the national economy." This admission of lack of competence plainly disregarded Malenkov's long years of experience in the detailed work of central administration, which in Soviet practice reaches down into the minute details of political and economic decisions.

Malenkov's resignation was accepted by the Supreme Soviet with its customary unanimity, and, upon nomination by Nikita Khrushchev, Marshal Nikolai A. Bulganin was elected chairman of the Council of Ministers. Upon the following day Malenkov was elected minister of electric power, one of more than 40 ministers. For the time being he remained officially a deputy minister and a member of the party Presidium. However, shortly after, when several high leaders were named as first deputy chairmen of the Council of Ministers, Malenkov was not among them.

Meetings of the all-powerful Presidium are almost never mentioned apparently in print, and only rarely is something known of its actions through later announcements. Under the rule of a conspiratorial dictatorship, which announces publicly only that which serves its own purposes, it is possible for Malenkov to be excluded from its deliberations or to be dropped entirely from its membership without any inkling reaching the Soviet public or the outside world for many weeks or even months.

The phrasing of Malenkov's letter of resignation resembles those "negotiated" recantations which Stalin imposed so frequently and so ruthlessly upon rival "Old Bolsheviks," whose claims to a share in Lenin's mantle had rivaled his own. Time and again in the 1930's Zinoviev and Bukharin, Rykov and Piatakov, and many others were compelled to confess their "mistakes" and to promise their unquestioning support to Stalin and "party unity." Eventually most of them were compelled in public spectacle to confess that throughout their careers they had been "spies" and "traitors" against both Lenin and Stalin.

There has been more than a hint that Malenkov's eclipse will be linked with the "traitors" of Stalin's earlier period of struggle for sole power. In his letter of resignation Malenkov assumed the heavy burden of responsibility for the poor state of Soviet agriculture, although Khrushchev has been universally regarded as the man chiefly charged since the War with the uphill struggle to raise the output of collective farms. In a speech to the Central Committee of the party delivered in secret session on January 25 and published on February 3, Khrushchev attacked the upholders of "the Right deviation, a belching of views which are hostile to Leninism and which, in their time, were preached by Rykov, Bukharin and their ilk." The way appeared open to attach the label of "traitor" to Malenkov if the course of the struggle for power should dictate it.

On the other hand, Malenkov has long been associated with Khrushchev, since the early 1930's, in a variety of important party jobs; and it is possible, though unlikely, that Malenkov, deprived of the means for further struggle, may continue as an influential member of the ruling group without holding a dominant post.

Nikita Khrushchev has long been known as a vigorous party and economic administrator. After World War II he carried through a drastic "purging" and reorganization of the reoccupied Ukraine, and his name has been associated with the strenuous post-war efforts to build up agriculture. In March 1953, at the end of Stalin's death, he headed the crucial Moscow party organization, which contains over 20 percent of the country's party membership. Immediately after Stalin's death Khrushchev was assigned to "special duties" in the Central Secretariat of the party. A few weeks later Malenkov resigned as party secretary, and Khrushchev was appointed to this post. In September 1953 he became "First Secretary," but he has not taken over Stalin's former title of "General Secretary."

During the second half of 1954 there was much debate among foreign observers over Khrushchev's role. Were he and Malenkov competing for power, or were they cooperating? Was either of the contestants likely to emerge in supreme control, or was power exercised by "collective leadership" of the "top party group"? In October and December Khrushchev paid well-publicized visits to Peiping and Prague and delivered several important statements on Soviet policy. These were, outwardly, visits to "fraternal" communist parties, and therefore he could appear as the logical representative of the Soviet party. At home his policy pronouncements were more frequent than those of Malenkov.

As the secret police have lost some ground within the Soviet power structure, have the armed forces gained in influence? Some commentators believe that the top party leaders, now consolidated around Khrushchev, share their power with, or perhaps owe it to, the armed forces, represented at the top by Marshal Bulganin, elected chairman of the Council of Ministers on February 8, and by Marshal Georgi K. Zhukov, promoted on February 9 from deputy minister to minister of defense. In early March several generals were also appointed to head-up important ministries.

Marshal Bulganin is primarily a "party general" rather than a professional military leader. After a career in party and secret police administration, he became the head of the Moscow party organization and then the head of the Political Administration of the Army, the party's eye and voice within the armed services. It has long been his duty to represent the military interests of the regime within the top agencies of the party and the state, and he has presumably had a strong say in the advancement of military and naval commanders during the past fourteen years or so. It is a long step from this, however, to assume that Bulganin or his successor, Zhukov, has direct command over the armed forces or can wield their might in any way opposed to the power and interest of the party leadership.

Marshal Zhukov rose from the ranks of Red Army and was considered one of the outstanding strategists of World War II. More than Bulganin, he might be supposed to represent a military viewpoint, but, after all, he has been an active member of the Communist party since 1922. It must be assumed that his rise has been due at least as much to his loyalty to the party as to his military talents. In becoming minister of defense, Zhukov has not been appointed to the party Presidium, the inner seat of power.

Much has been made of Zhukov's "exile" from the central seat of power after the close of World War II, and of his return to Moscow since Stalin's death. In Soviet practice there is no way in which a successful general can keep his name in the public eye once the fighting is over. In a party-ruled state he is not expected to give interviews on all or many subjects or, for that matter, on any subject. If Zhukov's command of the Odessa Military District represented some kind of "exile," it must be pointed out that in view of the Soviet pressure against Turkey and Greece and, after July, 1948, its bitter threats against Tito's Yugoslavia, that area was the most important single military district, and an "exile" would hardly have been entrusted with its command. The notion that "the party," "the army," "the secret police," "the economic apparatus," is each a self-contained, self-directing organization, a separate "piece" of power and that one is about to "destroy" the other persists abroad. In the West each would represent a more or less separate professional career, with its own loyalties. Within the Soviet system the party strives to permeate and direct all activities—and largely succeeds. Many of the top positions in the military hierarchy are held by "party-generals," like Bulganin. Other commanders, who made their way to the top through primarily military achievements, have also been drilled in party loyalty and ideology and have been advanced higher and higher only with the active approval of the party's military control apparatus.

A striking aspect of the last two years has been the deflation of Stalin and the re-emergence of the Lenin image. Only recently the "greatest leader," "most brilliant coryphaeus of science," "greatest genius of strategy," even "master of Russian style," Stalin's name soon began to appear less and less frequently in the carefully calculated propaganda media, and then primarily as "the pupil and continuer of Lenin's cause." A long manifesto on the fiftieth anniversary of the founding of the party published in (*Pravda*) on July 26, 1953, mentioned Stalin six times, always without hyperbole, and referred dozens of times to Lenin and to the party as the directing force in Soviet Society. The manifesto simply scrapped the elaborate legends which over the years had built up Stalin as a leader as wise as Lenin and definitely superior to him in practical achievements. The celebration of Stalin's birthday in December, 1954, brought forth renewed paeans of praise for his historic role, but they were sober and modest indeed compared with the extravagant praise which he had demanded and received in his own lifetime.

Whether or not Soviet rule, unprecedented in its scope and secrecy, is being gathered into one man's hands or whether it is being exercised by a small, closely knit group, there is no measurable sign of a serious disruption or weakening of the machinery of authority. The party structure, the secret police, the armed forces, the great economic machine carry on their work. The prediction, so freely made after Stalin's death, that the structure he had built would fall apart in disorder and mutual murder has not been borne out. A personal struggle for control has been going on at the top, but there is no sign that it has weakened the Soviet regime, which remains a powerful, centralized, secretive and determined force in world politics.

Professor Hans Kohn has a reputation on two continents for scholarly study and evaluation of trends in modern history. Well known particularly for his work on nationalism, especially Russian nationalism, his most recent work, THE MIND OF MODERN RUSSIA, *from which the following selection was taken, has received respectful attention from those who wish to understand more clearly the international scene. In the portion presented below, Professor Kohn states this thesis: From the end of the Middle Ages Europe has been divided into a West and an East. For centuries Russian Tsar-autocrats had kept Russia isolated from the West. Finally, however, there dawned for Russia a Great Age when, around the middle of the nineteenth century, breaches were made in the wall of autocracy; Russia and Europe began to come together in a kind of cultural detente. The March Revolution of 1917 signaled a great advance toward a real "marriage." The Bolshevik Revolution in October–November, however, cut this short and reëstablished a new autocracy on the old traditions; once more the old wall was erected. According to Professor Kohn, the Bolsheviks have turned back the clock of world history, plunged Russia into a Communist autocracy, and sundered the world anew.*

FROM

Hans Kohn

THE MIND OF MODERN RUSSIA

THE Anglo-American revolution in the seventeenth and eighteenth centuries developed against a unique background of English traditions of self-government and individual liberty. Thus they could lead to a continuous flowering of freedom under law. The French Revolution took place in a nation strongly absolutist in a political sense but at the same time culturally the most advanced of the period. Karl Marx expected his revolution to happen in the socially and economically most progressive countries of the time. The Russian revolution turned into a disaster because its stage was set among the politically, culturally, and socially most backward masses of Europe, where the traditions of liberty were just beginning to take root. Thus Lenin's total rejection and contemptuous hatred of "bourgeois" Western civilization could strike a responsive chord in many Russian hearts. The masses were not prepared for constitutional liberty; many of the intellectuals harbored an eschatological faith in revolutionary utopianism. The greatest Russian poet of the period, Alexander Block, succumbed for a brief moment to the nationalist missionary appeal of the Revolution. On January 30, 1918, before the misery of the Revolution cut off his voice, as it was to cut off so many other voices in creative Russia, Block wrote his last poem, presenting the Russians as "Scythians" prepared to embrace Europe in fraternal love or to destroy her in an apocalyptic struggle.

The Westernizing revolution of March 1917 wished to continue Russia's great age on a more popular and enlightened level, but the sudden relaxation of the restraints of traditional authority mobilized the un-Europeanized masses and released forces which Lenin with masterly and ruthless strategy harnessed toward a revival of the old Muscovite unity of state and church: the state founded by Lenin soon became more totalitarian than Ivan's had been, and the Communist party line showed itself more comprehensive and exclusive than the Orthodox Dogma. Masaryk, who was then in Russia, saw from the beginning that Lenin's revolution destroyed the hope of Russia's integration into Europe. He found in Lenin more of Bakunin than of Marx. "Unpolitical, wholly unscientific infallibility is the basis for the Bolshevik dictatorship," he wrote in 1920, "and a regime that quails before criticism and fears to recognize thinking men stands self-condemned."

True, the Marxist dogma came from outside Russia, and many of its elements originated in the German idealist philosophy and in the English political economy of the early nineteenth century.

But like Byzantine Orthodoxy, Marxism was soon nationalized and became a Russian church. The new regime took over from Marxism not so much its economic theories, which the development in the West had proved wrong and which were inapplicable to a backward agrarian community, as an eschatological expectation of the coming perfect social order, the faith in revolution through which the absolute ideal would be realized and this corrupt world saved. Marx's secularized eschatology promised salvation according to the tenets of science and through the means of technology. It offered to the descendants of the Russian nihilists an apparently utilitarian and rational religion, to the service of which all thought and art, all life and labor, could be directed.

When Lenin left Switzerland during the First World War to return to Russia, he wrote a farewell letter to the Swiss workers on April 8, 1917, in which he said, "To the Russian proletariat fell the great honor to inaugurate the series of revolutions which are being produced, with objective necessity by the imperialist war. But we do in no way harbor the thought of regarding the Russian proletariat as a chosen revolutionary proletariat among the workers of other countries." From the beginning Lenin proclaimed his "one world goal," and his movement promised to realize some of the desires and programs of the working class of nineteenth-century Europe. Under Lenin, Russia seemed to reach that position of world leadership which some of the extreme Russian nationalists of the nineteenth century had claimed for her. The forecast was impressive to many, but close observers, familiar with Russia and with socialism, saw from the beginning how alien Leninism was to the main trend of the European tradition, especially to its democratic tradition. How could Lenin harmonize his insistence upon the complete dependence of the people on the party as the "vanguard" of the proletariat and upon the total discipline within the party, with democracy? Leon Trotsky, Lenin's principal assistant in the Bolshevik seizure of power, wrote in 1904 that Lenin's method means that first the party substitutes itself for the people or the proletariat; then the party organization substitutes itself for the party as a whole; then the central committee of the organization substitutes itself for the organization; and finally a single dictator substitutes himself for the central committee. In 1870, the year of Lenin's birth, Bakunin described the organization of the revolutionary party which "will put itself at the head of the popular masses during the so vividly near destruction of the Russian empire." It will have nothing in common with political or socialist parties as known in the West. It will be a party

. . . strong by its discipline, by the devotion and passionate self-denial of its members and by its passive obedience to all the orders of a Central Committee . . . in which it is not the individual who thinks, desires, and acts, but the collectivity. A serious member will understand that only such a discipline can create a collective revolutionary force which, supported by the elemental force of the people, will be able to overthrow the formidable strength of the state. . . . Whoever is for this program, will come with us. Whoever is against us, is a friend of the enemies of the people, he is a henchman of the Tsar, he is our enemy. Whoever is not for us, is against us.

Lenin followed Bakunin's lead. His party was not, as parties in Western society are, part of a society, but a dominant all-embracing totality. In reality, it was nothing but the militant instrument of an omnipotent and omniscient autocracy. Masaryk asserted in 1921: "The Bolsheviks have accepted Marxism and pride themselves on being its only orthodox adherents. They do not realize how much they owe to Bakunin, the adversary of Marx. From him they took over their mystic faith in the revolution, in the Russian people, in its unique socialist and communist ability. . . . All the shortcomings which characterized the Russian state, the Russian school, the Russian church, and so on characterized also the Bolshevik state and regime because they had come from the same people and have undergone the same formation."

Even some of the most orthodox or radical non-Russian Marxists opposed Lenin's method. Rosa Luxemburg, a leader of German extreme socialists, wrote in September 1919:

Each democratic institution has its limits and shortcomings, a situation shared by all human institutions. But the remedy which Trotsky and Lenin found, namely the annihilation of democracy itself, is still worse than the evil which it wishes to cure; to bury the life source itself, from which alone all the innate insufficiencies of a social institution can be corrected, the active, unrestrained energetic political life of the masses. It is a manifest and incontestable fact that without a free press and without the free right of association and meeting the rule of the masses is entirely unthinkable. Liberty only for the adherence of the government, only for the members of one party—be they ever so numerous—is no liberty. . . . Public life gradually dies off. Several dozens of party leaders, men of inexhaustible energy and boundless idealism, direct and rule, but in reality not more than a dozen brilliant men are in real control, and the working class is called from time to time to attend the meetings, to applaud the speeches of the leaders and to adopt unanimously resolutions proposed by the leaders—this is truly a dictatorship, but not the dictatorship of the proletariat, but one of a handful of politicians.

Once only in their history the Russian people were allowed free elections. These were instituted by the provisional government which originated in the revolution of March 1917. The elections were held in November of that year. The Constituent Assembly thus elected was the realization of the hopes and efforts of many decades, the result of Russia's contact with Europe in her great age. But hardly had the assembly met in Petrograd in January 1918 when Lenin dispersed it by armed force. Two months later, Russia's capital was transferred from the maritime periphery where Peter had placed it at the beginning of Russia's great age, to Russia's ancient capital behind the hallowed walls of the Kremlin. At the very moment when to all outward appearances, Russia professed to appeal to the whole world as never before, she withdrew into herself and again became a closed society, anxiously guarded from contact with the infidel world; once again she became the Third Rome, Holy Russia, which was to lead mankind to salvation. Haughtily she turned against Europe. The encounter between Russia and the West, which had been a period of high intellectual fertility and ferment for both, was closed. With it, Russia's great age was over, at least for the time being.

On the other hand, Maurice Hindus, a Russian-born naturalized American who has been writing books on Communism and its society for a quarter of a century, looks at the same scene and sees a different picture.

Mr. Hindus is neither a Communist nor a fellow-traveler. He writes about Russia with very much the same attitude de Tocqueville had when he wrote his now famous study of our own country in the early nineteenth century, DEMOCRACY IN AMERICA. *The selection given below, from Mr. Hindus'* MOTHER RUSSIA, *may seem chronologically out of place. But actually his judgments have little to do with chronology in a narrow sense; no apology is needed for including in this section a reading written just before the end of World War II. To the reader who has just finished Professor Kohn's account, Mr. Hindus might well say, "And here, now, is the other side of the penny."*

FROM

Maurice Hindus

MOTHER RUSSIA

IT was just twenty years since I had first gone to Russia to write a series of stories on the Russian village and Russian peasantry under the Soviets. How different was the village then from what it was in the summer of 1942! How different was all Russia, city and village, peasant and worker, intellectual and official, Bolshevik and non-Bolshevik, the men and the women, the children and the youths! What a bewildering and galloping transformation had come over the very land of Russia—in the once-gay and fat Ukraine, in the hot and once-pastoral Central Asia, in the rough and turbulent Urals, in the immense and haunting Arctic . . . everywhere.

The vocabulary, the emotions, the aspirations, the very noises in the air, not only of guns but of machines, were new and epochal. Lenin had dreamed of the day when there would be 100,000 tractors on the land. There were over a half a million of them in 1940, nearly all manufactured on Russian soil by Russian men and women! Poorly fed, poorly clad, poorly housed (the civilians, not the Army), Russia in 1942 and 1943 was fighting the most momentous and most murderous war in her history, largely with her own weapons, from bayonet and rifle to armored tank and four-engined bomber—fighting, bleeding, dying—but never losing heart and with no thought of defeat! And in the Volga villages which I had visited school children were reading not only Pushkin and Tolstoy but Dickens and Mark Twain!

The transformation had wrung from the people the highest of sacrifices. They had been cold and hungry, weary and bewildered, masses of them had been, but they worked. They had no choice. If they did not work, they did not eat. If they grumbled, they were denounced. If they sabotaged or were suspected of sabotage, they were jailed, exiled, shot. Concentration, or as the Russians say, labor camps, were crowded. Jails were overcrowded. Late in the night men and women were awakened out of sleep and hauled away—to some far away and dreary exile or to their death. The days of the First Plan were among the most violent and the most agonizing the Russian people had known since the coming of the Soviets. In more than one sense it was a continuation and a reincarnation of the battle and the psychology of the Civil War.

Those were days of tumult and woe, but also of toil and more toil and still more toil. The slogan "socialism in one country" became the new gospel—not merely an article of faith but a plan of the most stupendous pioneering Russia or any other country, including America, had ever witnessed. It engulfed every person in the land. It rolled over every region, every hamlet, every hut. It struck hard at any obstacle, whether river, forest, swamp or sea; man or woman; intellectual, peasant, or worker; communist or counterrevolutionary.

Despite inexperience and privation, "socialism in one country" was forging a new Russia, not a Russia of black ties and white ties, of silk shirts and silk gowns, of ballrooms and drawing rooms, or even of good plumbing; not a Russia of free speech and free assembly except for those who made themselves an unswerving and implacable part of the behest and the will of the Kremlin—but a Russia of engines and blast furnaces, of iron and steel, of gigantic factories and mechanized farms; a

Russia that might not have enough glass to replace broken windowpanes and enough leather for new shoes, but which would possess the fire and the dynamite, the guns and the shells, the tanks and the planes, also the will and the skill to save herself from the tortured extinction which, with the support of Junkers and landlords, workers and peasants, Hitler's Germany would attempt to inflict upon her. With the rise of the factories, with the sweep of the tractors and the combines over the rich and fertile steppes, came a sobering of social thought, a stabilization of social ideas, morality and the family struck new and deeper roots, as deep as Russia has ever known. Gone were the literary firebrands who had heaped scorn and anathema on the men and women who beheld in art something more than the fighting slogan and the fighting passion of the moment. Some of these firebrands met their fate before a firing squad.

Pushkin became the hero, almost a deity, of the people. One by one the great dead of the past were lifted to living glory. Even the iconoclast Pisarev, who loathed Pushkin, became a voice of challenge and importance. Compared to America and England the people were poorly dressed. They lived in crowded houses. But the country resounded with the lilting tunes of folk melodies, the best that a many-nationed people had created in the past ages. *Predki* (ancestors) and *stariki* (old people) became words and personages of adulation and emulation. Young people gloried in the love letters they wrote and did not mind reading them to gatherings of friends, whether soldiers in a dugout at the front or girls in a dormitory of a rubber factory at Moscow.

Private enterprise was gone—hardly a shred of it remained— and youth especially was ready to spill its blood, oceans of it if necessary, to prevent its return. Russia was rediscovered, Mother Russia, old Russia, the Russia of yesterday and of the far away and hazy past, of legendary heroes and legendary triumphs. There were glory and goodness in this old and once-despised Russia. It had sinned and glutted, but it had worked and fought. It had also suffered and dreamed. It had bequeathed to future generations an array of scientists and statesmen, field marshals and conquerors, poets and novelists, literary critics and playwrights, and, yes, churchmen who were patriots which the new Russia was now only too happy to embrace, to make its own, to revere and to love with all the fervor of its tumultuous heart.

All this happened under the slogan and the dispensation not of "world revolution," but of "socialism in one country." It is this Russia that gave birth to the sixteen-year-old Shura Chekalin, the twenty-two-year-old Liza Chaikina, the eighteen-year-old Zoya Kosmodemyanskaya, whose heroic martrydom had made them as renowned as ancient folk heroes and who are now Russia's new saints!

How different was the Russia of 1943 from the Russia of 1917 of which I had only read and of the Russia of 1923, which I had seen! Uncertainty and chaos had given way to sober reflection and to deep-rooted stability. Class hate and class warfare, so flaming in former years, had yielded to love of country, love of the past, love of the people—and to immeasurable faith in the future. Talk and meetings, and more talk and more meetings, had given way to the most strenuous, the most gigantic pioneering that the world had ever known—pioneering for coal and iron, for steel and copper, for oil and potash, for wheat and cotton, for cows and sheep, for new cities and new schools, for a new life and a new destiny.

This Russia still has much to learn and to make her own. Superb as is the democratic eloquence of her constitution—which is assiduously studied in schools, factories, mining camps, collective farms—much of it, very much, still awaits fulfillment in every-day life. In political self-expression the pioneering is only in its infancy. Though the former method of elections is gone, though now not the show of hands but the secret ballot elects into all office Party secretaries, soviet officials, trade-union perfunctories, civil liberties, in the American and English sense of the word, are still a constitutional promise. In his speech of March 10, 1939, Stalin declared "Since our Party is in power, they (Party members) also constitute the commanding staff of the leading organs of the State."

In other words, the Party is supreme and will tolerate no

political opposition and no outside interference in any of its plans and programs. Thus, though Russia has won the battle of social and racial equality, the elevation of the individual to a condition of political self-expression, with the right to criticize the dictatorship or to speak his mind freely and adversely of its leaders, is still a matter of the future.

Nor in this writer's judgment is there much likelihood of there being serious relaxation of this condition until Russia has at least lifted production to a degree which permits a comfortable material standard of living and which in time of war insures ample industrial output for the fighting armies. All of Russia's industrial pioneering under the Soviets was achieved under the planning, the discipline, and the severity of a dictatorship. Only a dictatorship could have imposed on the people the sacrifices and the privations which the fulfillment of the Plan required. There are, of course, other motives and reasons for the dictatorship, but without it Russia never could have packed into the brief space of thirteen years, 1928–41, the amount of industrial pioneering it achieved. It knows what it can do, what it has done, under its own system of control, and it will take no risks with any other methods, particularly if Russia should be facing fresh hostilities in the outside world.

Yet stupendous have been the achievements of Russian pioneering, especially, I must repeat, since 1928. The methods, I wish to emphasize, are other than those which the American pioneers espoused and practiced. The times are different, the historical setting, the immediate national needs, the international relationships, the technological compulsions, the ideological aspirations are also different. But the one consciously directed ultimate aim —large-scale development of internal resources—is not dissimilar to that which America's "rugged individualism" sought and strove to fulfill. Most manifestly Russian collectivised pioneering under a dictatorship would have been unthinkable without the experience and achievements of America's "rugged individualism."

The greatest and most momentous triumph of this Russian pioneering is written large and red in blood and valor on the steppes and in the forests of Mother Russia.

*Thus far in the chapter we
have considered, besides a summary of the new situation since
Stalin, an evaluation unfavorable to Communist Russia, and
one seeing merit and hope in it. The next selection probes the
future and suggests three possible lines of development.*

Dr. Barrington Moore, Jr., the author of TERROR AND
PROGRESS, USSR, *published in 1954 by the Harvard University
Press, is the distinguished young scholar we met earlier in
our study of Soviet industry.*

*To one not familiar with the language of modern social
scientists, Dr. Moore's terminology in this section may seem
technical and involved. But if the reader will get a picture
of the three possibilities clearly established at the outset—
and have some patience with the language of modern scholarship—Dr. Moore's "three images" of the future come out
clearly and meaningfully. In non-technical language he considers a continuation of Communist totalitarian one-man rule,
control of Russia by Soviet "business and technical minds,"
(counterparts of America's "manager class") and the return to a non-totalitarian, neo-Tsarist despotism (sans Tsar,
of course) resting upon a socialist ideology.*

*The reader may or may not want to concur in Dr. Moore's
judgment as to which of these "images" is likely to emerge.
But his own thinking can scarcely help being stimulated
and clarified.*

FROM

Barrington Moore, Jr.
TERROR AND PROGRESS, USSR

[A STUDY of the present conditions in Russia reveals] an apparent range of three major possibilities for the future of Russian society. Though it is not possible to make a genuine scientific prediction as to which will actually take place partly on
account of an irreducible area of indeterminacy in human affairs, this viewpoint may still provide some rational basis for
estimating the probable course of future events.

In concrete terms, the first possibility facing the Soviet regime may be regarded as a continuation and possibly even some intensification of the dynamic, totalitarian, and expansionistic characteristics of a Stalinist system. . . . it is . . . doubtful that any great intensification of these features is still possible without seriously weakening social institutions that are necessary for the functioning of an industrial society. [Further, a] successful solution of the succession crisis and the emergence of an undisputed leader either through peaceful or violent methods or a combination of the two, appears to be an essential prerequisite for the continued operation of this system. . . .

The second possibility is that the technical-rational and formal legal features that exist in the Soviet system might come to dominate over the totalitarian one. This appears to be the central idea behind the predictions of a "managerial revolution" in the USSR. . . . I do not think that such a term could take the form of a parliamentary democracy if it were an outgrowth or extension of the Bolshevik regime. But a political system approaching a technocracy has more than mere plausibility. Probably the really discernible movement in this direction will stop somewhere short of its logical culmination. The absorption of the political Party official into the role of a technical administrator . . . is perhaps just as unlikely . . . as is the reverse process of making a political animal out of the technician.

Nevertheless the possibility of a pronounced technical-rational development does not appear out of the question. The system then would display roughly the following features. First of all, technical and rational criteria would largely replace political ones in the appraisal of economic activities, while the rapid pace of economic growth continues, but in a very different direction. Though the power of the central authorities would remain very great, enforced conformity to a code of law would replace the present device of frequent shakeups in the administrative apparatus as a means to which power and authority were exercised. By the same token, the importance of organized terror would greatly decline, though some aspects would unquestionably remain to enforce acceptance among the population of materialist and technical values held by the rulers. There would also be some increase in the personal security of the officials, inasmuch as conformity with objective roles in objectively appraised performance would become the chief basis for tenure in office.

*   *   *   *   *

The purpose of life would be expressed primarily in secular and materialist terms, emphasizing the society as a whole rather than the individual as the object to which benefits ought to accrue. Norms of behavior would be subject to change and display a largely rationalistic justification. What a person ought to do would be explained in terms of why a particular course of action brings certain results rather than in terms of more absolute standards. It might be described as a morality of "no smoking—fire hazard" signs. For the most part, its rules would be applied impartially. Industrialization exerts very strong pressures toward creating a society such as this. It could only come into full bloom however if industrialization and the creation of more material goods became more of an end in itself than has so far been possible for the Bolshevik regime.

For the latent traditionalist elements in Soviet society, to consider the third possibility, to assert themselves both the emphasis on industrialization and the power of the dictator, two elements now closely connected, would have to be sharply reduced. In this case too it might be expected that the process would stop far short of a disintegration into the European type of feudal society, but might remain a form resembling an Oriental despotism. That is to say, there would still be a central ruler and a bureaucratic apparatus that ruled the country, but it would do so with much less of an effective effort to control the details of daily life. Meanwhile, industry, the state of the technical arts and population would level off and remain more or less static. In terms used here there would occur a de-emphasis of political criteria in the appraisal of economic behavior and an end to the rapid pace of economic growth. There would also be an increase in the authority of local officials and a corresponding loss of power on the part of the Kremlin. An important part of this change would be manifested in the way personal connections took increasing precedence over merit in objective performance as the basis of allegiance and obedience. Terror as a major instrument of control and the enforcement of the writ of the center would diminish as this writ became weaker.

Corresponding to these changes would be an increase in personal security and tenure for officialdom for reasons that are very different for an improvement in their status under technocratic conditions. A much more rigid class system, with sharp educational and cultural distinctions that mark off one stratum from another, would also play a part in the allocation of political authority and material goods. Since the number of economic and other activities flowing through kinship and personal channels would increase, the importance of the family as the basic social cell would arise. The shrinkage of meaningful kinship ties, in other words, would very likely be reversed. . . . In a fully traditional society, the purpose of life is more or less defined as the maintenance of the (status quo). Though it may seem difficult to imagine Marxist doctrine in such a form, important features already serve this purpose. . . .

For the traditionalist forces to come to the surface and to take firm hold, the conflict between Moscow and Washington, which has governed international relationships since the end of World War II, would somehow have to be brought to a close. At first glance, therefore, it would appear that external pressures rule out this possibility. But it cannot be dismissed quite so readily. . . . If strong internal forces are at work in both the major antagonists to diminish expansionist pressures, there is at least a possibility of settling outstanding differences. Such forces are quite visible but do not predominate in the Soviet Union. At the moment, any extended American withdrawal runs too great a risk to be considered seriously by those who hold political responsibility in this country. In time, however, a growth of traditionalist forces in Russia might parallel certain American domestic pressures, such as a resurgence of isolationism and a demand for a smaller allocation of our national resources for foreign aid and the military establishment, to produce a slackening of international tension. Once begun, this reversal of the vicious spiral could have cumulative effects in both the United States and the Soviet Union.

. . . Though only time will yield a conclusive answer, I think it would be a mistake to dismiss the moves recently made by the new regime as a purely temporary and practical withdrawal, a feint without significance for the fundamental character and objectives of the USSR. So far these moves constitute a retreat, executed in good order but evidently in the face of strong and real forces.

. . . The key question, however, is not what the Communist leaders *want* to do about these forces but what they *can* do. With the Korean truce it appears they have had to cut their losses and to cease, at least temporarily, their external expansion in Asia, in a manner reminiscent of their actions in the West at the time of the Berlin air-lift. At home, by the early fall of 1953, it was evidently their judgment that pressure on the peasants would have to be relaxed, the industrialization drive somewhat slackened, more goods allowed to reach the population, the bureaucracy partly rationalized and the terror made less obvious. No single one of these steps is irreversible nor perhaps, is the series as a whole. But it is doubtful that the present "collective" leadership is strong enough to reverse them with the forceful and harsh methods of a Stalin, even if the leaders as a whole, or a dominant faction among them, wanted to. The concessions to the peasantry, particularly the stress on the private plot, favor traditionalist forces. The others favor primarily rationalist and technocratic ones. If peace should continue for a decade or more, the rationalist or traditionalist forces in Soviet society, or some unstable combination of the two, may do their work of erosion upon the Soviet totalitarian edifice.

Finally there remains the question, "What, then, shall we do?" To this question Professor John Plamenatz, of Oxford University, addresses himself in the concluding reading. Professor Plamenatz is justly respected for his powers of penetrating thought and lucid expression. His GERMAN MARXISM AND RUSSIAN COMMUNISM, *published by Longmans, Green in 1954, is marked by profound insights; from this work the following selection is taken.*

FROM

John Plamenatz
GERMAN MARXISM AND RUSSIAN COMMUNISM

THE Bolsheviks believe that we are their enemies. Their philosophy teaches them that it must be so, and our behaviour has ordinarily seemed to confirm what that philosophy teaches. Why did we engage so little with the enemy and husband our resources so carefully until almost the last year of the War, and then expend them lavishly at a time when Germany was already more than half beaten? Why did we, when Russian armies at last occupied most of the smaller countries of eastern Europe, countries whose docile friendship was necessary to Russia's security, show ourselves so anxious that democracy should flourish in regions where it had never existed? We had reasonable answers to these questions, but to the Bolsheviks they did not sound convincing. Not because the Bolsheviks are never amenable to reason, but because the habit of suspicion is so strongly upon them that it is almost out of their power to trust us.

What, then, must we do? Must we despair of peace, and make up our minds to a new war? Must we treat the Russians as enemies? That would be as foolish as to treat them as friends. We have no reason to believe that they want another war. Everything they have done since 1938 is as easily explained on the assumption that they are seeking to be secure against us as that they mean to attack us. Having defeated Germany—and with much less assistance from their allies than they felt themselves entitled to expect—they are now determined to push the outer line of their defenses as far westward as they can. The forces of their potential enemies are, they think, still much greater than their own. They must therefore, if they can, keep their enemies divided and occupied, and must use the Communist Parties of France and Italy to obstruct the western alliance that is directed against themselves. They no doubt welcome the triumph of communism in China, but have done less to insure it than the Americans did in the attempt to prevent it. Since the capitalist Powers are, they think, inevitably their enemies, and since they are still, when united, industrially and even militarily stronger than the Soviet Union and the satellite states, the Bolsheviks deem it mere prudence to make all kinds of trouble for them, domestic and foreign. The control of an international political movement that still claims to be revolutionary is the one great asset possessed by them and denied to their enemies, and they mean to take every advantage of it. That movement is their own peculiar weapon, but the use of it is not war; the more effectively it is used, the less likely—in their opinion—is war. Their hope and intention is, in any case, so to use it that they do not need to fight another great war.

The Bolsheviks are blinded by prejudice but are not without shrewdness. They know that their control of international communism makes them seem dangerous to the western Powers, and therefore that the use of their peculiar weapon may unite those Powers against them. On the other hand, they believe that the capitalist half of the world is exposed to recurrent and severe economic crises, causing widespread distress and disorder. The western governments, caught up in some such crisis, might seek relief from it by making war on the Soviet Union. Although the present intention of these governments may be pacific, there is no relying that they will always be so. While the western nations enjoy as much prosperity as capitalism allows of, there is no need for their governments to contemplate war. Most peoples most of the time, whether their states are bourgeois or not, greatly prefer peace to war. But the crises to which capitalism is liable grow more severe as the years pass, and are therefore more likely than ever to drive bourgeois governments to desperate courses. Soviet Russia, while the larger and richer part of the world remains capitalist, must always be in danger, and therefore always mistrustful and on her guard. She must use the Communist Parties everywhere to weaken and divide her potential enemies, bringing them into war with one another rather than with her. She must, of course, be careful how she uses the communists. She must not use them to threaten what they are too weak to perform; she must not exhort them to attempt revolution where there is, for the time being, no hope of success. She must not exasperate her potential enemies—who are potential enemies even when they seek to be friends—into union against her; she must look always to her own security and seek to strengthen communism everywhere. The rulers of the Soviet Union, whose empire was shaken to its foundations by Hitler are probably more interested in security than anything else. They are probably on the defensive; and yet that defensive is of a kind that can easily pass to offense. They still believe that the western world is capitalist in the old-fashioned Marxian sense of the word, and that it will eventually fall a victim to proletarian revolutions; and they perhaps still think it their duty to lend assistance to revolutionaries everywhere, not only for their own security's sake, but to hasten the coming of socialism. Their first leader greatly qualified historical materialism inherited from Marx and Engels, and they have not abandoned it. Indeed, Lenin's qualifications of it, which they still accept in principle, have served rather to multiply than to reduce the obligations imposed upon them by their creed. They do not deny these obligations, and, no doubt, were they to see signs of the imminent collapse of the capitalist economy they would work hard to hasten it. But at the moment they are probably more impressed by the immense power of their potential enemies than hopeful of their early downfall. They therefore use communism more to defend themselves than to overthrow the 'bourgeois' states they chose to consider most hostile to them. The present business of communist parties in the West (though not in Asia and Africa) is almost entirely to prevent an effective alliance against the Soviet Union, and hardly at all to prepare for totalitarian revolution. We must treat the Bolsheviks neither as friends nor as enemies. We cannot treat them as friends because they are still the victims of a creed teaching them that enduring friendship between us and them is impossible. But we need not assume that they mean to make war upon us, nor yet that they will, in their endeavours to get security, use methods that will make it difficult to avoid war. Lenin believed that the First World War would end with the collapse of capitalism, but Stalin lived to see it survive two such wars; and the Bolsheviks have now against them, in the United States, a country more prosperous and powerful by far than the Hitlerite Germany that nearly defeated them. Though they may still believe in the eventual downfall of capitalism, they have at least as much cause as the Western Powers to fear war. Historical materialism does not guarantee that, if they fight, they must win. The final triumph of the proletarian cause is assured, but not the victory of every proletarian state in every war. Just as several abortive revolutions may precede the last and triumphant one, so the first proletarian state may be defeated, and even abolished, before the time has come for the final and decisive victory of the world proletariat. Ever since he defeated Trotsky, Stalin made it his first duty to preserve and strengthen the Soviet Union; he did nothing to justify the belief that he would risk her destruction in a desperate attempt to make the world communist by war. He neither preached war to the Russian people nor imposed upon them a destiny not to be accomplished except by means of war. He may have thought himself the first servant of the proletariat, and therefore obliged to help them to victory everywhere; but he would not wantonly risk the destruction of the great society he so laboriously built up. He did not mind bloodshed; he did not officiously keep men alive when their living was no use to the cause he had made his own; but he did wish to preserve the new society whose structure is his monument. Like an Egyptian Pharaoh, he would sacrifice tens of thousands of lives to have his building, but his intention was that the building should endure.

The Bolsheviks are the dupes of a false philosophy, and are therefore blind and obstinate. They insist upon using an inadequate and obsolete vocabulary to describe the world, and are therefore bound to misdescribe it. They are pedantic, wearisome and rude, almost past endurance. They are abominably cruel. But they are not mad. They make their calculations according to known principles, which, though mistaken, are not altogether unplausible. Because these principles are mistaken, when the Bolsheviks calculate, they ordinarily miscalculate. We cannot hope that they will, while they retain their present philosophy, understand either our society or their own. We must therefore expect to be misunderstood by them, and also mistrusted and disliked. To imagine that we can collaborate with them to establish a solid world order is near illusion. They believe only in temporary accommodations with us, and while they hold to this belief, nothing more will be possible.

We can, however, since they have a philosophy and are also sane, so behave that it appears to them not worthwhile to attempt what does not suit our interests. If we avoid industrial crises and maintain a considerable prosperity, the Bolsheviks will not immediately conclude, either that capitalism will endure forever, or that our society shall cease to be capitalist; they will long continue to expect our ruin and to hope for it; but they will, at least for the time being (having as much cause for fear as for hope), leave our domestic affairs more or less alone, lest a premature attempt to subvert our social order should unite us in war against them. If we contrive to give generous assistance to Asian and African peoples bent on making their economies more productive and their poor less wretched, the Bolsheviks will no doubt predict our failures; but they will also refrain from exciting men to revolution so long as what they have been taught to consider the 'objective conditions' of successful revolution are not sufficiently apparent. We must, in short, knowing how they see our world and interpret it, make it look the sort of place where it would be unprofitable and even dangerous for them to make trouble. We must look formidable to them and yet not seem to threaten their security. We cannot rely on their goodwill, but we can, if we act wisely, rely on their patience. Their false philosophy teaches them that time is their ally; and the more they can be persuaded to let time pass quietly the better for us and for them. Let us at least thank God that Hitler is dead, and that the dictators we now have to deal with are sane.

INDEX

Achievements under Communism, 244–248

Agriculture, characteristics of, 108–123
   during NEP period, 108–109
   friction between Party and government officials in, 122
   from 1917 to 1929, 108
   People's Commissariat for, 120, 121
   place of government coercion in, 110
   post-1929 collectivization contrasted with earlier attempts in, 109–110
   socialization of, 109
     See also, *Kolkhoze*, Peasants, Serfs

Aktivs, as ancillary governmental units, 129

Alexander II, proclaimed emancipation of serfs, 8

Allied intervention in Russia, 21

American fascism, described by Soviet visitors, 209

Army, as an instrument of control, 124
   attempt made to increase its worker personnel, 157
   dependent on political forces, 155–157
   dissatisfaction watched for in, 160
   discipline tightened in, 164
   functions of, as outlined by Stalin, 156–157
   increased prestige of, 156
   not considered as a source of political opposition, 164
   Party control over, 161–163
   Party membership in, 158–159
   personnel in, in re age and education, 158
   political commissars in, 161–163
   principle of social selectivity used in recruiting for, 157–158
   share of, in political activity, 159–161
   traditional apparatus reintroduced in, 161

Bakhunin, Mikhail, as a forerunner of Lenin, 79
   works of honored by Soviets, 175

Belinsky, V. G., works of honored by Soviets, 175

Beria, Levrenti, considered as Stalin's successor, 231, 232–234
   first head of NKVD; member of Politbureau, 144
   nominated Malenkov as Chairman of Council of Ministers, 232
   reunited MVD and MGB, 234
   tried and executed, 232–233

Bernstein, Eduard, concept of revolutionary development, 63
   influence of theories of, 65

Bolsheviks, as branch of Social Democratic Party, 64
   called Communists after July, 1918, 21
   contrasted to Mensheviks, 67–68
   decided to take leading part in bourgeois revolution, 68
   formed own party, 1912, 73
   frustrated democratic trend in 1917, 78
   Kerensky's attitude toward, 19
   on necessity of forcing progress on society, 75
   origin and character of, 14
   slogans and strategy in March, 1917, 20–21
   telescoped two revolutions, 73–74
   unable, in 1917–1918, to precipitate world revolution, 74

Bolshevism, as administered by prejudiced but sane leaders, 255–258
   as compounded of Marxism and Bakhuninism, 242
   as species of distorted Marxism, 65–66
   as undemocratic creed, 67
   influence of agrarian conditions upon, 67
   necessary modifications of Marxist tenets of, 69–70

Bourgeois class, as creator of modern Proletariat, 45
   as civilizing catalyst, 43
   as exploiter of masses, 41–42

Set in Linotype Janson
Format by James T. Parker
Manufactured by Kingsport Press, Inc.
Published by HARPER & BROTHERS, *New York*